The Gospel-Perspective on Jesus Christ

The Gospel-Perspective on Jesus Christ

by Donald T. Rowlingson

The Westminster Press
Philadelphia

Published by The Westminster Press ®
Philadelphia, Pennsylvania

PRINTED IN THE UNITED STATES OF AMERICA

To C. F. D. Moule
Lady Margaret's Professor of Divinity
Cambridge University

PREFACE

THIS book has primarily in view the beginning student in theological studies, and any others with comparable interests and needs. Although it rests upon, and hopefully reflects, careful attention to the primary evidence and the work of scholars on the subject, it is more an introduction to a complex subject than a study in depth at any particular point.

Rather extensive footnotes are designed to serve three purposes: (1) in conjunction with Scripture references in the text, to indicate the evidence for positions that are taken; (2) to offer suggestions for further study; (3) to acknowledge indebtedness to others.

Among the latter I am particularly conscious of the contributions of my professional colleagues and my students at Boston University as well as those of other fellow workers in theological studies in general and in Biblical studies in particular. Due to the stimulation received during two sabbatical leaves in their midst, I wish especially to thank the Divinity Faculty of the University of Cambridge. Above all I am grateful to Prof. C. F. D. Moule, to whom I dedicate the book with appreciation and affection. I also wish to thank Mr. and Mrs. Hobert Farrell for assistance in typing and in preparing the index.

Except where otherwise noted, Biblical quotations are from the Revised Standard Version of the Bible.

D. T. R.

Winchester, Massachusetts

CONTENTS

CONTENTS

ABBREVIATIONS

BJRL	*Bulletin of the John Rylands Library*
IDB	*The Interpreter's Dictionary of the Bible.* Editorial Board: George A. Buttrick *et al.* Abingdon Press, 1962. 4 volumes.
JBL	*Journal of Biblical Literature*
JBR	*Journal of Bible and Religion* (since March, 1967, *The Journal of the American Academy of Religion*)
JTC	*Journal for Theology and the Church*
JTS	*Journal of Theological Studies*
LXX	Septuagint
NEB	The New English Bible
NTS	*New Testament Studies*
RIL	*Religion in Life*
SBT	Studies in Biblical Theology
SJT	*Scottish Journal of Theology*
TWNT	*Theologisches Wörterbuch zum Neuen Testament,* founded by Gerhard Kittel and ed. by Gerhard Friedrich. Stuttgart: Verlag von W. Kohlhammer, 1933 ff. (English tr. by G. W. Bromiley, *Theological Dictionary of the New Testament.* Wm. B. Eerdmans Publishing Company, 1964 ff.)

INTRODUCTION

THE New Testament consists of a collection of early Christian writings in two parts: Gospel and Epistle. Both units represent a selection from a larger pool of available literature. The choice of the four Gospels in question represented the solution of a theological problem caused by "the dual trend towards a multiplicity of Gospels and towards the reduction to a single Gospel."[1] The fourfold Gospel, *the* Gospel according to four different authors, discounted the trend toward harmonization on the assumption that the fullness of God's revelation in the incarnate Lord was too profound to be wholly grasped by any one Evangelist. At the same time it negated the trend toward an infinite proliferation of Gospels on the assumption that the four selected best represented the original deposit of the faith. This is the background for our use of the term "Gospel-perspective."

The distinction between Gospel and Epistle is in part a difference between literary forms,[2] but this is to a great extent determined by the difference in perspective on Jesus Christ. Both perspectives presuppose and proclaim a common faith in the resurrected and exalted Christ, and this central dynamic accounts for the creative aspects of each form. It led to the uniqueness of the gospel genre and the adaptation of the epistle form to the Christian experience and language. With respect to this dynamic center of faith the perspectives of Gospel and Epistle are the same.

They are different, however, with regard to the way in which history and kerygma are related to each other. This is largely a matter of emphasis on one or the other. Both combine historical and kerygmatic elements, but they differ in degree with respect to the emphasis that is placed upon each. The Gospels represent a maximum concern with the historical within a kerygmatic framework, whereas the Epistles represent a minimum concern with the historical in elaborating the kerygma. This distinction is not properly stated when Paul's concentration upon the Christ who is alive and present by the Spirit is too sharply contrasted with an alleged concentration on the part of other Christian leaders upon "the earthly *rather than* . . . the Risen Christ."[3] At least this is not the case as between Gospels and Epistles. It is a matter of degree, a matter of emphasis.

Granting that, the Gospels are unique in turning attention to the details of the preresurrection life and teaching of Jesus as a means of proclaiming the good news. This remains so even when it is acknowledged that the emphasis in the Epistles upon the death of Jesus implies more than is said about appreciation of the quality of Jesus' life, or when it is recognized that traces of Jesus' sayings exist in the Epistles. The two perspectives are still quite different in emphasis, and thus in method. It is this uniqueness of emphasis and method which justifies, as it gives body to, the conception of the "Gospel-perspective."

Not only is there difference here; there is tension as well. This arises inevitably out of the combination of historical and theological elements in the kerygmatic confession of faith in the Lordship of Jesus of Nazareth.[4] It is the tension characterized in current jargon by setting over against each other the Jesus of history and the Christ of faith or the Proclaimer and the Proclaimed. Beginning within the New Testament, the tension has continued throughout the history of Christian thought.

In the Christological thinking of early Christians an extreme form of the tension is illustrated by the differences between

Docetism and Ebionism. Derived from Hellenistic ideas of "divine men," the former held that Jesus Christ was only apparently human. The latter, influenced by Jewish ideas of divinely inspired human figures, considered Jesus Christ to be entirely human. One spoke of "Jesus *Christ*," the other of "*Jesus* Christ." Neither could bring the two together in synthesis.

Eventually, after much turmoil and debate, the theologians of the church arrived at the two-nature formula of the Councils of Nicaea (A.D. 325) and Chalcedon (A.D. 451). In this formula incarnation and resurrection were cemented together to declare that Jesus was both human and divine, both historical and transhistorical. This stated the problem without really solving it, but it had the advantage of tacitly acknowledging the inescapable elements of paradox and mystery in the person of Jesus Christ. Christians have never found it easy to maintain the paradox, however, and the tendency today, as in the past, is to emphasize either the human or the divine side of the equation at the expense of the other. More often than not it is the incarnational side that is compromised.[5]

This implies something about the relevance of the Gospel-perspective today, but it needs to be made more explicit. We are concerned with two levels of relevance. The first brings into focus the relationship within the New Testament between the perspective of the Gospels and that of the Epistles. It raises the question as to whether one effect of the Reformation in some quarters has not been virtually to decanonize the Gospels in favor of Paul, thereby losing the balance between them that is characteristic of the New Testament. To the extent that this is so, in whatever form, we wish to fortify the view that "the restoration of these Gospels to an important position in the canon is a return to the main stream of Christian tradition."[6]

The second level of concern is that of Jesus research. In this area the implications of the Gospel-perspective come into focus. The question is whether certain tendencies to minimize the value of Jesus research for faith are not another form of decanonizing the Gospels in favor of Paul.[7] To the extent that this is the case, we wish to encourage the view that "historical knowledge" and "faith-knowledge" should be clearly distinguished and that the former has an indispensable contribution to make to the latter.[8]

We shall leave until the last chapter any attempt to evaluate these issues. Before we are in a position to do so we must first see the Gospel-perspective by itself and in comparison with the perspective of the Epistles. It remains here only to indicate the general nature of our procedure. We are working throughout the bulk of the book at the level of what is called redaction criticism. That is, we are primarily interested in observing the ways in which the Evangelists relate historical and theological or faith factors in composing the Gospels. We are not concerned for the moment with deeper levels of source criticism and form criticism, except to the limited extent that they contribute to our main concern. Also, as against the usual concentration of the redaction critic on a single Gospel,[9] we are concerned, as we have said, with the common denominators of the picture as a whole. The individual Gospels will of course be involved, but as means to the larger end.

Following the precedent of the New Testament canon, as well as of John's choice of the gospel genre as the instrument by means of which to communicate his message, we include the Fourth Gospel within the Gospel-perspective. We hope to demonstrate that on intrinsic grounds as well this is a valid procedure. At the same time, since there are singular differences between the Synoptic and the Johannine perspectives, it is advisable to treat each separately. To encourage a false harmonization of the Synoptic and the Johannine pictures is as unfortunate as to ignore their common features.

Chapter 1

THE SYNOPTIC VIEW OF JESUS:
WHO WAS JESUS?

TRADITIONALLY, the subject of Christology divides itself into the rubrics of Jesus' "person" and "work." While assuming that the two cannot really be separated, we adopt this method of categorizing the materials as a framework for discussion. The precise question to be considered in this chapter is, "Who was Jesus?" That is, who did the Synoptic Evangelists think he was, and how did they express their views?

In attempting to answer this question we shall presuppose the general validity of the impressions of the Synoptics that a certain Jesus of Nazareth lived, carried on a public ministry, died, and was believed to have been resurrected in the early years of the first century A.D. Specific elements of that picture will concern us only to the extent that they contribute to the precise question being asked. The focal point will be the vocational and messianic terms or models applied to Jesus, by others or by himself, and related categories of thought that concern his nature or person. We are not concerned for the moment to determine the extent to which the views of the Evangelists are "authentic." We wish only to see Jesus, as far as we can, as the Evangelists saw him in the context within which they reacted to him and wrote about him.

Before taking up the various terminological items that are relevant, let us consider the general atmosphere of the Synoptics, their prevailing presuppositions with regard to Jesus. For them he is a figure of commanding authority, a person of unique dimensions. Although focusing upon the human aspects of his earthly life and death, they see him through the eyes of the resurrection faith. They are anything but "objective" witnesses. They are convinced that the period of his existence upon which they concentrate was but one facet of a total saving act of God, as is presupposed in the New Testament as a whole. The question of who Jesus is, therefore, stands at the center of attention. It does not come in as an afterthought.

Two features of the Synoptic accounts may be cited by way of illustrating and reinforcing this generalization in a preliminary way. One consists of the introductions of the Gospels. In each case they state a conclusion about Jesus' person, telling the reader that he of whom the Evangelist is speaking is no ordinary individual. Mark's opening sentence is, "The beginning of the gospel of Jesus Christ, the Son of God." If, as some texts have it, "Son of God" did not stand in the original, before the introduction is ended Jesus' Sonship, his endowment with the Spirit, and his victory over Satan are emphatically stated. Matthew and Luke open their accounts with the theologically interpreted report of Jesus' unusual conception and birth, followed by a reiteration of Mark's portrayal of the baptism and temptation of Jesus. Although it is more relevant in a later chapter, we may note also that John parallels, as he goes beyond, the Synoptics by opening his Gospel with the stately sentence, "In the beginning was the Word."

The other illustrative feature is the use of the term *exousia*, "authority," in the Synoptics.[1] Two references in Mark's first chapter are particularly significant. The first one sets the tone for all Jesus' teaching in the Gospels: "And they were astonished at his teaching, for he taught them as one who had authority, and not as the scribes" (Mark 1:22). The other reference reflects the atmosphere of all the miraculous activity of Jesus: "With authority he commands even the unclean spirits, and they obey him" (v. 27). Interestingly enough this action is referred to as "a new teaching." Not only does Jesus possess this authority, but he transmits it to his disciples (e.g., ch. 3:15, etc.).

Certain sayings of Jesus himself reinforce this reaction of the crowd. His authority, like that of John the Baptist, is "from heaven"—from God (ch. 11:27–33). This means, according to one saying, that "the Son of man has authority on earth to forgive sins" (ch. 2:10). The sweeping affirmation in Matt. 28:18, "All authority in heaven and on earth has been given to me," has a postresurrection exaltation setting, but it is a condition that, as far as the Evangelists are concerned, characterizes the stature of Jesus during his earthly ministry.

These segments of the accounts prepare us to consider the traditional models and patterns of thought that are employed in the Synoptics in order to delineate Jesus' authority. We find that in each Gospel they are combined into something of a patchwork quilt, not always in a tidy manner or with complete consistency. This is because the Evangelists are not systematic theologians involved in a process of precise and self-consistent definition. They are what the term "evangelist" connotes, proclaimers of a good news. They are less interested in explaining than in asserting their convictions about the salvation that God has effected in Jesus Christ. They are less concerned with causes (beyond the assumption of God's initiative) than with the effects of God's act. At the same time, as current redactional criticism is saying, they are self-conscious authors adapting their reports to specific situations and doing so with precise circumstantial purposes in mind. They are not Evangelists in general, but, like Paul, Evangelists geared into the life of specific Christian communities and influenced by a context of traditions peculiar to their particular circumstances. We shall presuppose this as we consider specific vocational and messianic categories or models which they use with reference to the question of who they believe Jesus to be.

RABBI

Under this heading we have in view not only the precise title of the Jewish teacher of the Law, "rabbi," but the roughly equivalent term "teacher" (*didaskalos*) and references to Jesus' teaching activity in general. We are not concerned here with the content of his teaching. The only point for the moment is that, among other patterns in the Synoptics, that of Jesus as rabbi or teacher is prominent.

We may take for granted certain characteristic impressions of the records: that Jesus considered himself to be a teacher and was generally recognized as such, that he taught in various places (in synagogues, in the fields and by the sea, in the Temple court) and in various ways (privately to disciples and publicly in friendly or in polemical situations). Against that background we want to observe the relevant titles and related items. Jesus is referred to often as a *didaskalos* ("teacher"), but this term is seldom used by Jesus himself. Three times he is addressed as "Rabbi": by Peter, a blind man, and Judas. Only once does Jesus use this title.

These statistics tell us little about the important concern of the Evangelists to picture Jesus as no ordinary rabbi. This is the consideration of chief interest in this area of thought. More important than the use of the title for Jesus is the clear implication that the Evangelists considered it quite inadequate as a means of expressing the kind of authority that Jesus was believed to possess. This is suggested in the references in which it is as "Son of man" that he forgives sins and is "lord . . . of the sabbath" (Mark 2:10, 28). Pointing in this direction as well is the characterization of his public utterances by other terms: preaching and evangelizing or proclaiming the gospel. There is a subtle portrayal of authoritative utterance in the expression at critical junctures in Mark, "He was preaching the word to them" (chs. 2:2; 4:33), along with the speaking "plainly" in ch. 8:32.[2] In Matthew the one who makes the pronouncements of the Sermon on the Mount is no ordinary rabbi. There is also something weighty and of more than customary importance in Jesus' "saying" or "sayings," as when the Nazareth neighbors are impressed or the crowd is astonished at the conclusion of the Sermon on the Mount. This is a dominant feature of Matthew and Luke.[3]

Sayings of Jesus himself cap the climax of these observations of the Evangelists. The parable of the houses, in Luke 6:47–49 and Matt. 7:24–27, stresses the wisdom of hearing and acting upon Jesus' "words." Even stronger is the crucial saying, "For whoever is ashamed of me and my words . . . , of him will the Son of man also be ashamed, when he comes" (Mark 8:38), or the one about the indestructibility of Jesus' words in ch. 13:31. In all of this the words of Jesus approach the status of that "word of God" which demands complete dedication: "My mother and my brothers are those who hear the word of God and do it" (Luke 8:21). In the subsequent section on the term "prophet" and in Chapter II on Jesus' message these impressions will be reinforced.

On a small scale this is the first example of a characteristic dialectical interrelationship between the context, which provides a term by means of which to interpret Jesus' status, and the Christian consciousness, which finds the term useful only as it is considerably upgraded, even transformed, when applied to Jesus. A specific example is seen in Matt. 23:8. To the disciples Jesus is reported to say, "But you are not to be called rabbi, for you have one *didaskalos* ["teacher"], and you are all brethren." The Jewish rabbi taught the Torah to his pupils in a memorizing procedure, the relationship between teacher and pupil being quite formal and temporary. Jesus also taught his disciples, but something more than the memorization of content by rote was involved. What was offered was Jesus himself in a binding and warm relationship, even beyond death, and, in addition, the transfer to the disciples of his authority to teach. The call of Jesus to his disciples was not so much to become pupils as to become sharers of his way, especially since Jesus as a person was one with his way.

PROPHET

Under this heading we have two models in mind: that of the classical prophet in the Old Testament and that of the eschatological prophet which comes to view in the intertestamental period. Also involved are John the Baptist and the concept of the Servant of the Lord in Second Isaiah. We shall assume the fact of Jesus' designation as "prophet" in the Gospels, but leave the discussion of the pertinent references until we have portrayed something of what that term meant in first-century Judaism.

The official view in ancient Judaism was that the authentic voice of prophecy had long since ceased.[4] Because of this and because the idea of an eschatological prophet was in the air, anyone who spoke of "a" prophet or "the" prophet would usually be taken to be referring to a messianic figure who was related to the ushering in of the new age.[5] Over against this we need to consider the fact that the ancient prophetic tradition existed in the Scriptures, "the law and the prophets," and that for many Jews, God was not so much of an absentee landlord as the religion of the Book officially presupposed.[6] This being so, the model of the classical prophet remained a live option for anyone sensitively inclined in that direction, and it should be included in the context of the Gospels. With the model of the classical Hebrew prophet in mind, then, we are concerned at this point only with his call and self-understanding, including his way of looking at his suffering.

What is of central importance here is the prophet's sense of the direct, personal, and highly individual nature of his reception of revelation from Yahweh, and the awareness that his main function is to proclaim God's word. Not only is this to be done verbally, but with his whole being, employing symbolism in each case. There is as well the sense of being invaded by Yahweh without regard to his personal likes or dislikes in such a way that his normal life is abruptly disrupted. The experience is deeply intense and shattering, because the divine invasion of his consciousness amounts to his sharing the emotions of Yahweh himself. The formulation of Yahweh's word in his mind is thus not the result of premeditation, whatever the form of its reception (ecstatically in visions or less dramatically) and regardless of how politically astute he is. Nor is his message a simple rearrangement of traditional doctrines, even though it presupposes Yahweh's saving acts in the past. It is Yahweh's startlingly new word regarding his purpose in world history as applied to the concrete and particular situation of the prophet and his contemporaries. At one and the same time the word is tremendously dynamic and completely relevant.[7]

Jeremiah introduced a new element into the conception of the prophet's self-understanding when he shifted the center of attention from the message to the messenger's suffering as an integral part of a prophet's service. Baruch's narrative in Jer., chs. 37 to 45, goes beyond the idea of painful solidarity with the nation expressed by the first phase of Jeremiah's preaching. In chs. 37 to 45 the idea is amplified that the prophet's whole being, not just his voice, is absorbed in the service of prophecy. Although the idea is a restricted one within the Old Testament as a whole, here suffering is a kind of unique witness-bearing, and the sufferer is a human, vicarious mediator of God's message and salvation.[8] This idea is present as well in the Deuteronomic picture of Moses and, above all, in that of the Servant of the Lord in Second Isaiah.

The other prophetic model, that of an eschatological prophet, was the form in which some envisaged the return of prophecy. As in Joel 2:28 f., this return of prophecy would mark the dawning of the new age. Various sources suggest that in pre-Christian Judaism the idea of one prophet arising in connection with the dawning of a new age was developed. Some of the references speak of this figure in general terms, but in other references specific individuals are mentioned, notably Elijah and Moses.[9] We shall confine our attention to these two figures.

The idea of a second Moses or a Moses redivivus originated with the prediction that the Lord would raise up a prophet like Moses whose function is described as that of authoritative spokesman for Yahweh (Deut. 18:15–19). Moses is called God's "servant" some twenty-five times in the Deuteronomic materials (out of a total of forty in the Old Testament). When this is connected with the report of his vicarious death for the sins of Israel, a possible connection between the Deuteronomic tradition and that of the Servant of Isa., ch. 53, is apparent. However that may be, in later Judaism the words of Deut. 18:15–19 were taken to refer to the eschatological prophet, and this idea was variously interpreted.

The Rabbinic literature has a human figure in mind, sometimes a known figure and sometimes an unknown future figure.[10] In the Qumran Scrolls, however, Moses is taken to be one of three eschatological figures, the prophetic forerunner of two messiahs. The discussion of this triumvirate with reference to certain texts, inclusive of Deut. 18:18 f. and 5:28 f., provides clear evidence that the hope was alive in the popular expectations of Palestinian Judaism at the beginning of the Christian era.[11]

The functions of the prophet like Moses are not exactly clear in the sources. The Samaritan *Ta'eb* "performs miracles, restores the law and true worship among the people, and brings knowledge to the other nations."[12] This is largely an inference, however, from Rabbinic sources in which by a process of fusion Mosaic functions are attributed to the Davidic messiah. The most consistent feature of this figure, perhaps due to some fusion with Elijah, is his preparatory function in relation to the priestly and kingly messiahs. If he was identified with the founder of the Qumran community, this becomes even more apparent.[13]

A few additional items in this area of thought may be cited. The term "righteous one," preeminently true of Moses, is used of the eschatological Servant in Isa. 53:11, but also of the Davidic messiah (Jer. 23:5; cf. Ps. of Sol. 17:35), and even of the devout Israelite (Hab. 2:4). The term "holy man of God," again characteristic of Moses, is employed in a Mosaic context to characterize Elisha (II Kings 4:9). In Hellenistic Judaism, Deut. 18:15–19 was apparently not interpreted eschatologically. On the whole, although there was a very lively interest in Moses, it took the form of his idealization as the epitome of all human virtue (cf. Wisd. of Sol. 2:18; 11:1), along with a Moses-redeemer typology in such legendary embroidery of the Biblical accounts as Philo's *Life of Moses*.

The idea of Elijah as the eschatological prophet owes its origin to the commentary in Mal. 4:5 f. upon "the messenger of the covenant," a different figure in ch. 3:1–4. In the former passage Elijah is pictured as being sent by Yahweh to inculcate repentance before "the great and terrible day of the LORD comes." In Ecclus. 48:10, undoubtedly dependent upon the Malachi passage, the idea that Elijah will "restore the tribes of

Israel" is added, perhaps an indication of the influence of Second Isaiah. This reference also indicates what made the Elijah expectation so persuasive, namely, the belief that he had not died as men do, but had been "taken up by a whirlwind of fire, in a chariot with horses of fire." Other references to Elijah need not be cited, except to note the coalescing of Elijah traits with Enoch and the Son of man in I Enoch 90:31, and to suggest that the Elijah tradition may have been influential in relegating the Mosaic prophet to the role of forerunner in the Qumran Scrolls (cf. "Elijah with Moses" in Mark 9:4).

With this background in mind what shall we make of the relevant Synoptic references? The picture is not completely self-consistent, but it is weighted heavily upon the side of the conclusion that, especially in Luke,[14] it is John the Baptist who is pictured as the eschatological prophet, with Jesus represented as the culmination and fulfillment of the ancient prophetic line. The evidence for this is as follows.

Certain features of the Gospel accounts are consistent in tailoring John the Baptist to the model of eschatological prophet, essentially the forerunner of the Messiah. The insertion in Mark's opening sentence of the quotation of Mal. 3:1 before that of Isa. 40:3 and the picture of the Baptist in the Lucan infancy narrative suggest this view on the part of Mark and Luke (cf. Luke 1:17 and 3:2). Mark 11:32 and Matt. 14:5 picture the general public's estimate of the Baptist as "a prophet." Jesus is also portrayed as considering the Baptist to be the fulfillment of the role of Elijah. Matthew 17:13 and 11:14 alone make this explicit, but this would appear to be the reasonable interpretation of Jesus' words in Mark 9:11–13. The ambiguous expression, "more than a prophet," which Jesus uses to characterize the Baptist, issues immediately in his delineation as the "messenger" of Mal. 3:1 (Luke 7:26 = Matt. 11:9 f.). The Baptist's eschatological role in the ushering in of the new age is specified in Luke 16:16 and Matt. 11:12 f., despite the difficulties of the terms about violence in these verses.

Although the Baptist himself is silent on this subject, what he *does*, as Charles Scobie so convincingly points out,[15] speaks louder than words. His wilderness setting and his asceticism, his dress and his message, all fit the picture of the precedent of Moses or Elijah. John's fearless criticism of Herod Antipas recalls many ancient prophetic actions, but none more applicable than Elijah's denunciation of Ahab. John's baptizing activity does not necessarily fit into this scheme, but the fact of its once-for-all administration by John himself, with reference to the moral requirement of repentance, contrasted with the Qumran baptism solely for ritual uncleanness, suggests a very high self-understanding of his role.

When we compare Jesus' action with this picture of the Baptist's activities, the case for John as the eschatological prophet in the eyes of the Evangelists is even stronger. There is a wilderness theme in the Gospels with reference to Jesus,[16] but not to the exclusive extent that John's ministry is characterized by it. In contrast to John's asceticism Jesus comes "eating and drinking" (Luke 7:33 f. = Matt. 11:18 f.), and there is no indication that Jesus' dress is very different from that of his contemporaries. Jesus does not baptize; he is, instead, the one who is endowed with and who bestows the Spirit at the End time. The message of Jesus has certain features in common with that of the Baptist, but it is strikingly different as well. The delivering up of the Baptist prior to Jesus' public ministry is theologically consistent with John's foreordained role as forerunner to Jesus (Mark 1:14).

This does not settle the question fully as to how the prophetic model is applied to Jesus in the Gospels. References to Jesus on the lips of the crowd label him "a" or "the prophet," and there are ambiguous references to Elijah's relationship to Jesus. However, Jesus nowhere speaks of himself in this frame of reference. As we have seen, what he does imply is that the Baptist is Elijah or the eschatological prophet.

There is a Mosaic strain in the Gospels, partly involving Jesus' own assumptions and outlook. In every instance, however, it is not the inference that Jesus is a prophet like Moses but, instead, that he far transcends him as he is pictured in the eschatological prophet tradition. As the new Moses of the Sermon on the Mount, for example, Jesus is the agent of God's new revelation and not simply the interpreter of the old.[17] He fulfills both Moses and the prophets. He is as well, in a climactic sense, the vicarious sufferer for all God's people, and not simply for Israel. Although the miracles of Jesus bring him into legitimate comparison with the Biblical Moses, they are not relevant to the Qumran picture of the Mosaic forerunner any more than they are to John the Baptist.

Jesus' own self-designation as "prophet" occurs only twice in the Synoptics, although several sayings of Jesus, primarily in Q, present him as being aware of the whole prophetic tradition in Scripture. If we take this set of references as a whole, two ideas stand out. One is that Jesus associates himself with the ancient prophetic tradition, but not simply as another prophet, nor as the eschatological prophet, since that role is assigned to the Baptist. Instead, especially in Matthew and Luke, Jesus views himself as bringing the prophetic line to its culmination in the dawning new age.[18] As the eschatological prophetic forerunner, the Baptist belongs in this End time as "more than a prophet," yet still so much a part of the old order that the "least in the kingdom of God is greater." This is the force of sayings previously mentioned in connection with Jesus' views of the Baptist as well as of Jesus' reply to the Baptist's question in Luke 7:22 f. and Matt. 11:4–6. It is probably with this in mind that the transfiguration pictures Jesus as God's "Son" in contrast to Moses and Elijah. It may also be a way of justifying the passion predictions by a reference to the Scriptures symbolized by these two figures. This carries with it the idea of Jesus as fulfilling the "law and the prophets."

Exactly how Jesus is viewed as fulfilling the "law and the prophets" with self-conscious content, beyond what has been implied, need not concern us at the moment. The only point here is that neither the model of classical prophet nor that of eschatological prophet, as the Evangelists see it, can fully contain Jesus' significance or self-understanding. His authoritative bearing is due to something more than the prophet's sense of divine invasion by God, even when it is similar, and something more as well than the confidence of the eschatological fore-runner of the Messiah in the End days.

The other significant idea that asserts itself in the sayings of Jesus in this area is implied in the two sayings in which he speaks of himself as a prophet, joined by several other sayings about the fate of the ancient prophets. These all suggest that Jesus finds the prophetic model relevant to his rejection and humiliation. In the face of his rejection by his fellow towns-men he says, "A prophet is not without honor, except in his own country, and among his own kin, and in his own house" (Mark 6:4, par.). Just before the reference to Jerusalem as the killer of the prophets Luke has Jesus say, obviously with a self-application, "It cannot be that a prophet should perish away from Jerusalem" (Luke 13:33 f.). The other references simply reinforce the idea that the suffering of the prophets was an acute thought in Jesus' mind.

In presenting this view of Jesus, did the Evangelists have in mind the vicarious suffering of Moses, or of Jeremiah, or of the Servant of Isa., ch. 53, or even more contemporary tradi-tions or memories? The critical question here is the possible influence of the Suffering Servant of Isaiah. This question belongs more properly with the passion story to be considered in the next chapter. Leaving until later pages the full discus-sion of the problem of the Servant in the New Testament, we shall simply make two observations at this point. First, the fifty-third chapter of Isaiah, granting its unique grandeur, was not the only precedent available to the Evangelists. Second, the paucity of explicit appeal to that tradition in the New Testament as a whole in connection with the rejection of Jesus is one of the anomalies of New Testament Christology. There are a few indications that the Suffering Servant may have been in the minds of the Evangelists, notably in Mark 10:45 and 14:24, but the title *pais* is used only once in Matt. 12:18, and not with reference to rejection and death.[19] In any case, the Gospels picture Jesus as finding the model of prophet mean-ingful with reference to his own rejection and death, whatever the specifics may have been.

Perhaps the most significant thing about the use of the prophetic model in the Gospels is the way in which it stays so close to the religious depth and moral earnestness of the classical tradition. This is true of John the Baptist as eschatological prophet and of Jesus as the rejected yet ultimately triumphant culmination of that worthy heritage. This sets them both over against the politically oriented Theudas and Egyptian "false prophet" whom Josephus tells us about,[20] the former of which Gamaliel mentions along with the well-known Judas of Galilee in Acts 5:36 f.

One of the postresurrection phenomena issuing from the Spirit's dynamic influence was the prophetic office, which Paul ranked as second only to that of apostleship (I Cor. 12:28). The model of the classical prophet, however, played no significant Christological role outside the Gospels, despite a general awareness of the prophets and their writings and also of their suffering and its bearing upon Jesus' suffering.[21] The reason for that is clear enough, as the tone of the whole New Testament is summed up in Heb. 1:1 f.: "God spoke of old to our fathers by the prophets; but in these last days he has spoken to us by a Son." Since the prophetic succession was brought to an end, models of more messianic significance were alone adequate to express the convictions of Jesus' followers about him.

CHRIST AND SON OF DAVID

We turn now to more explicitly messianic categories, beginning with "Christ." This is the translation of the Greek *Christos*, which is in turn a translation of the Hebrew *māshiah* ("messiah" or "anointed one"). It is a general term signifying, as suggested, one who is "anointed" as king or priest. Under this general heading the idea of a messianic king (*basileus*), more particularly a "Son of David," and that of a messianic priest are found in the relevant sources. The Gospels do not consider Jesus within the framework of priestly messiahship. All the references carry the connotation of kingly messiah either in the use of the general terms "Christ" and "king" or the title

"Son of David." A brief review of the non-Christian background should help us to appreciate the Gospel usage.

In preexilic times the historical king, such as Saul or David, was titled "Christ" or "Anointed One." A series of Royal Psalms (Ps. 2 and 110, e.g.) celebrate this fact. With the classical prophets following the time of David there arose the future expectation of an ideal king like David, the expression usually being a "shoot" or "sprout" of David. Evidence of this is most obvious in Isaiah (chs. 7:10–16; 9:1–7; 11:1–9), Micah (ch. 5:2–4), Jeremiah a generation later (chs. 23:5 f.; 22:30), and, with qualifications, in Ezekiel (chs. 21:25–27; 34:23 f.). Second Isaiah departs from this by viewing the Persian Cyrus as the agent of Yahweh (Isa. 45:1) and, even more, by abandoning the idea of an ideal king altogether in favor of the prophetic Servant of the Lord. Ezekiel, chs. 40 to 48, also introduces the idea of a priestly messiah in a time when, following the dethronement of the monarchy, the high priest virtually took the place of the king.

After the exile the Davidic hope revived temporarily in the figure of Zerubbabel in Haggai and Zechariah, although in the latter the picture is confused by the substitution of a priest for Zerubbabel in ch. 6:11. Not until immediately pre-Christian times, however, is the Davidic hope dynamic again. The expression "son of David" appears for the first time in Ps. of Sol. 17:20, to be followed by its use in post-Christian Judaism generally. The interesting thing is that this revival of the hope of a kingly messiah is combined with that of a priestly messiah in the Testament of the Twelve Patriarchs and in the Qumran Scrolls.[22]

Two things about this are particularly relevant to our subject. First, despite the emphasis upon a priestly messiah, the revival of the Davidic kingly hope is emphatic. Although in the Scrolls the priestly messiah seems to be exalted above the kingly messiah, this is not completely certain. At least when the term "anointed" is used alone it is applied to the kingly figure, and the picture of the Davidic warrior messiah in the Scrolls is that of the Psalms of Solomon. Second, the messianic figure, whether kingly or priestly, has now become a future eschatological one in contrast to earlier conceptions of a historical personage. Apparently an original aspiration to restore a legitimate high priest in Jerusalem shifted to the supranatural plane and tended to make the messianic figure more warlike when the hope of a genuine restoration receded under the impact of events. We may believe that historical circumstances conspired to bring this kingly hope to the surface again: the dethronement of the non-Davidic Hasmonaean house by the Roman conquest of 63 B.C. and the Hellenizing policy of the Herods.

In any case the paleness of the kingly messianic hope in the apocalyptic tradition of Daniel and I Enoch is confronted with a dynamic eschatological hope centered in a Davidic messiah who is anointed with the Holy Spirit. Traits of the prophet like Moses are assimilated in the Davidic figure in Rabbinic forms of this hope. In Hellenistic Judaism this type of messianic hope did not strike fire for several reasons, primarily because the national-political atmosphere was different from that of Palestinian Judaism.

With this background situation, and also the abundant references to "Christ" in the Epistles, in mind, we are struck by the paucity of relevant references in the Gospels. The pattern is there, but not as a major one within the whole. Traces of the use of the general title "Christ" or "Jesus Christ" as almost a proper name, so abundant in Paul, are present. Expectations on the part of the people that Jesus fulfilled the kingly hope, employing the term "Christ" or "King," are present in several places as well, as in the scene of Jesus entering Jerusalem. Excepting the infancy stories, which will be treated later, there is no suggestion that Jesus is of Davidic descent. However, the title "Son of David" is employed with reference to him (Matt. 21:9, 15) and in his own quotation of Ps. 110:1 (Mark 12:35 f.).

The most interesting aspect of the Gospel picture, aside from Jesus' own sayings, is the apparent merging of the Davidic ideal with that of the eschatological prophet. This comes out clearly in the plea of the blind Bartimaeus: "Jesus, Son of David, have mercy on me!" (Mark 10:47). Here the essentially nationalistic and political figure of the kingly messiah is assumed to have a saving function more characteristic of the Mosaic prophet. This merging of functions is also evident in several other passages, especially in Matthew. The response of Jesus to the Baptist's question, in the form of a quotation from Isaiah, points in this direction too (Luke 7:22 = Matt. 11:4-6). If there is any trace of the priestly messianic precedent in the Gospels, it is by inference in this connection, since both Moses and Elijah were priests as well as prophets.

The words of Jesus himself in Mark 12:35-37a are mainly significant for the way in which they negate the notion of Davidic messiahship. The meaning is ambiguous, but the apparent demoting of David as the Lord's son is consistent with the general picture of Jesus as being anything but prejudiced toward a narrowly nationalistic and favored-nation conception of the Kingdom of God. If the entry into Jerusalem does not imply this, the crucifixion does.

Additional references that directly involve the terminology being considered in this section implicitly tone down the Davidic emphasis. They represent the fusion of "Son of David" with other messianic patterns: the eschatological prophet or "Son of God" or "Son of Man." Or they associate the very un-Davidic idea of suffering with the "Christ" as in the letters of Paul. In contrast to the dynamic significance of the term "prophet" as applied to Jesus, the traditional idea of an Anointed One in a Davidic form associates itself with Jesus only in a symbolical and much transfigured way. In this respect the Synoptics tend to parallel and conform to the usage of Christ in the rest of the New Testament.

SON OF GOD

A more significant pattern of thought in the Synoptic Gospels consists of the use of the term "Son of God" in all the sources. If the "son" in the parable of the wicked husbandmen

(Mark 12:1–12) was understood by Mark to refer to Jesus, which appears to be a reasonable assumption, this too is evidence of a kind.

Once again, as a help in interpreting the Gospel data, let us consider briefly the non-Christian usages of the model of sonship. In the Old Testament the primary use of the term is for the empirical king. This follows the precedent of the royal mythology of Assyria rather than that of Egypt, with the latter's attributing of divinity to the monarch. That is, in the thought of Israel the king is adopted by Yahweh to fulfill his purposes, and the king abides in a filial relationship without metaphysical overtones. The covenant people are also so designated, as in Hos. 11:1, "Out of Egypt I called my son." In Ex. 4:22b–23a the king is the representative of the nation. In some sources the title is applied to angels and perhaps to the high priest.

Evidence that the term had crystallized as a messianic title before the Christian era is not abundant. The clearest indication of this is a summary of II Sam. 7:10b–14 in the Qumran Scrolls which equates "son" and "sprout of David" (4Q Flor. 10–14). Psalm 2 was interpreted messianically in Rabbinic Judaism, but the key verse was excepted from this: "You are my son, today I have begotten you" (v. 7). Some texts of I Enoch and IV Ezra read "my son," but "my servant" appears to be the more appropriate text. On the basis of the reference in the Scrolls the conclusion of Reginald H. Fuller seems reasonable, that "like son of David, son of God *was just coming into use* as a Messianic title in pre-Christian Judaism," signifying, "not a metaphysical relationship, but adoption as God's vice-regent in his kingdom."[23] There is no indication, however, that it was used in Hellenistic Judaism as a messianic title.

The question that arises with reference to Hellenistic Judaism is how we are to interpret the reference to "the righteous man" as "God's son" and "a child" or "servant [*pais*] of the Lord" in the Wisd. of Sol. 2:18, 13. Is this conception of sonship to be equated with, or assumed to be derived from, the Hellenistic divine man concept reflected in the *Letter of Aris-*

teas (140: "man of God"), Josephus (*The Jewish War*, VII, 344: "divine"), and Philo's *Life of Moses* (divinely inspired without sharing God's essence)? The Wisdom of Solomon at least does not suggest a positive answer, even though in a few formal matters it may reflect such an influence.[24] The burden of its picture of "the righteous man" reflects the actual circumstances of the persecuted Jew in Alexandria who is faithful to knowledge of God vouchsafed in the Law and who retains his confidence in God's ultimate vindication. What is suggested is the individualizing of the idea of sonship in application to Old Testament worthies in whose succession the righteous man believes himself to stand. The content is influenced more by Biblical precedents than by Hellenistic metaphysics. Fuller has also pointed out that in the extant literature the term "son of God" is never explicitly used of the divine man.[25]

In the highly syncretistic and, in some respects, quite untypical thought of Philo (not typical of Hellenistic Judaism as a whole, that is) the term "son of God" is used of the "Word" (*logos*).[26] In that setting it has all the supernatural overtones which "Wisdom" and "Word" possess in the Wisdom tradition. We may also remind ourselves that the emperor is at times called "son of God" (as well as "Lord," "Savior," and "God").

Turning to the Gospels, we observe first of all the distinct pattern that Mark imposes upon his materials. At baptism Jesus' Sonship is announced to him along with his special endowment with the Spirit. At the transfiguration, immediately following the announcement of his impending suffering, it is reaffirmed to selected disciples. And at the crucifixion a Gentile centurion, probably symbolizing the Gentile world, testifies to his faith in Jesus' Sonship.[27] Matthew reproduces this pattern exactly, except that he alters Mark's "Thou art" to "This is" at the baptism, thus making it more of a public announcement, as is done by all three Synoptics in the transfiguration scene. Luke follows Mark in the accounts of baptism and transfiguration, but he changes the centurion's acclamation at the cross to an "innocent man."

Two significant features of the Synoptic perspective are brought out by this pattern in conjunction with other Son of

God references. The first feature is the implication that the earthly work of Jesus, his whole history, is to be viewed under the terms of Sonship. The parable of the wicked husbandmen is relevant at this point, assuming that for Mark it was understood as an allegory of the church which justified the Gentile mission (as Matt. 21:43 makes explicit). There is in this parable the motive of the divine initiative in sending the Son, as in many texts outside the Gospels. This is the nearest that the Synoptics come to a conception of a pre-earthly pattern of incarnation or epiphany.

It is possible that behind the announcement of Jesus' Sonship at baptism and in the transfiguration there lies a shift from the exaltation and parousia contexts to that of the earthly life. The term "Son of God" is especially applied to the exalted Christ in many texts in the Epistles. Perhaps at any earlier stage, due to the delay in the parousia, there had also been a shift from a parousia context (as in I Cor. 15:28) to an exaltation context (as in Rom. 1:4).

Perhaps there has been a substitution as well of "beloved Son" for an original "servant" (pais) in Mark 1:11 and 9:7 under the influence of Ps. 2:7, the latter predominantly employed elsewhere in an exaltation context (as Heb. 1:5, e.g.). Perhaps the precedent of the Wisdom of Solomon has been influential. At least the best text of Mark 1:11 and 9:7 has overtones of Isa. 42:1 and its connection of Spirit endowment with the choice of "my servant." The Lucan parallel to Mark 1:11 has a textual variant that introduces Ps. 2:7, but the Lucan variant to Mark 9:7 echoes the "chosen" of Isa. 42:1. Matthew's quotation of Isa. 42:1–4, a substitution in fact for Jesus' recognition by demons as "the son of God" (Mark 3:11), suggests something of this interplay between the Servant tradition and Ps. 2:7.

At least it is evident that in the Synoptics the model of Sonship is used to make emphatic the idea that Jesus' preresurrection career is as much a part of God's act in and through him as are his resurrection and exaltation and expected parousia. Embodied within this conception is the prevailing Old Testament background and perhaps the kind of development that took place in Hellenistic Judaism as evidenced in the Wisdom of Solomon. The quotation of Hos. 11:1 in Matthew's infancy story and the appeal to Isa. 9:5 f. and II Sam. 7:12–16 in the Lucan infancy story belong within this framework of thought.

The second feature of the Synoptic use of the model of Sonship which stands out is its close connection, as in the baptism account, with the idea of Jesus' endowment with the Spirit.[28] In this sense we may say, recalling the previous discussion of the term "prophet," that Jesus embodies the revival of the prophetic tradition in two ways. His whole earthly ministry is carried on under the inspiration of the Spirit as a permanent endowment, at the same time that there are overtones of the idea that with the Spirit's activation the Last Days have been inaugurated (cf. Matt. 12:28). In this respect we may recall the way in which the parable of the wicked husbandmen represents Jesus as Son, bringing the prophetic line to its culmination and termination in the form of a fulfillment of Ps. 118:22 f. Echoes of this are seen in Acts 4:11 and I Peter 2:7.

In Mark's temptation story and in the picture of Jesus' being hailed twice by demons as "Son of God" (ch. 3:11; 5:7), we are introduced to his way of relating the activity of Jesus to the cosmic conflict that characterizes many of the Epistles. In Mark's view it is not only in Jesus' exalted reign, as the result of his death, that he conquers "the principalities and powers" under Satan's control. The conflict is being waged during his lifetime, and the outcome is already a foregone conclusion. This is the point of his victory over Satan in the temptation, as well as of his eminent success in exorcizing demons.

As James M. Robinson points out, this aspect of the cosmic conflict is but part of the total pattern of conflict in Mark inclusive of the polemical situations involving the Jewish leaders and Jesus' ultimate crucifixion.[29] The fact that Jesus is hailed by the demons as "the Holy One of God" in Mark 1:24 and Luke 4:34 suggests the influence of the Mosaic prophet tradition. This is also true of the way in which the Matthean and Lucan versions of the temptation turn upon the question of Jesus' sensitivity to God's sovereignty against a background of Deuteronomic quotations. Perhaps here an original "Servant," characteristic of the Mosaic tradition, has been replaced by a Sonship concept in the course of the development of the tradition (also in Matt. 27:40).

The Q version of the temptation in Matthew and Luke introduces a series of specific alternatives which raise the question as to whether it is the person or the work of Jesus that is in the forefront of attention, granting that this is only a matter of emphasis.[30] That is, is Jesus involved in subjecting his consciousness of Sonship, about which he may have some doubts, to convincing criteria? Or, taking it for granted, is he concerned with a program by means of which to implement it? It hardly seems likely that the Evangelists considered seriously the possibility that Jesus may have doubted his selection as Son of God. It looks as though their main concern was to reinforce Mark's view in an elaborated form by means of Scriptural precedents related to current messianic speculation: in the cosmic conflict Jesus decisively repudiated Satan. What they add to Mark is an emphasis upon the obedience of Jesus, so characteristic of Paul's view, thus giving Jesus' Sonship a decidedly ethical cast. He is not Son of God only because of his obedience, but he obeys because he is Son of God.

We should not minimize in this respect the concern of the Evangelists to oppose the idea that the Roman emperor could in any sense compare with Jesus as God's Son, even though on the surface the former appeared to have the upper hand. To the eyes of faith Satan and his battalions, including his earthly representatives, are already defeated by the true Son of God, even though one must wait for the full demonstration of this fact in the final consummation. That it is a Roman centurion who acknowledges Jesus on the cross as the Son of God may say something with reference to the imperial cultus, although he probably is a symbol of the Gentile world in general.[31]

Several additional factors may be treated briefly. Matthew has a few editorial additions to Mark that mainly serve to heighten the Son of God motif in that Gospel.[32] The famous Q saying of Jesus about his unique relationship with the Father emphasizes the intense and intimate filial relationship that is taken to be the secret of his authority (Luke 10:22 = Matt. 11:27). Here the connotation is not so specifically that of Messiahship as of complete oneness in understanding with reference to Jesus' revelatory significance.[33]

Mark 14:61 f. represents Jesus as giving an affirmative reply to the high priest's question, "Are you the Christ, the Son of the Blessed?" This is in contrast to the ambiguous and equivocal response that the other Synoptists report. Since this reference involves two additional questions, that of a messianic secret and the use of the term "Son of Man," we shall delay its consideration until we deal with those subjects. It is sufficient for our purpose simply to note that whereas in Rom. 1:3 f. Jesus is Son in his exaltation and in I Thess. 1:9 f. he is Son in his expected parousia, here he is Son during his earthly ministry. In this respect, although the saying in Mark 14:61 f. is complicated by the Son of Man addition, it is consistent with the Marcan pattern and emphasis as a whole. The saying about the Son's ignorance of the exact time of the parousia in Mark 13:32, although concerned with future events, is also consistent with the idea that on earth Jesus speaks as God's Son. The difference between this and the Q saying about the fullness of Jesus' knowledge, however, is striking.

In Matt. 28:19 the Son is linked with the Father and the Holy Spirit in a rather unique Trinitarian saying on the part of the resurrected Jesus in the exaltation context. Here the Synoptic tradition blends decidedly into that of the (probably more original) use of the "name" of Jesus Christ in writings outside the Gospels. On the other hand, in the Synoptics, in contrast to the Epistles, the concept of Sonship is not geared into a pre-earthly context in conjunction with the term "Lord." If the preexistence of Jesus is presupposed in the Synoptics, it is at least not made explicit.

SON OF MAN

This term is prominent in the Synoptics and its use is entirely on the lips of Jesus himself. Before taking note of its use in Jesus' sayings, we shall review briefly precedents in Jewish literature. This will enable us to observe more clearly its characteristic uses in the Synoptics.

It has two nonmessianic uses. One is as an equivalent of "man" or "humanity" in general. Psalm 8:4 illustrates the parallelism between "man" and "son of man" (*ben adham*), in each case mankind or humanity in general being meant. Translating another Semitic term (*ben enos*), the same signification is present in Ps. 80:17 and Ps. 144:3, although they are not quoted in the New Testament. In conversational Aramaic this latter term was employed as a self-effacing substitute for the first person singular: "one says" or "it is said," "*Mann sagt.*" The other usage is that of Ezekiel with reference to his capacity to read heavenly secrets, usually in connection with the Spirit's inspiration (ch. 2:1, etc.).

Of greatest interest to us is the way in which the term is used in the apocalyptic tradition. For the first time in Jewish literature the Son of Man appears as an eschatological figure in the second century B.C., in Dan. 7:13 f. In the night visions Daniel sees "one like a Son of man (*bar enos*), coming with the clouds of heaven and being presented before the Ancient of Days, who gives him eternal dominion over his realm. Apparently an individual figure in these verses, in associated verses he is given a collective interpretation, "the people of the saints of the Most High," that is, the remnant (ch. 7:15–18, 27). Probably we should take this to mean a combination of individual and corporate characteristics between which a clear distinction was not usually made. The individual's representative capacity is in view as in the picture of the four beasts in ch. 7. At least the Son of Man in Daniel is an eschatological figure whose exaltation ensues upon his faithfulness to Yahweh in persecution and rejection by men.

In the Similitudes of Enoch (I Enoch, chs. 37 to 71), a Son of Man is a prominent eschatological figure.[34] He is a composite figure, representing a syncretistic combination of several titles, but his essential characteristics as an individual Son of Man are clear. His designation as Son of Man is titular in nature and he is a preexistent divine being who is hidden in the presence of God from before all creation (chs. 48:2 f.; 62:7). He remains hidden until the End, when he will be revealed to deliver the elect from their persecutors (ch. 62:7 ff.), to judge the latter (ch. 46:4, etc.), and to preside as ruler in glory over the redeemed community throughout eternity. The figure of the messianic banquet also appears in this setting (chs. 69:29; 62:14).

In ch. 71, a variation on this appears. Here it is Enoch himself who is exalted to heaven as the Son of Man. There is precedent for this in Jubilees and the Wisdom of Solomon, where the righteous man is exalted at the End to play the part of witness in God's judgment. This is a peculiarity of I Enoch, however, rather than representative of the apocalyptic tradition in general. At a much later date, IV Ezra compares favorably with the tendency in the Similitudes to combine an original Son of Man with other elements from the Hebrew Scriptures.

Norman Perrin has recently proposed the view that Daniel's use of "one like a Son of man" as a cryptic figure was probably a pure accident, that any other cryptic symbol would have done just as well. What happened after that in I Enoch, IV Ezra, and in the talmudic and midrashic tradition represents a free and creative use of Dan. 7:13.[35] This is a radical and rather cavalier departure from the more generally accepted idea that some form of a Man or Son of Man tradition was a feature of the drama of the End time in ancient Judaism.[36]

In the New Testament outside the Gospels the term "Son of Man" is almost nonexistent. It is never employed by Paul, although some think that such a tradition is an ingredient in the background of his use of "the man of heaven" in I Cor. 15:47 ff. and at some other points.[37] The influence of Daniel (along with Ps. 110:1) is evident in Acts 7:56 and in Rev. 1:13 and 14:14. Psalm 8:4, however, informs the use of the term in Heb. 2:6, 9. The term also appears in Barnabus 12:10 and in Ignatius' Letter to the Ephesians 20:2.

In the Synoptic Gospels, Son of Man appears a total of 60

times in sayings of Jesus. They may be classified in three categories as follows:[38]

	Mark	Q	Matt.	Luke	Total
Eschatological orientation	3	6	6(3)	3(3)	18(6)
Suffering orientation	8	0	1(7)	1(6)	10(13)
Present orientation	2	3	2(2)	2(2)	9(4)
Total	13	9	9(12)	6(11)	37(23) = 60

The figures in parentheses denote parallels to Mark in Matthew and Luke. Deducting these repetitions of the term, the separate uses amount to 37.

Typical of the first group of sayings is that in Mark 13:26, "Then they will see the Son of man coming in clouds with great power and glory," with its apparent similarity to Dan. 7:13–14. All these sayings express the thought of the parousia of the Son of Man in one way or another. Certain variations in the interrelationships of the Gospels do not alter this impression.[39]

The second group embraces the three specific passion predictions in Mark and their echoes elsewhere in all three Synoptics. It is notable that Q lacks this type of usage and that Luke omits four of the Marcan references. The keynote of this type of saying is the prediction that the Son of Man will suffer and rise again. The several predictions portray various degrees of elaboration of the manner in which he will suffer, corresponding to subsequent details of the passion narratives inclusive of Scriptural confirmation. "A ransom for many" in Mark 10:45 echoes the Suffering Servant theme of Isa., ch. 53.

The third group applies the title to Jesus during his earthly career, as when as Son of Man he claims authority to forgive sins. In some of these sayings Son of Man is equivalent to "I." Matthew and Luke change "sons of men" in Mark 3:28 to "Son of man." If Mark 8:38 distinguishes between Jesus and the future Son of Man, we have a saying with an eschatological orientation. But it is relevant in a present context if this is an example of the parallelism between "man" and "son of man" in Ps. 8:4.

As we have observed, the first and third groups have precedents in the Jewish background. However, there appear to be no specific contextual materials to account for or to support the suffering orientation of the passion predictions. Some scholars, to be sure, on the basis of Mark 10:45 and 14:24 ("for many") and a few additional units, theorize that Mark self-consciously linked the Suffering Servant and the Son of Man traditions. However, the evidence is too scanty and too ambiguous to justify this conclusion, especially if we take seriously the evidence that a Servant suffering "for many" was not a live messianic alternative in ancient Judaism.

Morna Hooker has proposed the view that Daniel in fact offers a ready precedent for the suffering Son of Man as part of a precedent for a coherent pattern of Son of Man usage in Mark.[40] The crux of the question concerns the sayings with a suffering orientation. According to Hooker, if we ask not "*Why* must the Son of man suffer?" but "*How* can the Son of man suffer?" Daniel gives an immediate and unequivocal answer. When the rightful position of the Son of Man and God's authority are denied, the result is the inevitable suffering of the Son of Man. In Mark his suffering is caused by the opposition of the beast, who represents rebellion against the authority of God. "This is the theme which underlies the whole gospel: the suffering and death of Jesus, like the whole of his ministry, represent a conflict with the satanic forces of evil and rebellion against God."[41]

When the other types of Son of Man sayings are placed in juxtaposition with the suffering sayings the conclusion logically follows that Mark "has set clearly before us in logical sequence the three aspects of the authority of the Son of man: Jesus claims authority as Son of man—a claim which is not understood by the people, and which is rejected by the scribes and

Pharisees; their rejection of his authority leads to a plot to destroy him, but his claim will be vindicated—the Son of man will be seen in glory. Authority claimed, rejected, vindicated —in Mark the three groups of 'Son of man' sayings belong together."[42]

An alternative to this is Borsch's view that the idea of a suffering Son of Man came out of the prevailing baptismal sectarianism. This is to be preferred to Hooker's view, he thinks, because the idea of suffering is not prominent in Daniel's (or Enoch's) picture of the Son of Man, even though it is implied in the background of the Man tradition in general.[43] On the other hand, the idea of suffering is by no means absent from the picture in Daniel, and Hooker's proposal is consistent with Perrin's reasonable assumption that the imagery of Dan. 7:13 was used "freely and creatively by subsequent seers and scribes," and that "a similar but completely independent thing happened in the Christian tradition as a result of the interpretation of the resurrection of Jesus in terms of Dan. 7.13."[44]

Perhaps this but implies that the problem is as complex on the level of the Gospel redaction process as on that of the self-understanding of the Jesus of history.[45] At least the views of Hooker and Borsch suggest that there is a more feasible explanation of Mark's suffering Son of Man sayings than his dependence upon an ambiguous, if not questionable, Suffering Servant messianic tradition. If we wish to be more cautious, we can say that the solution of the problem need not be expressed in a rigid either-or on the grounds that different traditions (Son of Man, Servant, etc.) were not always, if ever, sharply separated in Jewish messianic thought.

LORD

It is not necessary to deal extensively with the use of the term "Lord" (*Kyrios*) in the Synoptics. In the context of the New Testament the term ranged from a form of address equivalent to "Master" or "Sir" to its use in the LXX to translate Hebrew words for God. In the Epistles it is applied to the exalted Jesus mainly in a worship context and, chiefly in The Acts, it appears ambiguously in application to Jesus and God.

The Synoptic Gospels illustrate its increasing use as a means of designating the authority of Jesus' earthly activity and bearing. The term is used once in an address to Jesus in Mark 7:28. Matthew follows Mark at this point and adds eleven uses in address to Jesus, all but two being editorial changes of Mark. Luke has a total of twenty-four independent uses, ten of which are editorial changes of Mark. In contrast to the use of the term in direct address, as in Mark and Matthew, Luke employs the term in narration in the third person singular: e.g., "The Lord appointed seventy others" (ch. 10:1). Matthew and Luke together edit Mark at two points in the form of direct address to Jesus. All this evidence illustrates the upgrading of the term as applied to Jesus in order to signify the authority which he was believed to possess during the pre-resurrection period. If the confusion between "Jesus" and "God" in The Acts is implied in Luke's usage in the Third Gospel, it is not made explicit. However, we may believe that for the author of Luke-Acts, Jesus on earth is implicitly and potentially the Lord that he was recognized to be after the resurrection.

In contrast to the term "Son of Man," however, *Kyrios* is not a term used much by Jesus himself. Its use in Mark 11:3 is simply equivalent to "the teacher" or "the master," as in the parable of the absent master (Mark 13:35). Aside from this, there is only the Q saying, "Why do you call me 'Lord, Lord,' and not do what I tell you?" (Luke 6:46), the intent of the Matthean version of the saying being similar (Matt. 7:21). This is a stark expression of the view that Jesus' words have the authority of the word of God itself. Here the upgrading of the term *Kyrios* in application to Jesus' earthly work is made most emphatic.

In addition to the titles that have been considered, and a few others that appear sporadically,[46] we should also give attention to the pattern of Old Testament fulfillment, the so-called secret Messiahship (or secret Sonship) pattern, the infancy stories of Matthew and Luke, and the resurrection narratives. The question of miracles is relevant here, but we shall delay its discussion until the next chapter.

Old Testament Fulfillment

This is an extensive subject which involves subtle and allusive as well as overt factors. We shall deal with some of the former in the treatment of the passion story in the next chapter. Attention will be confined here to explicit data. The main question is the extent to which the Scriptural apologetic characteristic of the postresurrection proclamation, as in I Cor. 15:3 f. and Acts 1:16 ff., characterizes the picture of Jesus in the Gospels.

This subject falls naturally into two parts: the usage of the Evangelists and that of Jesus. Mark 1:2 f. illustrates the former approach in quoting Mal. 3:1 and, followed by Matthew and Luke, Isa. 40:3 with reference to the appearance of John the Baptist. The words, "as it is written," imply a fulfillment motif. Aside from Luke's extension of the quotation from Isaiah at this point, it is Matthew's Gospel that makes this view of fulfillment explicit and emphatic. Twelve distinct references explicitly state that a facet of the life and activity of Jesus fulfilled a Scriptural prediction. Five of these are in the infancy narrative, as when it is said with reference to the flight to Egypt: "This was to fulfil what the Lord had spoken by the prophet, 'Out of Egypt have I called my son'" (Matt. 2:15).[47] The remainder, with the exception of Matt. 27:9 f., represent editorial additions to Mark.[48] One of these places the quotation on the lips of Jesus himself (Matt. 13:14 f).

The purpose of this technique in the use of the Hebrew Scriptures is to set Jesus in right relation to the Old Testament, which for the Evangelists means in relation to God's purpose as set forth in the Scriptures. Mark's solitary reference accomplishes this with regard to John the Baptist, but Matthew extends the application to the whole career of Jesus.

Turning to the usage of Jesus himself, except for Matt. 13:14 f., there is only a faint echo of this kind of fulfillment mentality. The use of Isa. 29:13 to characterize the hypocrisy of his opponents (Mark 7:6 f. and Matt. 15:7) is simply argument by analogy. Three references indicate a more profound understanding of the idea of fulfillment: Matt. 3:15; 5:17; Luke 4:21. Let us consider them in order.

Confronted by the hesitation of the Baptist to baptize him, Jesus says, "Let it be so now; for thus it is fitting for us to fulfil all righteousness" (Matt. 3:15). The Gospel according to the Hebrews reflects the problem that Jesus' baptism by John created for some Christians; the sinlessness of Jesus appeared to be put in question. In Matthew's pericope the answer is that Jesus himself had ordered it as consistent with God's intention for him, although it is not exactly clear how we should take the expression, "to fulfil all righteousness."

In the other reference from Matthew, Jesus says, "Think not that I have come to abolish the law and the prophets; I have come not to abolish them but to fulfil them" (ch. 5:17). Judging by the context, Matthew understands this type of fulfillment as a deepening of insight into what it means to observe the great moral commandments about murder, adultery, perjury, and the like. Jesus fulfills the intention of these universal moral laws by internalizing them, that is, by turning attention from the act to its seat in the imagination, from symptoms to the cause of the disease. If one wishes to avoid murder, let him refrain from murderous thoughts! Better, let him think positively of the value of every person before God!

The saying in Matt. 3:15 would appear, compared with this emphasis, to be a self-application, a testimony to Jesus' complete obedience to God's purpose for himself. It implies something much more positive with reference to God's plan for himself in relation to John than the apologetic of the Gospel according to the Hebrews in which Jesus' sense of sinlessness is in focus. In both references it is not a proof-texting procedure that is contemplated. Instead it is an appreciation of God's purpose in the Old Testament as a whole.

The saying in Luke 4:21, Jesus' statement after reading the Scripture at the Nazareth synagogue, is in the same category: "Today this scripture has been fulfilled in your hearing." What is fulfilled is the anticipation of the kind of ministry depicted in the quotation from Isa. 61:1–2 and 58:6. Luke employs this to set the tone of his whole portrait of Jesus, especially the emphases upon Spirit endowment and concern for the poor and underprivileged. Perhaps he assumes that the Scriptural reference has Jesus specifically in mind. At least the point is that with the coming of Jesus this kind of ministry can be envisaged realistically. It is this kind of ministry rather than some other kind which marks Jesus' thought and activity. Above all, it is messianic in nature. Jesus self-consciously brings God's profoundest hopes and purposes to expression in himself.

SECRET MESSIAHSHIP

Over sixty years ago William Wrede popularized the idea of a secret Messiah motif in Mark's Gospel, attributing it to the Evangelist rather than to Jesus himself.[49] What is the evidence for the theory?

The evidence is of three kinds. According to some references, on the assumption that the demons know who Jesus is, he forbids them to divulge the information. The narrative references in Mark 1:34 and 3:12 (using "Son of God") are confirmed by Jesus' own words in Mark 1:25 and Luke 4:35 (using "the Holy One of God"). A second group of references implies Jesus' desire to avoid publicizing other types of healing: the raising of Jairus' daughter, curing a deaf mute and a blind man. A third group relates to the confession at Caesarea Philippi, the transfiguration, movements through Galilee—all in narrative—and Jesus' saying about the "secret of the kingdom of God" in Mark 4:11.

The pattern of secrecy, however, is by no means completely dominant in Mark. The motif is broken at the trial before the high priest when Jesus openly affirms that he is "the Christ, the Son of the Blessed." In the parallel versions Jesus' answer to the question put by the high priest is noncommittal: "You have said so." In addition, a leper is told to certify his healing to the priest and make an offering "as a proof to the people" (Mark 1:44, par.); the Gerasene demoniac is advised to return home and tell his neighbors "how much the Lord has done for" him (Mark 5:19). On one occasion Jesus deliberately heals a paralytic in order to fortify his claim of authority to forgive sins, and on still another occasion he intentionally defies the authorities by healing a withered hand. The climactic statement of Jesus in this respect is the insertion of Matthew and Luke into Mark's report of the Beelzebul controversy: "If it is by the finger [Spirit] of God that I cast out demons, then the kingdom of God has come upon you." Although nothing here corresponds to the situation in which knowledgeable demons are silenced, the accent upon complete secrecy is qualified.

Still the pattern as such remains. It serves the purpose of answering in one form the question why it was that not until the resurrection was Jesus' messianic dignity recognized. Even more, it may have been an inevitable result of Mark's view of the cross and the resurrection. That is, Mark turns his back upon the divine man idea with his "God-given power to display and a gnosis to reveal," refusing to "put down a collection of epiphanous acts" of the divine man. In the words of L. E. Keck: "Mark seems to realize that a series of revelatory epiphenomena, even if they made a deep impression on the beholders, is no gospel because such a narrative would not be good news but merely spectacular news. What makes Jesus good news for Mark is the fact that he is the Son of God who lived and taught and called men to follow their crosses precisely as he portrays in his narrative. Because the gospel is the call to believe this deeply enough to follow Jesus, Mark's whole narrative is *euaggelion* [gospel] and the story of Jesus is its *arche* [beginning]." If one does not want to transform the Son of God into a divine man after the Hellenistic model, he has to take the idea of secret Messiahship seriously. "It is the inevitable result of writing about Son of God at all," if "the Cross is central to the gospel."[50]

THE INFANCY NARRATIVES

Our attention here is limited rather narrowly to the Christological motifs, with reference to items treated in previous pages. Almost in passing we may note that the parents of Jesus are clearly designated in both sets of stories as Joseph and Mary. Matthew is untroubled by the question of the actuality of Joseph's participation in conception due to the virgin birth idea, but Luke's "as was supposed" in Luke 3:23 may reflect such a question. We may also recall that four of Matthew's fulfillment references occur in his infancy narrative.

Luke provides strong support for the idea that John the Baptist was viewed as the eschatological prophet, the forerunner of the Messiah. The story of his birth, including the unusual nature of his conception, parallels that of Jesus, with the intent of showing that he was ordained by God to participate in the divine drama as forerunner of Jesus. Zechariah's words about God having "raised up a horn of salvation for us in the house of his servant David," if meant to apply to John, are inconsistent with his priestly origin, but the emphasis falls upon his function of going before and preparing the way of the Lord (Luke 1:76). In Luke 1:17 the figure of Elijah in Mal. 4:5-6 is taken to be the appropriate designation of John's person and function.

Various Christological motifs which we have observed previously appear as threads in the narrative, such as Christ and kingship, Son of God and Lord. The major note, however, is that of Davidic messiahship combined with these Christological threads and, quite distinctive of the infancy stories, the idea of conception by the Holy Spirit.

Both sets of stories appear to be based upon a Son of David Christology with the intent of setting Jesus' earthly ministry in proper perspective.[51] Matthew and Luke gather up and elaborate traditions which move forward from the baptism (as Mark has it) the precise time of the designation of Jesus' career as messianic. Each has reshaped the basic idea of Davidic sonship in the direction of his own interests. Both employ a genealogy as a means of substantiating Jesus' Davidic descent, but each does so in his own way. Luke expands his genealogy in the interests of an Adam-Christ typology (ch. 3:38), but the basic Davidic motif remains, even though he traces Jesus' descent along a different intermediate line from that in Matthew. In Matthew the Hellenistic concept of Old Testament men of God is combined with the Davidic theme by references to Abraham, Isaac, and Jacob (ch. 1:2). Matthew's inclusion of four women who participated in rather unusual ways in the fulfillment of God's purposes may reflect an apology against slanderous insinuations with regard to Mary by Jewish opponents of Christianity.

Both Matthew and Luke record the birth as taking place in Bethlehem, even though they differ about the circumstances that caused Joseph and Mary to be there. This confirms Jesus' descent from David. It is noteworthy that the Davidic accent in Luke 1:32–33, as in Mark 11:10, is eschatologically oriented, pointing to the parousia as the moment in which Jesus will be exalted as Son on David's throne. The term "Savior" in Luke 2:11 and the view of Jesus as destined to be "a light for revelation to the Gentiles" bring out characteristically Lucan traits, as they also point toward the fusion of the Davidic ideal with that of the eschatological prophet. Davidic traits appear in Matthean and Lucan stories which have other interests as well. Whatever the problem created by the virgin birth idea, in strict logic eliminating the reality of Jesus' descent from David through Joseph, the concern is to give messianic dignity to Jesus' whole career.

The point of the virgin birth is that Jesus is viewed as conceived by, not just endowed with, the Spirit. Palestinian Jewish and Hellenistic Jewish conceptions appear to be mingled in this area of thought. In the Qumran Scrolls the Spirit is normally conceived eschatologically as granted at the End time. In Matthew's account the angel informs Joseph that "that which is conceived in her is of the Holy Spirit" (ch. 1:20). Its reinforcement from Isa. 7:14 depends upon the translation of 'alma by the Greek parthenos (Matt. 1:23). The idea of the

Spirit of God as creative power, applied in Luke to the birth of Old Testament figures such as Isaac, is Hellenistic Jewish. This is still different from the idea of "second marriage" in pagan thought. The Sonship motif is also more characteristic of the Hellenistic Jewish atmosphere. This is suggested by the absence of the Bethlehem birth in writings, such as The Acts and Paul's letters, which at the same time presuppose Jesus' Davidic descent. To the extent that conception by the Holy Spirit has ontic connotations it has something in common with the epiphany motif characteristic of the divine man idea. On the other hand, the retention of the Davidic motif, even though it does not fit securely into this frame of reference, suggests the inability of the Evangelists to go over entirely to Hellenistic-Jewish points of view.[52]

The Old Testament influence better serves their intention to assert that during his entire earthly career, from his birth onward, Jesus is equipped to act uniquely for God. In both Matthew and Luke the point of the Spirit's influence is that Jesus is endowed to perform a saving function as "Emmanuel . . ., God with us" (Matt. 1:23), "Son of God" (Luke 1:35), and "Savior" (Luke 2:11). Like the New Testament as a whole, the Evangelists are more concerned to establish Jesus' authority for salvation than to explain him in ontic or ontological terms.

THE RESURRECTION

The resurrection stories in the Synoptics elaborate certain aspects of the formula in I Cor. 15:4–7. The general emphasis falls upon the resurrection as a stage beyond death and burial, with Luke implying the ascension. The exaltation as a stage beyond resurrection is implied, but it is the resurrection event as such that is at the center of attention. In a single, unelaborated sentence Paul mentions the burial which in the Gospels is presented in some detail. The Gospels reflect the change from the more general and flexible "after three days" of the earlier passion predictions to the more specific "on the third day" of Paul, although Matthew once retains the earlier form.

In contrast to Paul's view, the Gospels begin with the empty tomb tradition. Mark's basic account is elaborated and supplemented by Matthew and Luke in several ways. Matthew introduces two apologetic stories in order to make emphatic the reality of Jesus' supernatural resurrection from the tomb, and this idea is augmented by his reference to an earthquake and the descent of an angel to open the tomb. Whereas Mark and Matthew support the idea of Galilean appearances, Luke, consistent with The Acts, alters the prediction of Jesus' appearance in Galilee to a reminiscence of what was previously said in Galilee. All three Evangelists, however, stand in marked contrast to Paul's silence about an empty tomb.

Paul and the Evangelists agree on the report that Jesus "appeared," having in common reports of appearances to Peter and the rest of the Twelve. In addition, Luke reports an appearance to two disciples on the Emmaus road. The Synoptics know nothing of appearances to James and five hundred disciples as reported by Paul.

We are not concerned here to analyze the puzzle that is created by the "tension between the singleness of the Easter *message* and the ambiguity and historical problems of the Easter narratives."[53] We are concerned only with the Christological motifs that inform the narratives. Despite the differences between Paul's formula and the Gospel accounts, they agree in the juxtaposition of death and resurrection, with the latter emphatic in its reversal of the verdict of Jesus' crucifiers. The idea that the death of Jesus has atoning significance, so emphatic in Paul, is but hinted at in the Synoptics. That which is common to the Synoptics and I Cor. 15:4–7 is mainly the view of the resurrection as reversing the human verdict that Jesus was an impostor. In both instances this is rooted in the appearances. Summary references to Jesus' postresurrection authority (Matt. 28:18 f.) and the promise of the gift of the Spirit (Luke 24:47–49) anticipate the development of the exaltation theme in the rest of the New Testament.

No predominant pattern of Christological terms or categories dominates the narratives. The three main New Testament titles

(Christ, Son of God, Lord) appear sparingly. The eschatological prophet theme is evidenced in Luke, and in both Matthew and Luke an emphasis upon the value of Jesus' teaching appears. Luke especially introduces a strong strain of Old Testament fulfillment with reference to Jesus' death and vindication.

Taken as a whole the resurrection accounts serve as a means of marking the transition to the area of thought about Jesus' exaltation and Lordly reign. They are necessary to a complete portrayal of the earthly life and death of Jesus, simply because it is this resurrection event which sets the preresurrection days in proper focus for Christian faith. Except for this, the portrayal of Jesus' authoritative bearing, which characterizes the preresurrection portraits, would appear anomalous. Without this sequel the crucifixion in particular would justify its characterization as a stumbling block to some and folly to others. In the light of the resurrection, however, the whole face of the events is changed. The unbelievable becomes creditable. That at least is what the Evangelists believed and sought to convey to their readers.

Chapter II

THE SYNOPTIC VIEW OF JESUS: WHAT DID JESUS DO?

HAVING considered impressions of the person or nature of Jesus in the Synoptic Gospels, we focus attention in this chapter on his work. This involves three general items: his message, his miracles, and his suffering and death. The authoritative bearing of Jesus previously assumed and elaborated is presupposed here as well. Although the emphasis falls more upon what Jesus did than upon who he was, it is only a matter of selective attention. Of necessity the status and significance of the Messenger and the question of his self-understanding are forced into prominence even when they are not explicitly in focus. Actually, the concentration upon Jesus' message and actions serves to complete or to amplify impressions of the functional nature of titles and categories of thought previously considered. Both approaches must be combined in the interests of a full picture of the Gospel-perspective.

THE MESSAGE OF THE KINGDOM

By way of prolegomena to the message of Jesus two questions should concern us briefly. The first is the question raised with respect to Mark's view of Jesus by Eduard Schweizer's thesis that "the fact of his teaching is decisive, not its content." What is important is not what Jesus taught, "the words which can be handed down and repeated," but the authority of God's power manifested in his teaching. "What Mark states is simply

the fact that God himself encountered men in Jesus' teaching."
The teaching is thus "often paralleled with Jesus' miracles" as
demonstrations of Jesus' authority over the demons, both
teaching and miracles representing "the heavenly dimension
in which God himself breaks into the world."[1] The one exception to this in Mark is the prediction of the passion at Caesarea
Philippi viewed as "the divine revelation hidden from the
blindness of the world."[2]

There is something to be said for this view. Mark does emphasize the "authority" of the teacher, and the pattern of blindness to Jesus' real meaning is prominent. Jesus' failure to teach
as systematically as in Matthew and Luke also provides support. However, the theory rests upon too narrow a base, that
is, the alleged vocabulary of Mark peculiar to the connecting
links between his pericopes. It does not stand up when the
Gospel as a whole is considered, and especially when Mark's
prologue is taken to include, as it probably should, the summary of his preaching in ch. 1:14–15.[3] When full weight is
given to Mark's "discourses" in chs. 4 and 13, to the varieties
of themes that appear in various stories, sayings, and parables,
it is not reasonable to discount the value for Mark of the content of Jesus' message. Although Matthew and Luke obviously
concern themselves more systematically with the content of
Jesus' teaching, it would appear that they but develop an interest that is also present in Mark.

The real question with regard to the Evangelists is not properly posed in setting the "fact" of Jesus' teaching over against
its "content." The real question is the *kind* of content that it is
believed that God authoritatively reveals in and through Jesus.
The unique contribution of the Synoptic Gospels within the
total complex of the New Testament is to provide content from
the preresurrection days for the good news. For Mark as well
as for Matthew and Luke this includes the specific substance
of Jesus' message. The impression of the finished Gospel of
Mark, as of the other Synoptics, is that the fact of Jesus' teaching and its substance belong together like hand and glove,
neither one of which makes sense without the other.

The second consideration is that of the form of Jesus' teaching, primarily as it bears upon the message and the Messenger. Three facets of this subject will concern us here. First, there is the typical nature of what has been called the "pronouncement story," providing a narrative setting for a general saying of Jesus, such as the word about the Sabbath or about paying tribute to Caesar. Addressed by the Evangelist to his specific readers in a circumscribed situation, Jesus' authoritative view on the point at issue takes on the nature of a summary or typical teaching which covers later situations as well as the original one. Other sayings and parables also share this characteristic. Narratives as well, such as the healing of Bartimaeus, sum up Jesus' offer of salvation in a miniature gospel as it were.

Second, there is also the concern to systematize Jesus' teaching topically, as in Mark, chs. 4 and 13, Matt., chs. 5 to 7, and additional discourses, Luke 9:51 to 18:15; and Luke, ch. 15. Combining the proclamation of the gospel in general terms with attention to specific teaching relative to issues confronting the readers of the Gospel, this tendency is widespread throughout the three Synoptics, if most extensively in Matthew and Luke.

Third, as Amos Wilder points out, there is the significant factor of form of utterance in relation to content, the former being indicative of the experience and thought that seeks expression.[4] As this applies to the Gospels we have the writing down of what was originally oral communication. Jesus' oral communication presupposes a face-to-face confrontation, a "naïve and *extempore* language" directed to the occasion. As against an antiquarian interest or one completely absorbed in the future, this very manner of address in oral form reflects an intense awareness of God in the present. On the other hand, "the act of writing presupposes continuities and a future."[5] Something of Jesus' spontaneity was lost when his oral utterances were transmitted to the written page (in translated form) and adapted to later sets of circumstances.

This can be exaggerated, however, since the records as they stand bespeak a unique person who, while employing some forms of utterance common to himself and his Jewish contemporaries, is markedly different as well. Especially in the parables, we sense a uniquely consistent tendency to keep eternal considerations relevant to the real world of the present. As compared with Jewish teachers there is a newness in Jesus' thought which carries the Jewish outlook to a new stage due to the form of utterance as well as to its content. In this sense the mystery of Jesus' person is reflected in his modes of speech as well as in what they contain.[6] Despite their adaptation of Jesus' message to later and different situations, the Gospels retain impressions of this fact.

The Eschatological Crisis

The title of this section comes from Mark's impression of the message of Jesus: "The time is fulfilled, and the kingdom of God is at hand; repent, and believe in the gospel" (ch. 1:15). This note of eschatological crisis also permeates the reports of Jesus' message in general and is indicated in many of his actions. The question of eschatology, however, is not uncomplicated, since the Gospel portraits are not completely self-consistent. Our main concern here is to ask what impressions the Gospels give when all the relevant data are brought together and classified.

The source material should not be limited narrowly to Kingdom of God sayings. The criterion is the relevance of any saying or any event to the eschatological crisis that the Gospels assume to have been created by Jesus' appearance and work. The question may be refined further to focus attention upon the relationship between sayings that envisage a future development or event and those which concern God's activity in the present. In this latter sense the term "Kingdom" or "reign" of God is taken to mean his "effective action."

We shall proceed by classifying the sayings into two groups: those with a future emphasis and those with a present emphasis. We shall ask what is said in the former group about the time and the nature of the future event that is envisaged. With the latter sayings in view, we shall ask what is said about God's effective action in the present. We shall also consider the place that Jesus is portrayed as having in each type.

Considering the future references first, we take for granted that any reader of the Gospels is aware of the many sayings of Jesus which come under this heading. Some are of a quite general nature, whether referring to "the age to come" (Mark 10:30) or simply to a future time, whereas others are very specific about a future consummation as in the judgment scene in Matt. 25:31–46.

The temporal question is simply whether the future judgment or consummation is expected in the imminent future or whether the element of time is indefinite or ambiguous. The bulk of the material belongs in the latter category. The future tenses of the Beatitudes, for example, do not specify when the meek "shall inherit the earth" or when the pure in heart "shall see God." The original Aramaic verbs make no distinction between present and future tenses. The judgment scene in Matt. 25:31–46 is in the future, but we are not told whether it will come soon or late. To a great extent this is the case with the data as a whole, and we assume it as a fact.

The important question is that of the extent to which the materials suggest an imminent event. This question is complicated by the fact that sayings that carry a note of urgency may not so much have in view a sequence of time as the pressure of God's sovereignty for radical action. Granting this ambiguity in many instances, some sayings appear to imply a temporal element. Typical examples may be cited in support of this view.

The interpretation of the verb *engizō* in its perfect tense is a crucial matter in this area. In Mark 1:15, for example, should it be taken to mean "is at hand," just around the corner but still future, or "has come," is now here? Scholars are divided on the answer, but those who argue the case for the future emphasis appear to us to have the better of the argument.[7] There are several parables that emphasize the crucial importance of being alert for the unexpected return of an absentee master or ruler (e.g., Mark 13:33–37; Luke 12:35–36; Matt. 25:1–13).

If the emphasis upon an unexpected crisis means anything, it has the immediate future in view. One does not get excited about an unexpected event that is to occur vaguely in a distant future. In addition there are the Marcan sayings which are explicit about the imminence of the Kingdom's coming: "There are some standing here who will not taste death before they see the kingdom of God come with power" (Mark 9:1); "This generation will not pass away before all these things take place" (ch. 13:30); the lesson of the fig tree that "when you see these things taking place, you know that he [the Son of Man] is near, at the very gate" (v. 29); and the implication of the fact that "Elijah has come" (ch. 9:12–13).

Matthew and Luke add other sayings. From Q is the saying about the blood of the prophets being required "of this generation" and about the day of the Son of Man.[8] Matthew 10:23 adds, "You [the disciples] will not have gone through all the towns of Israel, before the Son of man comes." The parable of the rich fool in Luke 12:13–21, like the statement of Jesus to the thief on the cross about being in paradise with him "today" (ch. 23:43), may have any kind of imminent crisis in view, but the sense of temporal urgency is present. Many other sayings stress the urgency of decision without explicit reference to the End.

Leaving this body of material as it stands for the moment, let us consider impressions of Jesus' views about the nature of the future consummation. This breaks down into two interrelated questions: Is Jesus' teaching imbued with an apocalyptic cast in form and content, comparable to that of typical Jewish apocalypses and the Revelation of John?[9] Second, in the final judgment what criteria will be employed to distinguish between good and evil? Specifically, will they be nationalistic or universalistic in character?

With regard to the first question, there are evidences of the apocalyptic world view and methodology. This is particularly true of the "Little Apocalyse" in Mark, ch. 13, and parallels in Matt., ch. 24, and Luke, ch. 21, but it is not limited to these. Here we observe the apocalyptist's habit of thinking in cosmic dimensions as against the prophetic concentration upon this world in terms of the future of national units. There is a transcendent dimension including supernatural beings such as Satan, angels, and demons. There is a conception of a future life for the individual along with the consummation and its judgment. The presuppositions of demon possession and exorcism are consistent with this. The conflict between cosmic battalions in heaven has its earthly counterpart in the form of persecution of the faithful and of warfare between nations. Some of these characteristics are reflected in Mark, ch. 13, and parallels. This is the case even with Luke's seemingly more specific historical reference to "Jerusalem surrounded by armies" and to its eventual destruction (ch. 21:20, 24).

Apocalypticism is characterized as well by a predeterminism which involves a rather inflexible program of events leading up to the consummation. We have observed something of this in Jesus' sayings about the imminence of the Kingdom's coming and in the passion predictions. Mark, ch. 13, as a whole represents this pattern. The shortening of the days for the sake of the elect (v. 20) does not contradict this, since God may make some slight deviation in the schedule without altering the plan as a whole. Ignorance of the exact day or hour (v. 32), since it probably means the split second of the time of the consummation, does not change the overall pattern.

With all of this, the Gospels do not represent a consistent picture in this respect. As has been said, the bulk of the future references are ambiguous as far as the time factor is concerned. They need not be read within an apocalyptic frame of reference. Jesus' call to repentance, to be treated later, does not necessarily presuppose the apocalyptic tension, despite the urgency of the call to decision. And there is the report of Jesus' refusal to give a sign (Mark 8:12), at least not beyond "the sign of Jonah," which refers to the religious and ethical import of his message without apocalyptic overtones (Luke 11:29–32 and Matt. 12:39–41).

The case against the view that Jesus is pictured as a thoroughgoing apocalyptist can be more decisively stated. This is as true of Matthew's heightened apocalyptic picture as of the other Synoptists. Almost completely absent from the Gospels are any indications that Jesus employed the methodology of apocalypticism: visions and voices as the means of divine-human communication, the fulfillment of esoteric prophecies, the weird symbolism of beasts and numbers. His use of parables constitutes a completely different medium of communication, with connotations of God's self-revelation in "natural" ways. Furthermore, as against the tendency to exaggerate the remoteness of God, Jesus assumes his approachableness and his knowledge of our needs before we ask.[10]

Turning to the question of the criteria of judgment in the consummation, we remain for the moment within the framework of the apocalytic question. Apocalypticism often tended toward a sublimated nationalism, viewing the judgment as a vindication of the holy community that was being persecuted by the enemies of God. This is the situation in Daniel (e.g., ch. 7:22). The earlier prophetic conviction that God used foreign nations to punish Israel is necessarily absent from this outlook. Paradoxically there is implied in the apocalyptic view an individualism in judgment with reference to faithfulness under fire.

As portrayed in the Gospels, the attitude of Jesus touches the apocalyptic perspective only at the point of individualism. Although the Gospels picture Jesus' judgment of a group, as in the parable of the wicked tenants, generally the perspective is that of the individual standing alone before God. The judgment scene in Matt. 25:31–46 is typical, and it is especially significant because of its transcendental setting. This is consistent with the undeviating impression of Jesus' teaching that, like the prophets, he viewed the final judgment as a moral trial without any favored-nation bias whatsoever.

This brings into focus Jesus' attitude toward Gentiles in general. With the possible exception of the sending of the Seventy in Luke 10:1 ff., Jesus does not undertake a mission to Gentiles. Isolated sayings in Matt. 10:5 f. and 15:24 expressly forbid it. However, there is no hostility to Gentiles, and, when they come to him, they are received with sympathy. The story of the Syrophoenician woman in Mark ends with the healing of the woman's child. In the story of the centurion's servant in Q the faith of the Gentile is contrasted with the lack of faith in Israel. The Nazareth sermon and the parable of the good Samaritan speak for a major emphasis in Luke.

This note is stressed in Jesus' sayings about the criteria of judgment. "Men will come from east and west, and from north and south, and sit at table in the kingdom of God," and in many instances judgment will be unfavorable to the Jews (Luke 13:27-29 and Matt. 8:11-12). As in Matt. 25:31-46, the judgment will be a moral trial where everything having to do with earthly status is irrelevant in the face of God's concern for obedience to his moral will. Many sayings of Jesus reinforce this, and behind them stand others completely consistent with them, such as those about loving one's enemies. The latter stand in sharp contrast to the outlook of the Qumran community. This trend of thought in Jesus' sayings is too self-evident in the Gospels to require further documentation.

Consistent with this as well are the few references to a Gentile mission in the interval between Jesus' resurrection and parousia, such as Mark 13:10, "The gospel must first be preached to all nations"; or Matt. 28:19, "Go therefore and make disciples of all nations"; or Luke 24:46-47, "Thus it is written, . . . that repentance and forgiveness of sins should be preached in his name to all nations." (Also see Acts 1:8.) Within the context of Mark's situation the pericope about the Syrophoenician woman was probably intended to encourage such an outlook as well. In these and other ways the Gospel portraits are consistent with the universalism of Paul and other missionaries to the Gentiles. To that extent they cannot be understood as placing Jesus entirely within a rigid apocalyptic pattern.

In this section it remains only to ask about the place in the final events which is envisaged for Jesus himself. The Son of Man sayings with an eschatological orientation need not be reviewed here, except for the reminder that in this form of the tradition Jesus is understood by the Evangelists as the Son of Man who comes in judgment. The vital question is that raised by J. A. T. Robinson in distinguishing between what he calls the themes of "vindication" and "visitation."[11] That is, does the emphasis in the Gospels fall upon the idea of Jesus' "coming" a second time, a parousia, or upon his vindication and exaltation after death? Except for the Son of Man sayings, especially in the form of Matthew's editorial revisions of Mark and Q, practically nothing in Jesus' teaching refers to his coming again. Mark 9:1 and Luke 9:27 speak of the Kingdom of God coming, with Matthew substituting the term "Son of man" for "kingdom of God." Other Kingdom of God references are similar, without the return of Jesus being contemplated. That is, the idea of visitation is largely confined to the Son of Man tradition, predominantly in its Matthean forms.

Over against this, many references to the future envisage Jesus' vindication. This is the force of the reference to Jesus' resurrection in the passion predictions and related sayings. In Mark other sayings point in this direction. Whether or not Jesus and Son of Man are to be distinguished in Mark 8:38, acceptance of Jesus' person and words is the criterion of future judgment, as is also the case in ch. 10:29–30, without a reference to the Son of Man. The promise of Jesus' redemptive significance as a "ransom for many" belongs within this frame of reference along with the idea that his death will be heralded throughout the world (ch. 14:8–9). References to Jesus' being made the head of the corner (ch. 12:10 f.) and participating in the messianic banquet (ch. 14:25) also cohere at this point. Speaking for the Evangelist, the sons of Zebedee anticipate Jesus' future "glory" (ch. 10:37).

The most distinctive Q saying is that about Jesus and the disciples sitting on twelve thrones in judgment (Luke 22:28–30), with Matt. 19:28 including a Son of Man reference. Implications of Jesus' vindication also appear in reference to the blood of the prophets required of this generation and the lament over Jerusalem. The parable of the houses is consistent with this theme too.

The idea that Peter is the rock upon which the church will be erected, Matthew's addition to Mark's Caesarea Philippi pericope, is his main contribution beyond Son of Man sayings. Luke adds the idea that the time has come for Jesus, setting his face toward Jerusalem, to be "received up" (ch. 9:51) and the words to the thief on the cross, "Today you will be with me in Paradise."

With all this evidence in mind, we may perhaps say that in the Gospels the emphasis falls upon the idea of vindication rather than visitation. The implications of Jesus' authority while on earth buttress this impression. However, for the Evangelists the visitation theme is woven into the pattern in such a way as to suggest that they considered the two to go together. Both elements inform the Gospel picture of Jesus, with Matthew more emphatic than Mark and Luke about visitation without materially altering their perspectives.

We may now turn from futuristic sayings to consider those with a present emphasis and orientation. By way of transition let us recall the saying in Luke 17:20–21. Replying to the question of the Pharisees about the time of the Kingdom's coming, Jesus says: "The kingdom of God is not coming with signs to be observed; nor will they say, 'Lo, here it is!' or 'There!' for behold, the kingdom of God is within [in the midst of?] you." The ambiguity of the preposition *entos* does not permit us to be sure which translation to prefer, "within" or "in the midst of," but either one implies an act in the present. If we employ the latter, another ambiguity arises. Is the reference to the effective power of God in general being present or to his power working uniquely in Jesus—or both? On the whole the Kingdom of God sayings largely, but not entirely, support the former. When all the relevant material is included, however, a good many sayings indicate Jesus as the one in whom the effective power of God is being uniquely manifested.

But let us classify the data and thus see what the picture in the Gospels is. We shall consider first references to the present which assume God's direct action and then consider testimony to Jesus' unique position within this framework. The material may be classified in three main groups.

Several sayings speak about entering the Kingdom of God, the precise time of this action being often ambiguous. The saying in Mark 9:47 may have the future judgment in view, but, if the entering is a present act with future consequences, this is not certain. The same question attaches to Mark 10:15, but a present possibility is suggested in the context of the saying which follows about the difficulty of rich men entering the Kingdom. In the ensuing conversation between Jesus and his disciples he explicitly contrasts rewards "now in this time" and "in the age to come."

A present possibility is implied in Matthew's form of the Q saying criticizing those who prevent others from entering the Kingdom by their own failure to practice what they preach (Matt. 23:13). Even more emphatic on entrance as a present act is the Lucan form of another Q saying: "Since then the good news of the kingdom of God is preached, and every one enters it violently" (Luke 16:16). Uncertainty as to a present or a future experience remains in three additional Matthean references. It would appear that the scales have to be tipped, if at all, by other sayings that are more definite about the possibility of entering into an effective relationship with God now. That there are such sayings we shall see presently.

The parables of the seed growing secretly and the mustard seed, along with the parable of the leaven in Q, all "Kingdom parables," join with the parable of the sower in Mark, ch. 4, to call for faith in the effective action of God in the present (and in the future). Each parable has its own specific point, but they have this feature in common. Whether the idea be that the Kingdom is a growing thing or that God can produce wondrous results, the theme of God working here and now is clear. The saying in Luke 12:32 about the Father's intention to give the Kingdom, supported by the Q saying about God's overwhelming graciousness in giving the Holy Spirit to those who ask (Luke 11:13 and Matt. 7:11), cohere with this.

Several sayings imply the idea of realized discipleship in the present, which is another way of saying that the power of God's reign can be experienced now. Various specific teachings are expressed, but it is the realized feature that alone concerns us here. In Mark are the sayings about the Kingdom belonging to little children (ch. 10:14) and the approval of the scribe who is "not far from the kingdom of God" (ch. 12:34). Two of the Beatitudes imply realized discipleship in more than the tense of the verb: "the poor in spirit" and the "persecuted." Also in Q is the reference to "the least in the kingdom of God," Jesus' disciples at the moment in contrast to the Baptist. To seek the Kingdom implies that it is something that can be found here and now. The injunction to be alert to the signs of the times implies something that is active at the moment.

Matthew's parable of the weeds that are allowed to grow along with the good grain until the harvest implies that the good grain bears symbolically the mark of God's operation in the present. The parables of the pearl of great price and of the treasure hidden in the field, stressing the supreme value of the Kingdom, take for granted its potency in the life of the disciple at the moment. And unless something is expected to happen in the contemporary circumstances of the pray-er, why should one be expected to pray, "Thy will be done, on earth as it is in heaven"? For Matthew there is a sense in which the Kingdom comes when God's will is done, even if that does not exhaust the meaning of the petition.

When we set these sayings with a present note alongside many others with religious and ethical connotations for life in the present, it is obvious that in this type of expression God's effective action has a present as well as a future significance. This is reinforced by references, now to be considered, in which the teaching and activity of Jesus are taken by him to be indicative of God at work in a unique way in the present time.

In order to avoid needless repetition in portraying the Gospel impressions of Jesus' sense of something unique happening in and through his ministry, let us presuppose everything of a relevant nature set forth in the preceding chapter. Let us also for the moment eliminate considerations subsequently to concern us regarding the urgency of Jesus' call to decision and the miracles, especially the exorcism of demons. Let us concentrate narrowly upon additional sayings in which Jesus appears to be aware of something new coming to expression in him or in which his intention is explicitly voiced with reference to the present.

Beginning with sayings in which "kingdom of God" is used, there is Jesus' consciousness of an authority consistent with one who holds and dispenses "the mystery of the kingdom of God" or who gives "the keys of the kingdom of heaven." Consistent with this are sayings, in addition to those previously cited which employ *exousia* ("authority"), about Jesus' gratitude to the Father for delivering "all things" to the Son, about the reception of a child being equivalent to receiving him and the One who sent him, and about his ability to give "rest" to weary seekers. Cohering with this is the divine approval of Jesus voiced at baptism, at the transfiguration, and implied in the cleansing of the Temple. The call, instruction, and sending out of the disciples also belong in this category.

The newness of what is being accomplished in and through Jesus in the present comes out in the thought that since John the Baptist "the good news of the kingdom of God is preached." The new era is sharply distinguished from that of "the law and the prophets" which reached its culmination in the Baptist. This is the kingdom of God "in your midst." The "I came" sayings relate to this theme, echoing the Son of Man saying in Luke 19:10. They are: "I came not to call the righteous, but sinners" (Mark 2:17); "I came to cast fire upon the earth" (Luke 12:49); "I have not come to bring peace, but a sword" (Matt. 10:34). More positively, Jesus has come to fulfill the Law and the Prophets, as his baptism by John was a fulfillment of all righteousness.

Corresponding to the figure of children playing in the marketplace among the Son of Man sayings, in Mark 2:19 f. Jesus likens himself to a bridegroom whose very presence bespeaks a joyous occasion. More directly Jesus speaks of himself, or of that which is embodied in him and expressed through him, as "something greater than Jonah," greater even than "the temple" (Luke 11:32 and Matt. 12:41; Matt. 12:6). Summing up much of this type of appraisal are the words of Jesus to the disciples: "Blessed are the eyes which see what you see" (Luke 10:23 and Matt. 13:16).

Looking back over this entire section, it is easy to see how several schools of thought could arise with respect to what the historical Jesus actually taught about the relationship between the future and the present aspects of the Kingdom of God. Norman Perrin has traced this story since the beginning of the century in *The Kingdom of God in the Teaching of Jesus*.[12] Three major views emerge. Two take extreme positions, emphasizing either the future or the present element to the virtual exclusion of the other, whereas the third maintains tension between them. The Gospels as they stand mainly provide support for the tension hypothesis. This is the Synoptic perspective. As we shall see in the next chapter, it is not the Johannine perspective. Whether or not it is the view of the Jesus of history is not for the moment our concern.

Religious and Ethical Content of Jesus' Message

Whether the Kingdom's coming be expected, temporally speaking, soon or late, the message of Jesus contains a clear-cut call to decision. To this extent it involves action to be taken in the present. This applies particularly to the element of urgency which comes to expression on many occasions. This is most evident in the parables in which the admonition to watch for the unexpected coming is the thought, but it is not confined to them. Among sayings of Jesus not previously considered are the following, which are typical of others. In Mark there is the demand for radical obedience, even to the extent of sacrificing a vital member of the body (ch. 9:47), and the implications of the demand that the rich young man dispose of all his worldly possessions on behalf of the poor (ch. 10:21). Q adds several more under the general heading of the thought that "you cannot serve God and mammon" (Luke 16:13 and Matt. 6:24). Most emphatic is the admonition to settle a dispute out of court before it comes to trial (Luke 12:58 f. and Matt. 5:25 f.). The parable of the ten virgins is typical of much in

Matthew relevant to this theme. In Luke the parable of the rich man and Lazarus carries the sense of urgency in its closing words to the rich man who has asked that his brothers on earth be warned to avoid his fate while there is still time: "If they do not hear Moses and the prophets, neither will they be convinced if some one should rise from the dead" (ch. 16:31). The parable of the fig tree in ch. 13:6–9 bespeaks the same urgency.

We may consider these evidences of urgency in Jesus' call to decision as a sort of transition to the subject of religious and ethical content in his message. Remaining for the moment within the context of the call to decision, we ask more particularly about the nature of the response that Jesus is represented as expecting.

A predominant theme in Jesus' teaching in Mark is the imperative: "He who has ears to hear, let him hear" (ch. 4:9). In every source there are abundant echoes of this theme. The force of this in the Gospels, corresponding to Paul's emphasis upon faith, is the idea that, however gracious God may be, his gift of salvation must be accepted by man if it is to be effective. Negatively expressed, man is capable of what is called blasphemy against the Holy Spirit, which so disables his sensitivity to God's offer that he cannot respond to it. When this terrible condition exists man remains unforgiven, not because God ever stops offering his mercy, but simply because man fails to recognize it and accept it.

Within this large framework of response in general, it is interesting to observe how overwhelming is Jesus' insistence upon the need for insight, the need to perceive what is observed, to understand what is heard. This is the thought of Isa. 6:9–10 taken up into the Gospel materials, especially with reference to the parables. As with David when confronted by Nathan's parable of the ewe lamb, the story as such has an application that may be missed without insight and imagination.[13] Evidences of Jesus' demand for this qualitative kind of response are abundant in the Gospels, so much so that a few typical examples will suffice by way of illustration.

The Beelzebul controversy in Mark 3:24–30 turns on this point. Even a modicum of imagination should make it self-evident that Satan would not be trying to destroy himself. The rejection of Jesus at Nazareth is due to the failure of Jesus' neighbors to look beneath the surface of their familiarity with his family. The inability of the disciples to overcome their traditional ways of thinking in the face of Jesus' passion predictions and the request of the Zebedee brothers for preferred status in the future highlight the need for insight.

Q sayings are consistent with this. In the parable of the houses the contrast turns upon wisdom and foolishness, a way of saying that insight is required. The failure to be self-critical in exaggerating the faults of others, employing the symbols of log and speck, illustrates the same blindness (Luke 6:41 f., par.). Sensitivity to the meaning of the "sign of Jonah" requires that one's eye be "sound" (ch. 11:29–32, 34, par.). The prospect for Jerusalem is a desolate one because of inability to be discerning about history and the meaning of Jesus (ch. 12:34 f., par.).

In Matthew the purity of heart prerequisite to seeing God bespeaks sincerity, but this in turn presupposes insight. False piety in almsgiving, prayer, and fasting illustrates an undiscerning mind and spirit (Matt. 6:1–18). Many of the criticisms of the scribes and Pharisees enumerated in ch. 23:1–36 presuppose this kind of failure. In Luke, discernment is required to apply rightly to oneself the lesson of certain current events such as Pilate's slaughter of Galileans or an industrial accident in Siloam (ch. 13:1–5). The elder brother's attitude in the parable of the prodigal son represents something more than a lack of discernment, but it is included.

Even in the resurrection narratives the true significance of what is happening in the appearances might be missed until eyes are opened to *perceive* the reality (e.g., Luke 24:31–32; Matt. 28:17). Those who continued to oppose the Christian movement after the resurrection were persisting in the same kind of blindness about which Jesus had had so much to say before his death.

There are more specific characterizations of the kind of response that is required in order to rise to the challenge of the gospel. Two of these are set forth in Mark 1:15: repentance and faith. Comparatively speaking, the direct appeal to repentance is relatively rare, whether employing the term *metanoein* ("repent") or *epistrephein* ("turn about"), but the thought underlies much else. The idea of turning about, reorienting oneself about a new center, is the basic idea, inclusive of but not exhausted by remorse at past failures.

References to belief or faith are much more abundant. In some instances this is the positive thrust that implements healing. In other examples it is the trust thta enables God's power to flood the person's spirit to such an extent that, as with Paul and his thorn, mountainous difficulties are reduced to manageable proportions (Mark 11:23, par.). In Matthew the refrain of "O men of little faith!" versus its positive counterpart is a major theme, notably with reference to trusting God's intention and capacity in creation (cf. Matt. 6:25–34). In most cases to believe or to have faith is to combine discernment with commitment in such a way as to overcome the inhibiting force of doubt, doubt about the good news in general or about Jesus' capacity to channel God's power for healing.

Another type of appeal emphasizes obedience to God's will. The petition in Matthew's version of the Lord's Prayer comes immediately to mind: "Thy will be done, On earth as it is in heaven." This is Matthew's commentary on the equally God-centered petition, "Thy kingdom come." In the contrast drawn between lip service and obedience, the version in Matthew explicitly introduces the thought of doing God's will (ch. 7:21). Two Marcan references typify much else in employing the term "will." One is Jesus' own example in Gethsemane: "Not what I will, but what thou wilt." The other consists of the words of Jesus with reference to his family: "Whoever does the will of God is my brother, and sister, and mother." Various references to bearing fruit cohere with these statements. References in which the term "righteousness" is employed are also relevant, as when seeking the Kingdom first is equated with seeking God's righteousness. Capping the climax is the great commandment: "You shall love the Lord your God with all your heart, and with all your soul, and with all your mind, and with all your strength."

These sayings are perhaps the most explicit evidences of Jesus' emphasis upon the necessity of doing God's will as an adequate response to him, but the idea is rampant throughout the Gospels in less explicit forms. The disobedience of the tenants in the parable of the wicked tenants, for example, indicates this, as well as Jesus' own positive example in the temptation narratives. Since the list is endless, it is unnecessary to cite further illustrations.

Closely related to this is what is said about following Jesus. Aside from many uses of the verb *akolouthein* ("to follow") in general, there are specific applications of the word to Jesus' message on discipleship. The narrower sense is illustrated in the call of Peter, the Zebedee brothers, and Levi. In each case Jesus commands, "Follow me!" Luke 22:28 records Jesus' statement addressed to his intimates at a later time: "You are those who have continued [followed] with me in my trials."

With the larger group of disciples in view Jesus says, "If any man would come after me, let him deny himself and take up his cross and follow me" (Mark 8:34); and the imperative is repeated to the rich young man. The theme of following is found in three instances in which Jesus finds it necessary to warn the prospective disciple against thoughtlessness in taking up with him (Luke 9:57–62 and Matt. 8:19–22). Matthew's version of Jesus' offer to the weary stresses the relative lightness of his yoke without discounting its reality (ch. 11:28–30). When combined with other sayings these references suggest that to follow Jesus is to do God's will as he does.

Another type of response is prayer. That this is also evidence of a depth of spirituality and trust characteristic of the experienced follower does not make it less a way of reacting to God's offer of salvation. We take for granted evidences in the Gospels, especially highlighted in Luke, that Jesus was a man of prayer. Our interest centers upon what Jesus says about the subject within the present context.

Prayer is efficacious in the exorcism of demons (Mark 9:29), in facing seemingly insurmountable obstacles (ch. 11:24), in enduring persecution bravely and with insight (ch. 13:11), in the times of testing (Luke 11:4 and Matt. 6:13). One should pray for the Kingdom's coming (Luke 11:2 and Matt. 6:10a). Prayer is the proper mood with reference to the expected parousia of Jesus (Mark 13:33). If one is to deal properly with one's persecutors, it is essential that the whole issue be brought into the presence of God: "Pray for those who abuse you" (Luke 6:28 and Matt. 5:44). Only out of prayerful sensitivity to God's own forgiving Spirit can a forgiving attitude emerge (Luke 11:4 and Matt. 6:12).

It is prayer that chiefly demonstrates and stimulates other types of response. Sincere obedience to God's will is a prerequisite, as one prays steadily that God's sovereignty be acknowledged and that insincerity and false piety be eliminated. In this spirit the Temple becomes what it basically should be, "a house of prayer" (Mark 11:17). Faith in God is also prerequisite, prayer becoming truly vital in the realization that God offers more than we can possibly imagine (Luke 11:9–13 and Matt. 7:7–11). By contrast with the man who was reluctant to rouse himself in the middle of the night to help his neighbor, "how much more" can God be expected to be receptive to us (Luke 11:5–8)! Since God already knows our need before we ask (Matt. 6:8) and since he is already predisposed to meet that need, prayer is at root acknowledging him and opening our heart to him. In fact, it is the supreme means of responding to him, comprehending all other types of response.

In the treatment of Jesus' thought up to this point much has been implied about its religious and ethical content. It remains only, if somewhat more systematically, to indicate the staples of his teaching about God and the nature of discipleship as the Synoptic Evangelists portray them. This type of procedure in a topical way introduces theoretical considerations which are not fully overt in the Gospels, since there is little indication that Jesus systematized his teaching. On the other hand, it is not entirely inconsistent with the outlook and methods of the

Evangelists. There is a content attributed to Jesus' teaching and there is some attention to a topical arrangement of that teaching. It is the Gospels themselves that present Jesus' summary of the great commandments under the headings of love of God and love of neighbor. In discussing the content of Jesus' thought we shall follow that lead. What conception of God is implied? And what is implied about the nature of the ethical life?

Jesus gives no systematic teaching about the nature of God, but a content is implied in everything that he says and does. He does speak often of God. The specific terms are *Theos* ("God"), *Kyrios* ("Lord"), *Patēr* ("Father"). The unusual term *Abba* is employed once, in Mark 14:36, and only twice more in the New Testament. It is the use of the term "Father" which is most significant, especially the distribution of its use.[14] Whereas the term is used in material peculiar to Matthew some twenty-three times, and thirty-two times in Matthew as a whole, Mark has the term only four times, Q eight times, and Luke thirteen times, only six of which are peculiar to Luke. A further breakdown results in the following distinctions: "his Father" or "their Father" or "your Father": 15; "the Father" or "one Father": 5; "our Father": 1; "my Father": 19; "Father" in direct address: 6.

With reference to the views of the Evangelists these statistics suggest two basic things. While in some quarters a certain reticence was envisaged on the part of Jesus in using the term "Father," in other circles it was taken to be his most characteristic way of addressing and thinking about God. The unusual nature of employing the title in direct address, over against the tendency in Judaism not to pronounce the divine name at all and especially not to talk about "my Father," suggests the unique degree of intimacy that the Evangelists believed to be characteristic of Jesus' relationship to God. This fact has been correctly discerned and emphasized by outstanding books on Jesus, those by Bornkamm and T. W. Manson for example. As Bornkamm puts it: "The reality of God and the authority of his will are always directly present, and are fulfilled in him. There is nothing in contemporary Judaism which corresponds to the immediacy (*Unmittelbarkeit*) with which he teaches."[15] Manson's contribution is to emphasize the intensity with which the sovereignty and the Fatherhood of God are experienced by Jesus as a present reality, rather than as an article in a creed.[16] Since Fatherhood involves Creatorship as well as acceptance of responsibility for the creation, it is a comprehensive conception. While Bornkamm and Manson are speaking for the mind of the historical Jesus, they are also stating the mind of the Evangelists in this respect. The same may be said for J. Jeremias' view that in Jesus' use of *Abba* "we are confronted with something new and unheard of which breaks through the limits of Judaism."[17]

It is this intensity of Jesus' realization of God in his experience which leads into the heart of his message about God. It is this which makes it "new." An aspect of this newness may well be the announcement, according to Bultmann, that in "his presence, his deeds, his message," "God's Reign is breaking in."[18] It is even more the way in which God and man are "de-historized," in the sense that God "lifts man out of his worldly ties and places him directly before His own eyes."[19] Once again, while attempting to portray the Jesus of history, the writer is describing the impressions of the Gospels as they stand.

To say this still leaves the matter of content about God's nature uncertain, so that it is necessary to go farther. This opens up the question of newness or uniqueness in Jesus' thought in general. In order to lay bare significant ideas peculiar to Jesus, Norman Perrin applies a strict criterion of dissimilarity from the emphases of Judaism and of early Christianity.[20] This means discarding much material as not characteristic of Jesus of Nazareth. The Gospels make no such distinction, partly because they tend to identify Jesus of Nazareth and resurrected Christ to a certain extent. It is also in part due to the fact that they define newness or originality in a different way. For example, the new feature in Jesus' stance as contrasted with that of the scribe is not new at all. It is a recovery of the prophetic spirit and manner of response to God. With regard to Jesus' thought of God, he is but emphasizing features already expressed in the Hebrew Scriptures. What is new is the dynamic synthesis that he creates in deed as well as in word.

The result is that, while adding little that is essentially new to traditional ideas of God's sovereignty and mercy, Jesus takes them so seriously that they appear as a paradox in his message. On the one hand he states God's sovereignty, involving his justice, in absolute terms. God never compromises with Satan. Jesus reflects this in his own responses in the temptation narratives, in Gethsemane, and abundantly elsewhere. In the judgment scene in Matt., ch. 25, the line between "eternal punishment" and "eternal life" is sharply and uncompromisingly drawn. Blasphemy against the Holy Spirit "never has forgiveness" (Mark 3:29). This absolutistic rigidity runs through the records of Jesus' teaching. On the other hand, the graciousness of God in dealing with repentant sinners is just as intensely and absolutely stated. The parable of the prodigal son is typical of sayings in this category. Behind the demand to forgive "seventy times seven" stands God's own example (Matt. 18:22). Jesus' coming to seek and save the lost, embodied in his constant attention to tax collectors and sinners, bespeaks the God who seeks the lost sheep until he finds it. The cross reveals the extent to which God goes in offering himself and his salvation to mankind.

The result of all of this in the Synoptics is a paradox that is never resolved philosophically. The two extremes stand side by side, just as in Matthew a certain particularism and a broad universalism stand without logical resolution (cf. chs. 10:5 f.; 28:19). The Evangelists do not ask how this paradox is resolved, or even if it is resolved in Jesus' thought of the divine mind. They are content to portray Jesus' view of God as containing these extreme emphases. The essential point is that Jesus' intense awareness of and obedience to God is thereby set forth. There is something here of the Semitic temperament that is capable of pursuing "the logic of several incompatible opinions to absurd ends, without perceiving the incongruity."[21] Even more there is appreciation of a person who takes God so seriously and so realistically that no other result is possible, including the faith that is content to leave to God the ultimate resolution of what appears to be an insoluble paradox. Thus, despite the paradox, the note of joyful confidence in God is the prevailing atmosphere of the proclamation of the good news.

Perhaps the least unambiguous aspect of Jesus' message is its ethical content viewed as response to the will of God, as it is set within the context of Jewish legalism. The first facet of this question concerns what is implied about the nature of man and the nature of sin.

On the nature of man psychologically considered, Jesus is represented as assuming the basic premise of all Jewish theories of man's nature as expressed in Gen. 2:7: "Then the Lord God formed man of dust from the ground, and breathed into his nostrils the breath of life; and man became a living being." Whether this was viewed as a dichotomy of body and soul or as a trichotomy with a spiritual or vital principle added to a body and a soul, there was consistency in viewing man as a union of flesh and soul. That is, Jewish thought saw man in his totality or wholeness. The terms used to describe the psychological facets of man's being were those of the ancient world: heart, psyche, life, body, spirit, flesh, and the like. In ethical terms the psychological dichotomy expressed itself in contrasts between spiritual and carnal, inner and outer, higher and lower, moral and immoral, all related to the basic factors of obedience or disobedience to God.

Jesus is assumed to be thoroughly in line with this as implied in the Genesis precedent of man created in the image of God yet handicapped by his rebellion as mirrored in the myth of the Fall. If we look at the latter emphasis first, Jesus is realistic about man's capacity for sin. This is obvious enough from what has already been said about the unforgivable sin and about the judgment. The terms "sin" and "sinners" appear with relative frequency in his sayings, and his criticism of the Jewish leaders implies much in this respect. Although before God's holiness all men are inadequate, even he (Mark 10:18), and although on one occasion he speaks of mankind as "evil," Jesus simply assumes what we call the reality of freedom of choice. If men have a "sinful inclination," they also have the capacity to make right choices. In fact, as against the tendency to downgrade man in the face of a transcendent God, Jesus holds to a much less pessimistic view.

The emphasis of Jesus falls upon man's religious and ethical potentialities through a right relationship with God. Heightening the trend toward individualism, Jesus calls men to decision-making, as previously indicated, on the assumption that they can realistically seek perfection. As compared with God, man will always be the debtor (Luke 17:7–10), but he is capable of sincere and intelligent response. He has the capacity to accept responsibility in God's redemptive enterprise. If sin is basically disobedience to God, man is able to accept forgiveness and to turn about in obedience. Jesus' ethical teaching as a whole assumes this throughout. Since he does not attempt rationally to tie all the threads together into a theoretical construction, a paradox remains, but his emphasis, rooted in his own faith in and immediate experience of God, is on the positive side with regard to the nature of man. Man has been created for fellowship with God. It is reasonable for man to expect to fulfill that promise, if he does so in terms of Jesus' view of what the will of God requires.

The context of his elucidation of this matter is the legalism of ancient Judaism, with its religion of the Book. Into this static situation and its idea of an absentee God whose will is set forth in a complex system of precedents, Jesus introduces the living and present God. Jesus is not entirely alone in this, since legalistic Judaism has its more deeply religious and ethical side. But he introduces the living God in such a radical way as to bring him inevitably into sharp conflict with the upholders of the *status quo*. The record of conflict in the Gospels makes this self-evident. The conflict is not about the need for complete obedience to God, since all parties concerned take that for granted. It is over the nature of God. Nor is it about the need to love one's neighbor, since, once again, both Jesus and his adversaries teach that precept. It is, rather, over the definition of neighbor and the meaning of loving him.

The key to much else is the way in which Jesus absolutizes the two great commandments with reference to man's obligations, when his meaning is discerned in the light of his total ethical teaching. This means distinguishing between "the commandment of God" and "the tradition of men" (Mark 7:8), which is a way of saying that inner sensitivity to God's present word takes precedence over the lawyers' decisions about regulations of conduct. Or it means a discriminating and creative effort to implement the purpose of the Sabbath, for example, as against adherence by rote to scribal rules. As the Evangelists understand this, it means a response to Jesus' own creative way of defining Sabbath obligations: "The Son of man is lord even of the sabbath" (Mark 2:28). Because of the immediate presence of the divine will, this also means differentiating between things of greater and lesser importance and emphasizing "the weightier matters of the law" (Matt. 23:23-24). Allied with this is the abolition of the distinction between sacred areas and the profane world on the basis of formal rules of purity, so that the "unchurched" and the nonconformists are proper objects of direct concern. In the face of what God wills and does, to love one's neighbor completely is to become so responsive to him that one reproduces God's loving concern for every fellow being regardless of the accidents of birth and circumstance. The parable of the good Samaritan both defines one's neighbor as anyone in need and emphasizes the obligation of an outgoing love like that of God himself. The person who "showed mercy," whatever his formal status, has proved himself to be fully responsive to God as Jesus views him.

This kind of emphasis in Jesus' teaching is directed against those who cling to precedent and institutional tradition as adequate means of defining God's will for the present. The full force of Jesus' opposition to this view of things is expressed in the Sermon on the Mount. Responding to the charge that he is abolishing the Scriptural tradition, Jesus replies that he is in fact fulfilling it. He is thereby calling men to a higher level of devotion to God than is the case with the legalism of scribe and Pharisee. The implication of the examples that are employed to implement the idea of fulfillment, murder and adultery and the like, is that, in order to observe properly these basic moral laws, man must cleanse his heart of feelings and imaginings that lead to the acts in question. The implication is that evident failures in these respects are not being attacked at the source by a procedure of legalistic externalism. Thus Jesus appeals for a treatment of the disease rather than its symptoms. He calls for the kind of radical obedience to God's will that the rich young man could not face, even though he kept the commandments and thus qualified as a respectable member of his society. In sum, Jesus views God as concerned for the kind of obedience that arises spontaneously from a communion with him which reproduces inwardly, and thus outwardly, his own positive respect for persons.

Bornkamm discerningly points out that, in the Sermon on the Mount, Jesus attacks the tendency of man to retreat behind his deeds and achievements by separating the law from God in such a way as to make the law, rather than God, his real authority. Jesus "liberates the will of God from its petrifaction in tables of stone, and reaches for the heart of man which seeks seclusion and safety behind the stronghold of observance of the law." He forces man to confront the fact of his delusion "that his life is in order under the existing regime," offering him the paradoxical gift of captivity to the law of God now set free from "the traditions of men."[22] Even when Jesus is represented as reacting to as specific a law as that about divorce, his ultimate authority is his view of God as he finds it set forth in terms of his ultimate purpose (Mark 10:6–9), a purpose to be implemented creatively in the present under God's immediate inspiration and guidance.

On the other hand, as Bornkamm also brings out, the Sermon on the Mount is directed to another front as well, "the front of the fanatics who wish to claim Jesus for their own as the great revolutionary." Viewing Jesus as "the bringer of a new era, to which must be sacrificed all that has gone before," they become "obsessed by a picture of the future of the world" which is now "made the only valid law."[23] To this tendency Jesus demonstrates a basic approval of the law, whether we have in mind Matt. 5:18–19 or the implications of his attitude toward the laws against murder and adultery. In counseling inwardness with respect to the latter he does not deny their validity. In fact, he takes them more seriously than do those who are content with external observance alone. What was said to "the men of old" only becomes a hindrance when it is made into a formal substitute for acknowledging God's will in the present by means of which the lessons of the past may be rightly apprehended and implemented. The danger of the fanatic's position is that he depersonalizes man, making him "an anonymous cog in a world machine," instead of enhancing that sense of personal dignity and responsibility characteristic of Jesus' view of man. For Matthew the Christian scribe is open both to old and to new (ch. 13:52; cf. ch. 23:34).

The eschatology of Jesus in the Synoptics unites, as we have seen, a future and a present emphasis. There is no contradiction so far as his teaching about the will of God is concerned. Man's responsibility is to have confidence in the future without attempting to solve enigmas of the time and the manner of the consummation, at the same time that he is sensitive to the urgency of responding to God's challenge now. To be responsive is simply to acknowledge God's present reality in the radical obedience which has been described. To love God with all one's capacities, with the whole man, is so to enter into fellowship with God that one spontaneously prays for the Kingdom's coming as one does God's will in the present, loving the neighbor as the effect of knowing that one is loved. The reward is the confidence that God is with one now as he will be in the future, present and future being of a piece under God.

This description of the religious and ethical content of Jesus' message in the Synoptics might tend to imply that he is viewed as teaching in the abstract. This implication is heightened by the absolute way in which Jesus voices God's demands, without any attention to the problem of middle axioms, of making a decision when the alternatives are not in the form of a clear-cut choice between black and white but rather in various shades of gray. While the Synoptics do picture Jesus as absolutistic in his teaching about God and man's obligations, they do not picture him as voicing his ideas without reference to very specific and concrete issues. We may believe that this is so because the Evangelists were appealing to Jesus, remembered and still speaking, with reference to issues that were alive in their circumstances. This fact probably accounts for the selective interest that is displayed, some things being ignored or unstressed because they were not relevant while other things were emphasized because they were critical issues in the congregations addressed by the Evangelists. The impression is that Jesus was not less situation centered than John the Baptist when he addressed special groups, even though his message was not that of the Baptist but distinctly his own.

On this presupposition we may reconstruct much about the situations of the Evangelists and much about the way they understood Jesus as still speaking to conditions in the congregations familiar to them. Current redactional criticism reconstructs the situation of each Gospel with reference to its particular set of circumstances,[24] concern for the community in question being a predominant interest. If Matthew is most explicit in this respect,[25] the other Gospels are no less concerned with the issue. Some of the specific issues that were in view are indicated by the series of controversies with the Jewish leaders portrayed in the Gospels. Questions of Jesus' authority, Sabbath observance, fasting, defilement, marriage and divorce, were live issues. Political questions relative to Roman rule and the Temple authorities, while not exclusively political, had to be dealt with. It is significant that, quantitatively speaking, the questions that receive the greatest attention are those which concern non-Jews (an extension of Jewish nonconformists) and possessions. While the scribes and Pharisees are represented as being Jesus' chief opponents with regard to controversies about the Law, there is reason to believe that the excessive literalism of the sectarians was also in view. At least Jesus' "spiritualizing" of the Law, his protest against Sabbatarianism, and especially his call for love (versus hate) of enemies set him sharply in contrast to the Qumran teaching.[26]

This is not the place to expand the treatment of these issues. The only point is that, however adequately or inadequately we may observe the Jesus of history in the Gospels, we do see him as the Evangelists pictured him with reference to the concrete conditions of their communities. In this sense, at least, to the Evangelists "Jesus is not in the first instance a figure of the past, but rather the risen Lord, present with his will, his power, his word." The Evangelists relate past history, in this case "his word," but they are seeking to proclaim "who he is" and the significance that he has for their present and the future.[27] If in this process of relating the past to the present, Jesus' words, singly and as a whole, are readapted, colored, and applied in several different directions,[28] this is no more than we should expect.

THE SYNOPTIC GOSPEL MIRACLES

The work of Jesus was not confined to the proclamation of the good news; it also included the working of miracles. Since it was no problem for the Evangelists, the question of the credibility of the miracles does not concern us here.[29] Our concern is to classify the miracles and take note of various aspects of the tradition in order to determine what the miracles of Jesus meant to the Evangelists.

Four types of miracles come into view in the Synoptics: exorcisms of demons, healings, raisings of the dead, and nature miracles. We have already had occasion to consider cases of demon possession and Jesus' estimate of the significance of his exorcism of demons. The Synoptics report six specific cases of demon exorcism: the Capernaum demoniac (Mark 1:21–28); the Gerasene demoniac (ch. 5:1–20); the child of the Syrophoenician woman (ch. 7:24–30); the epileptic child (ch. 9:14–29); the dumb demoniac (Matt. 9:32 f.); and Mary Magdalene (Luke 8:2). In addition there are frequent references to this type of activity on the part of Jesus, as well as the very significant Beelzebul controversy with the Jewish leaders over the question (Mark 3:22–30, par.).

Fourteen specific cases of healing are reported without the mention of demon possession, and these are supplemented by frequent generalizations about Jesus' healing activity. The specific cases include the following: the fever of Peter's mother-in-law (Mark 1:29–31); a leper (vs. 40–45); a paralytic (ch. 2:1–12); a withered hand (ch. 3:1–6); a hemorrhage (ch. 5:25–34); a deaf mute (ch. 7:31–37); a blind man (ch. 8:22–26); blind Bartimaeus (ch. 10:46–52); the centurion's servant (Luke 7:1–10 and Matt. 8:5–13); two blind men (Matt. 9:27–31); an infirm spirit (Luke 13:10–17); dropsy (ch. 14:1–6); ten lepers (ch. 17:11–19); and a severed ear (ch. 22:51).

There are two raisings from the dead: Jairus' daughter in Mark (ch. 5:21–24, 35–43) and the widow's son at Nain in Luke (ch. 7:11–17). General references are very limited as compared with the generalizations about Jesus' activity in the two preceding areas (cf. Luke 7:22 and Matt. 11:5; Matt. 10:8; Luke 16:31).

What are called "nature miracles" include the stilling of a storm on the Lake of Galilee (Mark 4:35–41); two feedings of a multitude (chs. 6:30–44 and 8:1–10); walking on the water (ch. 6:45–52), supplemented in Matthew (ch. 14:28–31) by Peter's unsuccessful attempt to duplicate Jesus' feat; the blasting of a fig tree (Mark 11:12–14, 20–25); the coin in the fish's mouth (Matt. 17:27); and the catch of fish (Luke 5:1–11). Matthew's application of the Jonah miracle to the resurrection is irrelevant here (Matt. 12:40).[30]

Several terms and patterns of thought call for brief notice. The two main terms used to designate the miracles are *dynamis* ("mighty work") and *sēmeion* ("sign"). Both turn the mind away from the simply marvelous or from the tricks of the magician or conjurer. As a "mighty work" the act of Jesus turns attention to God's power at work through him. The "sign" points beyond itself as well to what is symbolized, rather than being a proof of one's authority, let alone being a prodigy.

This is most evidently the meaning of the Johannine miracles, but it informs the Synoptic tradition as well. The frequent references to the faith (*pistis*) of the patient is coherent with this. It implies insight and conviction of a Christological kind directed to the power of God uniquely working in Jesus.

The Christological aspects of the miracle tradition fit this view. This is especially so in the fusion of the eschatological prophet with the Davidic figure which we have previously considered, notably in the story of the healing of Bartimaeus. The influence of the Hellenistic divine man concept has also entered into the Synoptic tradition to a limited extent, especially in the infancy stories, but also in such an instance as that of the woman with the hemorrhage. Jesus perceived, it is said, that "power had gone forth from him" (Mark 5:30). However, this kind of divine epiphany is toned down and limited by the concept of secret Messiahship. The dominant conception here is the idea of the cosmic struggle in which Jesus is a participant through the power of the Spirit, centering in the exorcisms but by implication including other types of miracles. In this respect the exorcisms and healings of Jesus are linked up with his authoritative teaching as the proleptic presence of the reign of God to be consummated in the future.

We may profitably consider one other very important aspect of the Gospel picture, namely, the combination of negative and positive attitudes which Jesus is represented as taking toward his miracles. This corresponds to what we have already observed in the combination of secrecy and openness relative to the messianic secret. In passing we may note that the motive of compassion on the part of Jesus receives little explicit attention, even though we may assume its implicit presence with reference to needy and suffering people.

We need not repeat much that has already been said about the positive attitude that Jesus takes toward his exorcisms and some of his healings. We may simply recall the statement about the Kingdom coming upon his listeners in the form of his exorcism by the Spirit of God and his very emphatic statement about the authority of the Son of Man in connection with the healing of the paralytic. Most of the general references cohere with this, including the few references to raising the dead. The positive note in the nature miracles is also self-evident.

In the face of this positive side, what is said, aside from the theme of secret Messiahship, on the other side of the shield? There is a body of material constituting a very distinct pattern which pictures Jesus as repudiating miracle as a means of co-ercing faith. It turns its back upon considering the miracles as prodigies or as in any way designed to convince unbelievers of the truth and value of Jesus' message. The temptation nar-ratives portray this vividly, even though this aspect of the mat-ter may not exhaust their meaning. Mark's view of Jesus' vic-tory over Satan sets the tone for the more elaborate reports of Matthew and Luke. The keynote in the latter material is, "You shall worship the Lord your God, and him only shall you serve" (Luke 4:8 and Matt. 4:10). To perform the miracle of turning stones into bread or to expect miraculous protection by leaping off the pinnacle of the Temple is to tempt God rather than to trust him; in effect it is to acknowledge the worship of Satan.

This is consistent with the implications of the mocking at the cross, that Jesus cannot, morally as well as physically, come down from the cross as a means of coercing faith. It is consis-tent with the words of Abraham in the parable of the rich man and Lazarus: "If they do not hear Moses and the prophets, neither will they be convinced if some one should rise from the dead" (Luke 16:31). False prophets make an appeal to signs and wonders (Mark 13:22), and it is "an evil and adul-terous generation" that looks for such evidence (Matt. 16:4; 12:39). Even the ability to cast out demons in Jesus' name will not guarantee one a favorable judgment in the consummation (Matt. 7:22). Of greater significance is the recording of one's name in heaven, signifying a profounder obedience than facil-ity in exorcism expresses (Luke 10:20).

References to a "sign" show something of a progression, the word "sign" being taken to mean the kind of materialistic and magical demonstration that the superficial consider to be evi-dence of divine authority. In Mark 8:11–13 the reply to the request for such a sign is bluntly, "No sign shall be given to this generation." In the Q version the saying is qualified to add, "except the sign of Jonah" (Luke 11:29 and Matt. 12:39). The appeal here would appear to be in nature like that which we have previously observed in Jesus' constant call for insight, the ability, as another Q saying has it, "to interpret the present time" in the analogy of forecasting the weather (Luke 12:54–56 and Matt. 16:2 f.). Going beyond this, Matthew reports a version of the saying about Jonah which employs it as an analogy of the period between Jesus' death and resurrection (Matt. 12:40). However, both Matthew and Luke report the conclusion that "something greater than Jonah is here" (Luke 11:32 and Matt. 12:41). The implication is that there is less excuse now for the lack of spiritual insight which expects magical "proofs" for faith. All of this is consistent with other Gospel evidences, such as the Nazareth visit, that when faith in Jesus was absent his ability to perform a mighty work was curtailed or at least his willingness to do so was withdrawn. In general Matthew, more than the other Synoptics, tends to interpret the miracles as "signs" in the Johannine sense, but this places no less emphasis upon the necessity of insight into their meaning.[31]

We may now ask what all this adds up to so far as the perspective of the Evangelists is concerned. It would appear that the Jesus they picture is not simply the preresurrection figure, although the appeal is made to past events, but instead the resurrection and exalted Christ. They are proclaiming not only what Jesus once did, but, even more, what he continues to do. Perhaps one purpose that the theory of secret Messiahship served was to suggest that the miracles, so mysterious and indirect and paradoxical as revelations during Jesus' earthly life, are "revelations of the risen Christ addressed to him, the reader."[32] That is, the problem of the miracles as open manifestations of the divine glory when confronted with the story of the passion was solved by the device of secret Messiahship. In Phil. 2:6–11 Paul solved the problem by means of the theory of a self-emptying of Jesus' divine glory. At least the perspective of the Evangelists is that of postresurrection faith in Jesus Christ as Lord of the continuing church whose miracles bespeak his saving power in the present.

Within that frame of reference we may see an analogy to the two fronts addressed by Jesus in the Sermon on the Mount, the fanatics and the traditionalists, applied now to the miracle tradition in terms of the negative and positive emphases previously described. On the negative side the readers are warned against viewing the miracles as wonder stories disconnected from the Christian proclamation and its spiritual foundations or as displays of supernatural power that guarantee the truth of Jesus' teaching. On this side of the shield is Mark's deliberate aversion to the influence of the Hellenistic divine man concept in the form of the theory of secret Messiahship as prologue to the story of the passion, and also as inevitable in relation to his view of Jesus as Son of God. The Evangelists do not portray a Jesus whose miracles have an evidential kind of value which may be substituted for the risk of faith. To all such the answer is, "No sign shall be given!" As Jesus gave no sign to extricate himself from danger, evidenced most emphatically in the crucifixion, his followers cannot expect it to be different for them. In this sense the exalted Christ is also the crucified Lord whose call to follow after still involves taking up one's cross.

On the positive side, however, there is still much to be said, although the question relates not so much to any particular miracle as to that of belief in Jesus in general. The question concerns the Christological connotations relative to the total fact of Jesus as the sole sign of the gospel and the Kingdom of God. As M. E. Glasswell says, "We are not to ask for a miracle or a sign apart from Jesus himself, grasped and met by faith." Continuing, he points out that "even the Resurrection does not appear in Mark as a well-attested miracle in history." The risen Jesus, not the empty tomb, is "the sole sign of the Resurrection." It is this meeting which alone gives meaning to the empty tomb. When this is related to the Gospels as a whole it appears that "miracles are what happens when one believes in Jesus, and it is faith in Jesus which truly perceives a miracle and by that faith that the miracle becomes a sign."[33] If the "mystery of the kingdom of God," as Mark sees it, is revealed at Caesarea Philippi in the form of a prediction of Jesus' passion, the proclamation of a crucified Messiah still calls for a miracle of perception which is evidence of a faith such as this, faith despite the fact that Jesus did not avoid the cross or come down from it.

Probably the most positive thing to be said about the miracles is that they are tokens that the Last Days are at hand, that Satan, proleptically at least, has met his match in Jesus as God's Son. The form and content of the miracles are more influenced by this aspect of Jewish eschatology than by the Hellenistic concept of a divine man. The miracles are recalled by the Evangelists in order to awaken faith in the eschatological fulfillment of God's redemptive purpose for Israel, now transferred to the Christian church.[34] Within this context some of the stories, perhaps many of them, contain the gospel in miniature. As Wilder says of the cure of Bartimaeus, it was "a dramatic sign of what God was bringing to pass. . . . It conveyed the truth that God had bared his mighty arm and wrought salvation: being thus a small companion piece to the Resurrection-drama itself."[35] May we not also see such a significance in the nature miracles? For example, does the story of the stilling of the storm on the lake have in mind angry waves or disturbed emotions?

In this respect we can also include the motif of compassion, even though it is not explicitly stressed in the Gospels. God's acts in the Last Days, as envisaged in the Hebrew Scriptures, were compassionate as well as mighty acts, as when in imagination Ezekiel's valley of dry bones came to life. To proclaim the recovery of sight to the blind and good news to the poor implied a profound compassion, in part that of the physician, but even more that of a father longing for the return of his son from a far country.

Summing up, on the one hand there is protest in the miracle tradition against a superficial view of faith, declaring in effect that "the faith which will not believe until it has seen a miracle is no real faith" and that "to demand a miracle means to experiment with God."[36] On the other hand, the tradition bespeaks the power of God in Jesus to produce certain kinds of results when all human power fails. At the same time, as throughout the whole teaching of Jesus, there is a conditional element, since "miracles are what happens when one believes in Jesus," the effect rather than the cause of faith. This points toward a definition of miracle which informs the perspective of the Evangelists. It is more inclusive than healings and wonders as such, although it includes them. A miracle is "an event, whether natural or supernatural, in which one sees an act or revelation of God."[37] In the Gospels the miracles as signs serve to signify for faith an essential ingredient of the truly foundational miracles, namely, the incarnation and the resurrection of Jesus Christ.

The Death of Jesus

In the New Testament writings outside the Gospels, Jesus' death is treated as part of his work. It is viewed as "according to the scriptures" and as having redemptive significance. Our central concern in this chapter is to determine the extent to which the Gospel portraits share this perspective. To that end we shall deal with the question of responsibility for the death of Jesus, and then consider several patterns relative to the subject in general. In considering this subject we distinguish the passion story proper (Mark, chs. 14–16, par.) from earlier material, even though relevant material from any part of the Gospels is included in the analysis.

On the whole the Gospels represent the Jews as being primarily responsible for Jesus' death, especially by indicating Pilate's lack of conviction about Jesus' guilt. Luke in particular plays up this latter theme in a subtle way.[38] Jewish culpability is also reinforced by references, such as the parable of the wicked tenants, to the judgment to come upon the Jewish nation. The most important question is the degree of blame to be placed upon various groups of Jewish leaders. Those most clearly identified in opposition to Jesus in the portraits as a whole are the Pharisees, scribes, priests, elders, with some slight mention of Herodians.

Judging by the passion stories, it is the Temple authorities (priests and elders), supported by the scribes, who bring the plot against Jesus to culmination. With one exception (Matt. 27:62) the Pharisees do not figure in the final events. The Herodians appear only spasmodically prior to the Last Week, and, according to Mark (ch. 12:13), they are present on one occasion during the Jerusalem period. Luke alone reports a trial before Herod Antipas at the instigation of Pilate as a device to absolve himself of responsibility. This coheres with Matthew's version of Pilate's washing his hands of the whole affair. Sadducees as such are mentioned only four times in the Synoptics (Mark 2:18; Matt. 3:7; 16:1; 22:34), although it may be assumed that many of the Temple authorities were Sadducees.

The most interesting thing about the references to officials in the context of controversy with Jesus is the way in which the scribes span the period before and during the passion stories. As early as Mark 1:22 the contrast is drawn between Jesus and the scribes, and it is the scribes who figure most prominently in the earliest controversies in Mark. Along with the priests the scribes are also prominent in the closing events right up to the mocking of Jesus on the cross. The Marcan picture is in general followed and supplemented by Matthew and Luke.

It is noteworthy that Mark is more accurate than the other Evangelists in his assumptions about the nature of the scribal function and practice. The scribe was an expositor of Scripture who, as a cautious conservative, tended toward literalistic interpretation. Several Marcan references indicate the nature of the scribe's standing and influence in connection with the Pharisees and Sadducees. The reading in Mark 2:16, "scribe of the Pharisees," accurately reflects this. The concern for precedent in the same verse is typical of the scribe's outlook. At the same time only "some of the scribes" supported the Pharisees with respect to the oral tradition (Mark 2:6; 7:1). The allegiance of others to the Sadducees gave them authority in the administration of justice (cf. ch. 8:31 and other combinations of scribes with Temple authorities). The distribution of the references to the scribes in relation respectively to the Pharisees and to the Temple authorities (including many Sadducees) suggests that it was the scribe with leanings toward the Sadducees who figured in the plot against Jesus.

Zealots, or their forerunners, are nowhere mentioned in the sources. It may be presumed, however, that Jesus' failure to match their nationalistic jingoism would have turned them against him. Although Essenes are not mentioned either, to the extent that they are represented by the Qumran community we may also presume that they would have shared the hostile spirit of the Pharisees. Generally speaking, it would appear that, for one reason or another, every representative group found something disturbing in Jesus' manner and teaching. However, the Evangelists are more concerned to demonstrate the innocence of Jesus than to assess the degree of blame to be attached to these Jewish groups. The latter is elaborated because it is necessary in order to elucidate the former.

This takes us only part of the way, however, in assessing the extent to which the death of Jesus is viewed as part of his work. We must, therefore, consider other related patterns in the Gospels. In Mark the passion story is but the culmination of a plot which takes shape almost from the beginning of Jesus' ministry, even though the only explicit reference to a plot is in Mark 3:6. Four Marcan strands intermingle, however, to produce the impression of a preordained fate.

One is the series of controversies beginning with the charge of blasphemy in Mark 2:6 f., linking it with ch. 14:64, and continuing right down to Jesus' arrest. The second is the use of the verb *paradothenai* ("to hand over," "give up," "arrest"). Its first use in ch. 1:14 strikes the note of impending doom: "after John was arrested." Thereafter it appears in two passion predictions and with reference to the persecution of the disciples in the Little Apocalypse. Its use is continued in the passion stories, quite specifically with reference to Judas.

The third and most prominent thread in this pattern consists of anticipations of his suffering on the part of Jesus himself. In Mark these predictions begin with the Caesarea Philippi watershed, but prior to this is the saying about the bridegroom being taken away (ch. 2:19 f.) and the Evangelist's report of the fate of the Baptist (ch. 6:17–29). Following the Caesarea Philippi scene, anticipations of suffering appear explicitly or implicitly at several points. In the passion story certain items continue this predictive outlook, notably the references of Jesus to his body's being prepared for burial, "my blood of the covenant," and in his words in Gethsemane. Luke supplements this Marcan scheme by having Jesus "set his face to go to Jerusalem" when it is time for him to "be received up" (ch. 9:51). He also adds two important sayings: "I have a baptism to be baptized with" (ch. 12:50); "It cannot be that a prophet should perish away from Jerusalem" (ch. 13:33). In addition, he supplements the passion story on this theme in his resurrection narrative. Matthew reinforces the theme of the persecution of the disciples and adds a passion prediction to those in Mark.

Q apparently had no passion story, but it contains a number of sayings which carry this note of anticipated suffering, if only by implication. Set within the framework of the Gospels as a whole, they are significant. Among the relevant sayings are those about the persecution of the disciples; the expectation of offense, clearly present in the parable of the children in the marketplace; and the blood of the prophets. They are climaxed by the lament over Jerusalem, which bespeaks the rejection of Jesus in the judgment to be passed upon Jerusalem.

The fourth thread in this pattern emphasizes the failure of the disciples, like that of Jesus' family and opponents, to grasp his meaning. Even before the passion predictions this becomes evident in a series of sayings beginning with Mark 4:34. At Caesarea Philippi, Peter voices the theme of dissent from Jesus' anticipation of suffering. This is followed by continuous misunderstanding of Jesus on the part of all those closest to him, dramatized by the request of the Zebedee brothers for preferred status at the judgment. It is brought to a climax by the betrayal by Judas and the denial by Peter. The general impression remains in Matthew and Luke despite their attempts to exonerate the disciples in various ways.

With these patterns in mind we may now attempt, with the help of additional data, to reach conclusions about the perspective of the Synoptic Gospels in this area of concern. The historical facts, as seen by the Evangelists, have already been stated. An important ingredient in this picture is Pilate's reluctance to cooperate with the Jewish authorities. This probably represents an apologetic concern to appeal to Gentiles, perhaps, in Luke, to Roman officials.

The historical facts, however, are not stated for their own sake. They are a means to an end, instruments required to fulfill the specific purposes that the Evangelists have in mind. Thus we must ask what the records imply about their intentions. It appears that to a great extent they interpret Jesus' death as predetermined for some mysterious reason by God's redemptive plan. They do not engage in the subtleties of distinctions between God's primary will, which did not wish Jesus to suffer, and his secondary will which accepted Jesus' suffering as inevitable in this kind of world. They simply record the course of events and assume that, in Jesus' own words, "the Son of man *must* [*dei*] suffer" as part of the redemptive plan which concludes with his resurrection. They portray it as God's will without explaining why it is.

A sort of explanation exists in the way in which the passion stories are honeycombed with Scriptural allusions. This is the Evangelists' way of saying that Christ died "in accordance with the scriptures." Only occasionally is the fulfillment theme made explicit, as in Mark 14:27: "You will all fall away; for it is written, 'I will strike the shepherd, and the sheep will be scattered.' "[39] Usually the Scriptural apologetic is by allusion. This is evident in Jesus' cry of dereliction, using the words of Ps. 22:1 (Mark 15:34); in references to the dividing of Jesus' garments and the casting of lots (Mark 15:24 from Ps. 22:18); and the wagging of heads (Mark 15:29 from Ps. 22:7; cf. Ps. 109:25). This is a distinctive feature of all three Evangelists.

Although Jesus himself is portrayed as participating in this view of his death, it is a feature primarily characteristic of the narrative. Elements of narrative and sayings both emphasize another feature of the apologetic, namely, the crucifixion/resurrection pattern with its emphasis upon Jesus' ultimate vindication. This becomes explicit in the reference to rising again in the passion predictions, and it is the impression of the passion stories as a whole. The tragedy of the cross is redeemed by Jesus' resurrection. The portrayal of Jesus as the innocent victim of the blindness of the Jewish people, and of the disciples, contributes to this theme. There is an important Christological and soteriological connotation here. The vindication of Jesus' earthly message and career is of a piece with his resurrection, exaltation, and expected parousia. That is, the vindication consists of approval by God of all that Jesus had stood for during his earthly life.

The Evangelists do not go very far beyond this in the direction of the kind of theological interpretation of the death of Jesus which is characteristic of the Epistles. It is clear enough that there was a vicarious aspect to his whole life, of which his death is the seal, but explicit expressions of the idea that he died "for our sins" are few in number. The most obvious are Mark 10:45 and 14:24 with their references to "a ransom for many" and "my blood of the covenant, which is poured out for many." Characteristically Luke omits these two sayings, as in general he avoids the interpretation of Jesus' death as an atoning sacrifice.[40] Perhaps we should elaborate the implications of Mark 10:45 and 14:24 more than we are doing here, but the emphasis of the Evangelists lies elsewhere.

Perhaps more may be said for the Evangelists' intention of setting Jesus' death forth as the kind of "example" that is found in I Peter 2:21 and emphasized in the thought of Jesus' obedience in Paul's letters and in Hebrews. This is reasonable to the extent that we may think of any one of the Gospels as designed to inspire heroic discipleship in a persecution situation. All three of the Synoptics give indication of a desire to bolster the morale of the readers in the face of opposition, but it is Mark, especially, that implies a serious situation of actual or anticipated persecution. The placing of the Little Apocalypse just prior to the passion story proper suggests an appeal to the apocalyptic motif in conjunction with the martyr motif in order to inspire courage. As in all apocalypses, the former emphasizes God's faithfulness and certain victory in the near future, whereas the latter sets Jesus' heroic example before the readers. If the idea of the atoning significance of Jesus' death is one thread in this total picture, it is not as prominent as in the theological thought of Paul.[41]

This brings us to the end of the exposition of the "work" of Jesus in the Synoptics. It has been done in an impression-istic manner in the light of the purpose of the book as a whole. We turn our attention now to the perspective of the Fourth Gospel on the person and the work of Jesus, making compari-sons with the Synoptics as we proceed.

Chapter III

THE JOHANNINE VIEW OF JESUS

FOR our purpose there are some questions about John's Gospel that we do not have to settle. We do not have to determine the exact limits of overlapping between John and the Synoptics. We assume that, in addition to the explicit parallelism in 8 or 9 percent of the materials, there are many more subtle ways in which parallelism exists. Nor do we have to decide whether or not John knew the Synoptics, although a strong case can be made for his knowledge of Mark and Luke. Nor is it necessary for us to reach a conclusion about the identity of the author or possible editors. We shall use the name John to designate the author of the Gospel as it stands without presuppositions as to his identity. On the questions of date of writing and the location of the readers, we shall assume that the Gospel was written in Ephesus or Syria near the end of the first century.

Our attention is focused on the nature of John's interpretation of Jesus. Despite the similarity to the Synoptics in general form and to a certain extent in substance, the Fourth Gospel represents a divergent tradition about Jesus. Furthermore, the author has given a distinctly individual cast and tone to everything in his Gospel, not only in material peculiar to himself but also in material paralleled in the Synoptics. In narrative and sayings alike everything has been sifted through the writer's mind and expressed in his language and thought forms.[1]

Our procedure will be to portray the perspective of John with reference to the Synoptic perspective in the framework employed in the last two chapters, distinguishing, as far as possible, between Jesus' person and work. We shall look for similarities and for what is distinctly Johannine.

WHO WAS JESUS?

We need not pause long to consider the general tone of John's Gospel with reference to its view of Jesus. It is through-out emphatically on the side of respect for Jesus' authority and uniqueness. We have already noted the enhanced manner in which the Johannine prologue corresponds to the introduc-tions of the Synoptics. We shall have occasion to reconsider it before we are through. John, like the Synoptics, uses the term *exousia,* translated "authority" in Mark 1:22 and 27 and else-where. Four uses of the term in John denote the "power" which the Father has given Jesus to execute judgment and to give eternal life, or to decide what to do with his life. The other use of the term designates Pilate's "power" as given from above. As in Matt. 16:19 and 26:28, the Johannine Jesus con-veys to the disciples authority and power to forgive sins.

Generally speaking, in John's Gospel there is no place for such indications of human limitation as Jesus' inability at Nazareth to perform a mighty work, the struggle in Gethsem-ane, or the cry of dereliction from the cross. And one can hardly imagine Jesus asking in John: "Why do you call me good? No one is good but God alone." To be sure, John asserts that "the Word became flesh," and his major thrust is antidocetic.[2] But he represents a very advanced stage of the process that tended to tone down and eliminate human limitations in Jesus. He is not at the level of the apocryphal gospels,[3] but he is well beyond Matthew and Luke with their alterations of Mark.[4] As we shall see, the Johannine figure is consistently and un-equivocally a majestic one, with the glory of his resurrected status informing the whole even more obviously than in the Synoptics. This includes especially the interpretation of the crucifixion.

Rabbi

Several direct references are made in John to Jesus' teaching function, "the teaching" being used once. Two references appear on Jesus' lips, one similar to Matt. 23:8 in which he employs *didaskalos* ("teacher") as a self-reference, the other, as in the Synoptics, referring to his teaching in synagogues and in the Temple. Otherwise, as far as titles go, Jesus is seven times addressed as rabbi or *rabboni*,[5] with the explanation being added in two instances that this means *didaskalos*. This exhausts the Synoptic terminology in this area of thought, except for the use of "word" (*logos*). "To evangelize" and "to preach" are never used.

Aside from the plural "words," alike in John and the Synoptics, the singular "word" has three significant uses in John. It means (1) a saying or discourse; (2) collectively, Jesus' message of revelation and command, equivalent to the "gospel" in the Synoptics, on a par with God's word; (3) God's self-revelation to man in Scripture and through Jesus. In connection with this the "I say" of the Synoptic picture is employed and developed, but "I am" sayings are more typical of the Johannine Jesus.

Despite the enhanced forms of reference to Jesus' words and the incarnational motif of John 1:14, the Synoptic and the Johannine materials coincide in one important respect. This is to say that the title "rabbi" is of minor importance as compared with other ways of designating Jesus' person and function. The Johannine way of implying this is to say that Jesus' word is authoritative in a unique sense. Three additional references reinforce this. In one, John the Baptist, obviously subordinate to Jesus, is addressed as rabbi. In the other references this title is supplemented by others: Son of God, King, and Lord. The interplay between God's word and Jesus as the incarnate Word heightens all this.

Prophet

Traces of the expectation of "a prophet" and of "the prophet" exist in John's Gospel, and Jesus himself repeats the statement about a prophet's being without honor in his own country.

Two references to Elijah, combined with "Christ" and "the prophet" in John the Baptist's denial that he fits these categories, and several references to Moses, suggest a trace as well of the concept of an eschatological prophet. However, except for three references to Moses which belong under the heading of Scripture fulfillment, it is the contrast between Jesus and Moses that is brought out: "For the law was given through Moses; grace and truth came through Jesus Christ" (John 1:17). This statement in the prologue is echoed in Jesus' own words, and the contrast between Pharisees and Jesus in chs. 9:28 f. is set within this framework.

The concept of the Servant of the Lord plays no specific role in John. The term *pais* ("servant" or "child") is not used, and related ideas of service emphasize the subordination of the one who serves to the master (cf. ch. 13:16). The exception is Jesus' reference to his disciples as "friends" rather than as "servants" (ch. 15:15). Under the figure of the shepherd, however, the very distinctive Johannine idea of voluntary self-giving appears. The characteristic words are, "I lay down my life, that I may take it again" (ch. 10:17, e.g.). This is reminiscent of the passion predictions in the Synoptics. The shepherd analogy may reflect Isa. 40:11, although it may owe as much to Ezek. 34:11–16.

Recalling the view that in the Synoptics John the Baptist is regarded as the eschatological prophet, in the Fourth Gospel his subordination to Jesus is made emphatic. As in the Synoptics he is "the voice of one crying in the wilderness" to prepare "the way of the Lord," but everything else about the Synoptic picture is subordinated to his function of witnessing to the One who comes after him. Amplifying the implications of Matt. 3:14 f., the Baptist testifies to having seen the Spirit descend upon Jesus as a permanent gift, signifying that, in contrast to John's water baptism, Jesus "is he who baptizes with the Holy Spirit" (John 1:32 ff.). Two titles appear on John's lips as well: "the Lamb of God," whose function is to eliminate sin, and "Son of God."

Although in the Fourth Gospel, in contrast to the Synoptics,

Jesus' ministry runs parallel to that of the Baptist for a while,
the subordination of the latter to the former is consistently set
forth. Some of the Baptist's disciples become disciples of Jesus.
The Baptist himself climaxes a short discourse with the words,
"He must increase, but I must decrease" (ch. 3:30 with *dei*,
"must," as in the passion predictions). The last word on the
Baptist is that, in contrast to Jesus, he "did no sign" (ch. 10:41).
This general picture of John the Baptist may be informed with
the eschatological prophet motif, but the original concept has
been greatly adapted to the Johannine Christology.

Christ and Son of David

The traditional Jewish messianic conception of the Anointed
One plays a very small role in John. Only two references call
for attention. One is Jesus' identification of himself with the
"Messiah" ("called Christ") in response to the anticipation of
his coming on the part of the Samaritan woman. Before this
section is over, however, Jesus is being hailed as "the Savior
of the world" (ch. 4:42). In John 6:15 Jesus' aversion to a
concept of nationalistic messiahship is reflected. This is heightened by his declaration to Pilate later that his Kingdom is "not
of this world." Otherwise the term "Christ" is used almost as
a proper name.

It is likely, as C. H. Dodd has argued, that the expression,
"the Lamb of God who takes away the sin of the world" in
ch. 1:29 and 36, is "a symbol of the Messiah as leader of the
flock of God, i.e. as 'King of Israel.'"[6] This appears from the
context in which the Baptist's announcement of Jesus as "the
Lamb of God" is followed by Andrew's declaration, "We have
found the Messiah" (v. 41). It is supported as well by the
fact that, as the Lamb of God, Jesus does not bear sin in a
sacrificial sense. Rather, performing the function of the Jewish
Messiah, he abolishes it; he does away with it entirely. Other
strains of thought may be combined with this in John in a
sublimated sense, such as the idea of the Lamb being the
Servant who was a sin offering. This thought is not followed
through in the Gospel, however, as it is, for example, in the

Johannine Letters. The conquering Lamb of the apocalyptic tradition appears to provide the best precedent for John's usage.[7]

Son of God

"Son of God" or "Son" is John's favorite title for Jesus, it being the precise counterpart of his extensive use of "Father" for God. The Son-Father relationship dominates the portrait, often explicitly and always implicitly. All men, or all followers of Jesus at least, may be sons or children of God, but Jesus is so in a unique and exclusive sense. The prologue sets the pace by designating Jesus as God's "only Son," and this is followed up elsewhere.

In several ways the unique intimacy of Jesus with God and his unparalleled authority as a result are expressed. John 3:35 f. is typical: "The Father loves the Son, and has given all things into his hand. He who believes in the Son has eternal life." With the crucifixion primarily in focus, as in ch. 17:1, the language of the Son's glorification is employed. The Son is subordinate to the Father and absolutely dependent upon him (ch. 5:17 ff., e.g.). But, because of the absolute and permanent oneness of their relationship, to be the Son is to be much more than a prophet who functions as God's representative with a kind of delegated authority. As C. H. Dodd expresses it, "The absolute dependence of the Son on the Father being presupposed, it is impossible to overstate the extent to which divine powers and prerogatives are exercised by the Son."[8] This is all summed up in the idea that the Son gives life[9] and exercises judgment,[10] both of which are essentially divine prerogatives. In this respect the unity of the Father and the Son is complete, and the unique nature of Jesus' Sonship is manifested.

Jesus' ability to act as Son in this way, in contrast to all others, is due to the fact that he is "from above" and "not of this world" (e.g., ch. 8:23). Even though John retains the Synoptic perspective in saying these things about Jesus in terms of his historic mission, probably with a concern to counter docetic ideas, the Jesus of John's Gospel belongs in dualistic terms to the eternal world. In the prologue the Logos concept says this, but the language of Sonship also expresses it. This is why the Son alone can be designated in ch. 1:18 as the one who has seen God and can thus make him known. If the Son is not preexistent in a literal sense, he is viewed as at least non-temporal, having been sent by God and given up by him (ch. 3:16 f.). "The relation of Father and Son is an eternal relation. . . . The human career of Jesus is, as it were, a projection of this eternal relation (which is the divine *agapē*) upon the field of time."[11] The metaphysics of this relationship are not completely clear, although John's conception is more a step in the direction of ontological ideas later to inform Christological thought than is apparent in the Synoptics. At the same time there is retained something of the Hebraic idea of the Son as one who functions perfectly for and with God due to the quality of his obedience grounded in his perfect understanding of and sensitivity to God's will and purpose. In this sense, at least, Father and Son in John's Gospel are "one" (ch. 10:30).

Thus John aims at surmounting the inadequacies of a conception of the Messiah symbolized by John the Baptist and Nathanael, eliminating any narrow connection with Jewish nationalistic messianism.[12] However, the concept of Sonship is so all-pervasive in John's Gospel that a complete elucidation of its meaning calls for an exposition of the whole Gospel. Since its meaning is to a great extent derived from other categories, we shall leave further exposition to later treatment of the message of Jesus. This applies especially, recalling the Synoptic perspective on Sonship, to the relationship between the Son and the Spirit. To the extent that the Hellenistic concept of a divine man is relevant, it will be discussed under the heading of the miracles in John.

Son of Man

This term is employed thirteen times in the Fourth Gospel, all but two (in ch. 12:34) on the lips of Jesus as in the Synoptics. The almost complete absence of eschatological tones sharply differentiates these Johannine sayings from a major facet of the Synoptic usage. Jesus' authority to "execute judgment" in ch. 5:27 may be an exception, since the context appears to have the consummation in view, but the judgment that Jesus executes is usually a present rather than a future fact (as in ch. 3:19).

At the same time, despite the fact that no specific Synoptic saying is found in John, there are features common to both traditions, including the connection between the death and subsequent vindication of Jesus. In John these ideas are combined in the distinctive reference to the Son of Man's being "lifted up" (chs. 3:14; 8:28; 12:34). Typical of John's habit of giving double meanings to terms, "lifted up" combines the act of being elevated upon the cross with the figurative exaltation in glory. The unique feature of John's picture is the way in which the crucifixion itself exhibits Jesus' glorification. While John retains the death/resurrection formula of the Synoptics, unlike the latter, the glorification of Jesus occurs in John when his work is finished on the cross (ch. 19:30). This idea is governed by the view that Jesus' glorification is but the return to a former status consistent with his previously having come from above. Son of Man sayings with an ascend/descend motif cohere with this in implying that the correspondence between earth and heaven is manifested in Jesus.

There is a sense in which Son of Man in John is simply a variation on other titles, Son of God and Son in particular. In five Son of Man sayings, Son of God could just as well be used with reference to Jesus as salvation bringer (ch. 6:27, 53), as judge (ch. 5:27), and as being glorified (chs. 12:23; 13:31). On the other hand, all the Johannine titles are subservient to and influenced by reverence for the exalted Jesus without thereby justifying the conclusion that they are merely synonymous versions of the same thing.[13]

The distinctive features of the Son of Man terminology in John are not completely clear, but it may well be that one of its significant traits is portrayed in the view of Dodd, that this term "shows most markedly the influence of Platonism and of the more speculative Judaism" in the idea of a "Being who is the archetype of the human race, and at the same time the true or essential humanity . . . resident or immanent . . . in individuals of the human species."[14] If we grant this representative capacity in John's picture as a whole, Jesus, as a genuine human being, combines the particular with the universal in such a way that he cannot be confused with the idea of a heavenly man as a metaphysical abstraction. It is John's next term that most clearly evidences the way in which he views this combination in the thought forms of his milieu.

The Word

On first appearance the opening lines of John's Gospel, by introducing the concept of the Word (*logos*), place us more in the atmosphere and context of thought about the preexistence of Jesus characteristic of Paul than within the framework of the Synoptic perspective. The preexistence of the Word, his agency in creation, and his incarnation are clearly stated in ch. 1:1-3 and 14. We are reminded immediately of the Wisdom myth of Hellenistic Judaism, especially its tendency in Philo to fuse "Wisdom" and "Word," supplemented by or informed with a heterodox Jewish Gnosticism such as is expressed in the Odes of Solomon and the literature of Qumran and Nag Hamadi.[15] At the same time we are reminded of the dynamic Hebrew conception of the word of God as "the function of a conscious and moral personality," as against a force in nature, operative in creation and in revelation.[16]

Much of the discussion of the meaning of "Word" in John's Gospel revolves around the question of the relative influence upon the writer of Jewish and Hellenistic Gnostic conceptions. This is inevitable, but a more profitable approach to the question appears to be to ask first about other aspects of the matter, leaving until later the attempt to ascertain the meaning of *logos* in its explicit use in the prologue.

The first question to be asked then is whether the Logos concept in these opening verses is to be understood primarily with reference to the remainder of the prologue and the rest of the Gospel, or whether the reverse is the case. What is involved in this question is implied in the observation of C. H. Dodd: "It is only the first three verses of the gospel that necessarily refer to the pre-incarnate Logos. The rest *could* be understood as referring to the historical appearance of Jesus Christ."[17]

John A. T. Robinson has likewise raised this question in an analysis of the prologue in relation to the Gospel as a whole and to the Johannine Letters.[18] His basic premise is that, although the Gospel was prior to the letters, this does not apply to the prologue in all its parts (or to the appendix in John, ch. 21). It was the writing of the letters, with their strong anti-docetic tendency, that caused the editing of the original beginning of the Gospel in the form of the Logos content. Like Mark, John's Gospel originally began with a reference to the testimony of John the Baptist. This has survived in vs. 6–9, 15, 19 ff. On this assumption an important conclusion follows: "The timeless truths were not the matrix of the Gospel, but the fruit of meditation upon it." Even though the Gospel is theological, "history has its own primacy."[19] Whether or not the proposed reconstruction is valid or even necessary to establish the conclusion, the question that is posed is crucial. Both Dodd and Robinson suggest that Christian experience focused upon Jesus, rather than Hellenistic speculation, was the controlling factor in John's understanding of the Logos.

This is to raise the important question. In a search for its answer it appears feasible to examine the prologue first as a whole, inclusive of the Logos references, in relation to the rest of the Gospel, and then to consider the meaning of the Logos concept in its contextual relationships. Both approaches are required for fullness of analysis.

It is sufficient for our purpose to make certain summary statements about some rather self-evident aspects of the relationship. Certain themes, regarding both terminology and content, characterize the prologue and the rest of the Gospel. This is true of concepts portraying Jesus as revealer of God and as salvation bringer, such as life, light, truth. These concepts in turn draw to themselves "I am" sayings and the series of signs that dominate the first part of the Gospel. Along with this body of ideas is that concerned with the response to the gospel. Here again various conceptions are found in the prologue and in what follows it, such as receiving the gift, believing or having faith, knowledge as related to seeing or perceiving, which in turn involves rebirth. Adversely, the theme of rejecting Jesus and the contrast between Moses and Jesus appear in both sections.

With regard to the term "Word" or "Logos," the relationship is not so clear. There appears to be no further reference to Jesus as the agent of creation, except perhaps by implication. The Gospel as a whole, on the other hand, abounds in the thought of Jesus as agent of revelation and as the bringer of salvation. The incarnational theme of ch. 1:14 is implemented throughout the remainder of the Gospel, whether in the form of concepts previously listed or in the specific ideas of Jesus' coming from or being sent by or manifesting God. References to the "world" as the sphere of Jesus' operation on God's behalf are common to prologue and Gospel as a whole, whether the world be taken to mean human society or the opposite of the world above. The theme of Sonship in a sense binds together the Word made flesh and God's word uttered by and embodied in Jesus. There is consistency as well between the divine mode of being implied in ch. 1:1 f. and the idea of Jesus' being from above. However, for Jesus to say in ch. 8:58, "Before Abraham was, I *am*," is not the same thing as the idea of the preexistence of the Word in ch. 1:1 f.

One marked difference is the absence of the term "Spirit" from the prologue compared with its prominence at Jesus' baptism and the contrast drawn between spirit and flesh in ch. 6:63: "It is the spirit that gives life, the flesh is of no avail." This may indicate the validity of the view that it is the Spirit that is the unifying principle in John,[20] although the absence of the term from the prologue tells against it. At least its absence from the prologue is an exception to the rule of continuity between it and the rest of the Gospel. If we grant that, there is no necessary conflict between the idea of the Word's becoming flesh and the idea that at death Jesus gave up his spirit. The latter may say no more than when in Luke, Jesus commits his spirit to his Father. The only possible difference is that John's thought often moves on two levels, so that "spirit" in John 19:30 may go beyond the thought of mortal breath to include Jesus' dynamic life-giving power. However, this still leaves the reality of the incarnation untouched, especially if, asserting another Johannine habit of thought, spirit is a synonymous version of the truth, life, and light embodied in and imparted by Jesus, rather than an independent entity.

With these factors in mind let us return to the original question as to where the emphasis of John lies in his use of the term "Word." Its associations with the Hellenistic Wisdom tradition are clear enough. It would appear that the idea of the Word as the agent of creation and as the agent of revelation, resting upon a view of the Word as expressing the eternal thought of God characteristic of the Wisdom tradition, has influenced John. This still seems to be the case if we assume an influence as well from the Hebrew Scriptures. However, going far beyond anything that the Wisdom tradition could contribute, John's thought moves from the historical facts to cosmological considerations, from the experience of faith in Jesus to considerations of creation and eternal forms, rather than vice versa. Furthermore, the Wisdom myth is interpreted in the light of the history of Jesus, even when that history is explicated by means of symbols consistent with Hellenistic thought. The crux of the matter is that "the Logos *became* the *sarx* or human nature which He bore. The life of Jesus therefore *is* the history of the Logos, as incarnate, and this must be, upon the stage of limited time, the same thing as the history of the Logos in perpetual relations with man and the world."[21] What the contextual mythology does is to provide the instrument by means of which to confess one's faith that "the meaning which we find in Him is the meaning of the whole universe—that, in fact, that which is incarnate in Him is the Logos."[22]

If this is true, then the relationship between the prologue and the rest of John's Gospel, so far as the Logos concept is

concerned, is not that of a synonym for Jesus' life-giving effi-
cacy comparable to water, bread, life, light, and the like. Instead, "the Prologue is an account of the life of Jesus under
the form of a description of the eternal Logos in its relations
with the world and with man, and the rest of the gospel an
account of the Logos under the form of a record of the life of
Jesus; and the proposition *ho logos sarx egeneto* ["the Word
became flesh"] binds the two together."[23] The prologue does
not represent the whole Wisdom myth. It confines itself to the
ideas of preexistence and incarnation, the incarnate life portrayed in the rest of the Gospel concentrating in itself, as it
were, the saving effect of the resurrected and exalted Christ.
In portraying the life and death of Jesus from the resurrection
perspective in this way, John treats the historical tradition
with greater freedom than is the case with the Synoptics, but,
like them, he is still bound to the earthly circumstances of the
Word made flesh.

Other Traditional Titles and Categories

Brief attention may be called to three additional titles and a
few other items. Only once does the title "Savior" appear
(John 4:42). However, the self-evident character of Jesus'
work as directed to salvation is characteristic of the whole
Gospel. This is made explicit several times by the use of "salvation" (*sōtēria*) and "to save" (*sōzein*).

Once Jesus refers to himself as "Lord" (*Kyrios*) (ch. 13:13 f.).
The Johannine usage closely parallels the Lucan usage of the
term in narrative and in direct address to Jesus in the vocative.
Seven of the ten references in narrative occur in the resurrection story.

The exclamation of Thomas addressed to the resurrected
Christ, "My Lord and my God!" is the sole direct application
of the term *Theos* to Jesus (ch. 20:28). Although the distinction
between Jesus and God in John is often ambiguous, previous
discussions have indicated that the difference between the
Sender and the One Sent is maintained. Questions of a merging of natures as against distinctions of function arise to some

extent, but even when terms like "Word" and "Lord" and "God" are employed, the oneness involved is primarily functional in nature in an ethical and religious sense. The important idea of union with God, abiding in him, is more mystically and ethically, rather than metaphysically, conceived.

An echo of Mark 2:19 ff. may exist in the designation of the Baptist as "the friend of the bridegroom" (John 3:29).

As far as other categories of thought characteristic of the Synoptics are concerned, the idea of secret Messiahship is absent from John, and the miracles will be treated at a later point. John also has no infancy story, although he parallels the Synoptics in considering Jesus to be a Jew, the son of Joseph and a woman, obviously Mary, who is not named as such. The reference to being "born . . . of God" in John 1:13 is taken by Edwyn Hoskyns to contain a veiled indication of the virgin birth.[24] This more likely gains its meaning from the idea of preexistence in ch. 1:1 f. The discussion about the birth of the Davidic messiah in Bethlehem tends to tone down the idea of Davidic descent for Jesus (ch. 7:42 f.).

This leaves the subject of Old Testament fulfillment to be considered. Generally speaking, the view is similar to that of the Synoptics as against Paul's Rabbinic use of Scripture. John follows the tendency of Matthew, but more cautiously, in references to specific fulfillments.[25] The use of Isa. 6:10 in Mark 4:10–12 and Matt. 13:14 is paralleled in John 12:39 f. References to Judas and to casting lots over Jesus' garment recall Synoptic usage. The verb "to complete" (teleō), implying purposive intent, is used in ch. 19:28–30 in place of the usual word for fulfillment (plēroun). This corresponds to Jesus' dying proclamation, "It is finished" or "completed." Of particular interest are the references to the insight of the disciples after the resurrection (as in Luke 24:27, 46), which arises in connection with the Scriptures (John 2:22; 20:9). Quite distinctive of John are two references to the fulfillment of Jesus' own words (ch. 18:9 and 32).

John's view of the resurrection will be treated later when his passion story is considered.

Johannine Categories

If the person and the work of Jesus cannot be completely disconnected in the Synoptics, this is even more so in John's Gospel. For example, a whole series of symbolical terms are employed in connection with the expression "I am," such as "I am the bread of life." Additional terms include life, light, resurrection and life, truth, water of life. In addition there are references to "the name" of Jesus (e.g., ch. 3:18). To these terms may be added the various ways, some of which have already been considered, in which Jesus is viewed as intimately related to God. All of these have Christological implications at the same time that they refer to Jesus' saving work. Thus it would be artificial to treat them under the heading of the person rather than of the work of Jesus. Therefore, we shall proceed to the discussion of the work of Jesus, including, as in Chapter II, the message, miracles, and passion, on the assumption that in so doing we are at the same time continuing the discussion of his person.

What Did Jesus Do?

Although Jesus in the Fourth Gospel has a lot to say in the form of long discourses, that he is working is signified explicitly by the use of the noun *ergon* ("work"), singular and plural, and of the verb *ergazomai* ("to work"). This term is preferred by John to other terms, some of which have connotations of miraculous deeds.[26] The basic idea is that God is at work and that he is working in and through Jesus. "My Father is working still, and I am working," Jesus says (ch. 5:17), and Jesus' sole purpose is to accomplish God's work (ch. 4:34). Jesus' work is authorized by God and bears testimony to the fact that he has been sent by God (ch. 5:36, etc.). It signifies Jesus' definitive and unparalleled relationship to God (chs. 5:20; 15:24). At the same time it is envisaged that the disciples after Jesus' departure will do even "greater works" through his influence on them (ch. 14:12).

Two aspects of this usage are consistent with the Johannine

picture in general. Some uses of the term may appear to signify a particular deed of Jesus, such as the healing of a blind
man, but there is always the connotation of the meaning which
the deed has for spiritual renewal. The work is the total meaning that Jesus has for spiritual vitality. There is also the idea
of the word as an act characteristic of the Hebrew manner of thought as evidenced in the idea of creation by God's
word. The full meaning of the Johannine signs involves an act
or deed, such as the turning of water into wine or the healing
of a blind man, combined with a discourse or a dialogue which
brings out its symbolical meaning with reference to salvation.
That is, in the term "work" itself both aspects of the situation
are included.

The Message of Jesus

Jesus in John's Gospel is concerned to impart a content of
thought. The content may involve a relatively small number of
ideas reiterated in many different ways, but it is still a content.
This is indicated not only by the long discourses in the first
part of the Gospel, but also by the way in which John introduces long speeches by Jesus into the Last Supper setting (chs.
13 to 17).

The forms of Jesus' teaching in John differ considerably
from those in the Synoptics. Strictly speaking there are no
parables (*parabolen*), but "figures" (*paroimia*) instead, even
though these two Greek terms translate the same Hebrew
word in the LXX. These figures include birth, bread, darkness
and light, flesh and spirit, glory, life, sheep, water, and the
like, with a prevailing tendency toward their allegorization.
In place of short, self-contained sayings and parables Jesus
indulges in John in long discourses characterized by a subtle
complexity and an interweaving of themes, or he engages in
dialogue, both types of teaching being a means of elucidating
his signs. Furthermore, the Johannine discourses are not pieced
together, as in the Synoptics, from isolated sayings or groups
of sayings, resembling mosaics. Instead, they often grow out of
preceding narrative and "revolve about one or even more

themes, in part in the form of dialogue, so that with a certain correctness we may speak of the 'dramatic' character of the Johannine account."[27] Instead of the Synoptic "kingdom of God," used only twice in John, the expression "eternal life" dominates the teaching. Or the emphasis falls upon Jesus himself as the bearer of the gospel in the form of "I am" sayings in contrast to the reticence of the Synoptic portraits in this respect.

Eschatological Crisis. As in the previous chapter we are mainly concerned here with the eschatological content of Jesus' message and its religious and ethical substance. We may recall that the realized eschatology of some Synoptic sayings exists along with other sayings that point vividly to the future consummation. There is tension between the two emphases.

In John's Gospel, references to a future consummation are almost swallowed up by a concentration upon the activity of Jesus and its meaning for salvation in the present. This is an almost exclusively realized eschatology in full bloom. Both Kingdom of God sayings are within this frame of reference, including the ideas of seeing God and entering the Kingdom (ch. 3:3, 5). As we have noted, the Johannine Son of Man sayings drop out the futuristic eschatological motif. References to judgment, as in ch. 3:18 f., emphasize the division that results in the present between those who accept and those who reject Jesus. In this sense, as Bultmann says, "his coming is the eschatological event," as is most evident in the sayings about judgment.[28]

Furthermore, the eternal life that is bestowed upon those who respond to Jesus, although it contains an element of future time, is qualitatively the endowment of God's life within the believer now: "He who believes in the Son *has* eternal life" (ch. 3:36). By a positive reaction to Jesus the believer "*has passed* from death to life" (ch. 5:24). Some references to resurrection appear to have a future event in view, but the emphasis of John is suggested in the Lazarus story. Reference is made to "resurrection at the last day," but attention is focused upon the fact that, symbolically with reference to the raising of Lazarus, Jesus can say, "I *am* the resurrection and the life" (ch. 11:24 f.), or "The Son *gives* life to whom he will" (ch. 5:21).

In part the Spirit may be an eschatological sign, indicating that the Last Days have been inaugurated; it is the active agent in rebirth in the present, as in the case of Nicodemus. In the farewell discourses the Spirit, or Paraclete, is something to be received from the resurrected Jesus after his death, which eventually takes place (ch. 20:22). On the other hand, before the crucifixion the Spirit as a permanent gift inspires Jesus (chs. 1:32 f.; 6:63) and is bestowed by him upon believers (ch. 3:34). Despite the inconsistency there is no conflict for John, since in reality it is the resurrected Jesus who speaks throughout the Gospel.

There is, to be sure, a future ingredient in the midst of this realized eschatology. In ch. 5:25–29 a future consummation is envisaged in terms of "the resurrection of life" and "the resurrection of judgment." In the Lazarus scene "the resurrection at the last day" in Martha's words is taken for granted even when the center of attention is shifted to the present. In one breath Jesus says, "Now is the judgment of this world" (ch. 12:31), but in another breath he refers to judgment "on the last day" (v. 48). The judging function of the Counselor is reserved for the future (ch. 16:8–11), and the Son's function as judge has the future as well as the present in prospect. Some references to eternal life explicitly involve the idea of endless life (e.g., ch. 6:51, 58) or they link it with "the last day" (vs. 40, 54), even when the qualitative emphasis predominates. This line of thought is qualified, if "last" is used by John in the sense of "decisive," that is, "God's last word on the subject." Realized eschatology interprets the eschatological as final in this qualitative sense. At least John's picture is ambiguous as far as the temporal aspect of his eschatology is concerned.

It is not so much that John completely ignores or discounts the futuristic aspect of the eschatological picture. Three things appear to be determinative for his handling of this question with reference to his context and purpose. First, he is influ-

enced by the type of dualism characteristic of the Hellenistic
distinction between two worlds, the higher and the lower,
rather than primarily by the idea of two successive ages. In
this respect his outlook resembles that of the letter to the Hebrews rather than that of the Synoptics and Paul. Much that
has been said already about Jesus as the Logos, as sent from
above, as Son of Man ascending and descending supports this.
The contrast that is consistently drawn between this world and
the other world is emphatic: "You are of this world, I am not
of this world" (ch. 8:23).

Second, John wants to stress the present consequences of
accepting or rejecting the living Christ. In this respect he resembles Paul's view of the work of Christ as producing a new
life in the present. Third, he concentrates upon the individual's
relationship to God in terms of abiding in him. Thus the question of time becomes almost irrelevant, except for the matter
of making the proper response to the call to decision. To be
sure, there is a corporate concern for the inner life of the
church, but this is viewed as resulting from individuals com-
mitted to *agapē* in the present.[29]

We may say, therefore, that in John's Gospel, Jesus' coming
creates an eschatological crisis much as in the Synoptics, except that it is not viewed as comprehensively with reference
to the final consummation as it is in the Synoptics. The urgency
of decision is not at all conditioned by the thought of the master of the house arriving unexpectedly in the imminent future
but, instead, by consideration of the fateful significance of the
present moment. In this respect John takes to an extreme one
element in the Synoptic picture, probably under the duress of
the delay of the parousia. Perhaps we may say that he purifies
the element of urgency by eliminating any considerations other
than those of religious and ethical import. Whereas Paul retains both present and future elements in an uneasy paradox,
John puts most of his eggs in one basket. In contrast to the
inaugurated eschatology of the Synoptics and Paul, the present crisis envisaging its future transcendental consequences,
John tones down the latter in favor of a truly realized disciple-

ship with an indefinite future in view. In this way he provides a type of spiritualization of futuristic eschatology, also somewhat characteristic of Luke-Acts, which has continued down to the present time.[30] Expressed in another way, John represents a one-sided emphasis upon the realized eschatological element in the Synoptics and Paul, whereas The Revelation to John represents an equally one-sided emphasis upon the futuristic element in those traditions.

Religious and Ethical Content. Again following the outline of Chapter II, we shall consider first the call to decision and then questions of the nature of God and of ethics. The miracles as signs are closely bound up with any discussion of John's religious and ethical outlook, but we shall delay until the next section consideration of the miracles as such.

We may begin by considering the urgency with which decision is forced upon his listeners by Jesus. The note of urgency is just as great in John as in the Synoptics, except, as we have observed, it lacks the element of an imminent parousia. Although there is a future aspect to judgment and eternal life, the emphasis falls upon avoiding the former and enjoying the latter now. This will be implied in much that follows, so that it need not be elaborated further here. Suffice it to say that John stresses the urgency of responding to a love of God that is great enough to give his only Son for the world, so that one may in the present experience the power of God to overcome and to redeem the world (cf. ch. 16:33). The appeal lies in the intrinsic worth of what is offered in and through Jesus with respect to man's deepest spiritual needs.

In a bewildering variety of ways Jesus describes in John the kind of response that God expects as the condition for accepting his gift of salvation. A dominant conception is that of receiving what is offered. The verb is *lambanein* ("to take" or "to receive"), as in the prologue: "He came to his own home, and his own people received him not. But to all who received him, who believed in his name, he gave power to become children of God" (ch. 1:11 f.). Here, as elsewhere, "to receive" is equivalent to believing in Jesus. To receive Jesus is also to receive God, and to receive the one sent by Jesus is to receive Jesus (ch. 13:20). At the end the disciples are bidden to "receive the Holy Spirit."

Other general ways of expressing the receptive spirit include being born "again" or "from above," which is equivalent to being born "of water and the Spirit" (ch. 3:5-8), the latter also being associated with Jesus' words (ch. 6:63). Receiving Jesus is to be born "of God" (ch. 1:13). It is also a condition of salvation to worship God "in spirit and truth" (ch. 4:23) and to be "of the truth" (ch. 18:37). Those who are not open to truth are blinded to reality (ch. 8:43).

The need for insight is as emphatically portrayed in John as in the Synoptics. This is expressed by the use of different terms for seeing or perceiving, knowing, and hearing. "To know" is in some references "to understand," as when Jesus asks Nicodemus, "Are you a teacher of Israel, and yet you do not understand this?" The condition of experiencing eternal life is to know God and Jesus Christ (ch. 17:3). In ch. 6:69 believing and knowing are closely bound up together, as are seeing (perceiving) and believing in ch. 9:37 f. Echoes of Isa. 6:9-10 and its use in Mark 4:10-12 appear in John 9:41 (and ch. 12:40) in connection with the healing of the blind man, which turns upon the willingness of men to receive light. Echoes of the Beelzebul controversy in the Synoptics, with its statement about blasphemy against the Holy Spirit due to spiritual blindness, also inform this pericope. These are typical of many other uses of verbs for seeing and knowing. The ability to hear is equivalent to the ability to see or to perceive, and this is also equivalent to believing (ch. 5:24).

To believe or to have faith is a dominant thread throughout John's Gospel. Typical of many references are the words in ch. 3:16 ff., "whoever believes in him" and "he who does not believe." A summary example is v. 36: "He who believes in the Son has eternal life." The same verse includes an indication that believing means more than intellectual assent to a proposition, that it means commitment to the Son and his way of life: "He who does not obey the Son shall not see life." To believe in Jesus is at the same time to believe in God (ch. 5:24). According to the summary in ch. 20:29–31, the whole purpose of John's Gospel is to inspire belief in the significance of Jesus for salvation, especially on the part of those who have not seen him as his intimates have. The fundamental significance of faith is that it is the primary means of overcoming the offense of the incarnation.

Included in genuine faith is obedience to God's will. Referring to God, Jesus says: "If any man's will is to do his will, he shall know whether the teaching is from God" (ch. 7:17). The obedient spirit is linked significantly here with insight. God is to be worshiped "in spirit and truth," which includes sincere submission to his will. There are other ways in which John says this same thing, such as abiding in love, drinking the water that Jesus gives, losing one's life, responding to Jesus' love of God.

Since the inculcation of obedience to God is so often expressed in terms of following Jesus, we can carry this farther by taking note of ways in which Jesus is the object of attention. The characteristic Synoptic use of *akolouthein* ("to follow") is reproduced in John in the call of Philip and in the challenge to Peter to faithful care for those under his leadership (ch. 21:19, 22). As in Mark 8:34, Jesus says: "If anyone serves me, he must follow me," and he promises that his follower will not walk in darkness (John 8:12). The Johannine form of Peter's confession emphasizes following Jesus as the one who has "the words of eternal life" (ch. 6:68). To follow Jesus means to obey him and to keep his commandments (chs. 3:36; 13:34). This in turn is to abide in him (ch. 15:6). Other expressions of this idea are loving Jesus, eating his flesh, accepting his sending to others, believing and acting in his name.

Prayer as a form of response to God is indicated mainly in John by Jesus' example. The Synoptic terms for prayer (*proseuche* and *proseuchomai*) do not appear in John. "Asking" and "seeking" are the preferred terminology, as in ch. 14:13 f. The disciples are urged to approach God with their requests, echoing the saying in Q about asking and receiving, on the assumption that to ask in Jesus' name is to be assured of a responsive answer. In a sense prayer is its own answer. The "Our Father" of the Lord's Prayer in Matthew does not occur in John, and, except by implication, the model prayer is not repeated. Its exclusive God-centeredness without any reference to Jesus would probably not have been congenial to John. The characteristic emphases of John appear in Jesus' prayers, especially in the high-priestly prayer of ch. 17. Here Jesus addresses God as "Father," the intimacy of Jesus and God throughout the Gospel giving weight to the confrontation and communion. On two other occasions, one of them echoing the Synoptic Gethsemane scene, Jesus prays directly to the Father (chs. 11:41; 12:27 f.). This implies much for the practice of the disciples.

On the other hand, the language of indwelling and union with God, so consistently present in the picture of Jesus' relationship with God, keeps constantly to the fore the spirit of obedience to God as prayer's precondition. In the figure of the vine in ch. 15:1–11, in the references to works, and in much else it is evident that for John prayer does not lose its concern for doing God's ethical will in a vague and dissipated mysticism. Jesus' high-priestly prayer in ch. 17 emphasizes the absolute faith of Jesus in God, his complete commitment to God, and his concern for the outreach of the gospel among the disciples and, through them, to unbelievers. This is the typical universalism of John's Gospel with its view of God's concern for the world. Prayer for John is a life constantly devoted to the Father's interests as well as an act in the setting of worship or private meditation. Without repeating the Synoptic sayings in this respect, it is thoroughly consistent with the concern of the Synoptic sayings for genuineness in prayer.

Once again, with the outline of the preceding chapter as our guide, we turn to consider the ideas of God that characterize the Johannine portrait. Two things are most distinctive of John's views of God. First, the use of the term "Father" for God, some 107 times, far exceeds its use in the Synoptics. In two sayings the terms "God" (*theos*) and "Father" (*pater*) are brought together explicitly (chs. 6:27; 20:17), and their inter-relationship is evident in several other sayings. In a good many additional sayings God is used alone, as in the prologue. However, the predominate term is "Father," used by itself. In the preceding chapter statistics on the use of various forms employed for Father were cited, and a comparison with the Johannine statistics is in order. John does not employ "our Father"; this is confined to the Matthean address in the Lord's Prayer. "Your Father" occurs in John only twice, "his Father" only once, and "their Father" not at all, as against 15 examples in the Synoptics (mostly "your Father" in Matthew). While "Father" is used eight times in direct address to God in John, as against six examples in the Synoptics, the percentage in John is much lower. In terms of percentages "my Father" appears less frequently in John than in the Synoptics, although it is employed twenty-five times. It is at this point that John and Matthew come closest together, since this form of expression in the Synoptics is found mainly in Matthew. The expression "one Father" occurs once each in the Synoptics and in John. The predominant usage of John is the simple objective reference "the Father" (77 times), and this sharply contrasts with the five times that it is used in the Synoptics (one of which is in Matthew).

Several inferences might be drawn from these statistics, but we confine ourselves to a limited number of observations most pertinent to our concern. If there is a reticence on Jesus' part in Mark, Q, and L explicitly to publicize the intimacy of his relationship with God by the use of "Father," a reticence that in the M materials is dissipated, it has entirely disappeared in John. Although on a percentage basis Matthew exceeds the Johannine usage of "my Father," the whole atmosphere of John's perspective lifts this expression into prominence and even gives to the expression "the Father" a more personal connotation than it might seem to have. What is distinctive about Jesus' view of God, inclusive of his feeling of oneness with God, is primarily embodied in this term "Father."

Second, God's nature and activity are, with very few exceptions, portrayed in relationship to Jesus. This is so obvious that almost any saying picked at random can be used to typify the whole. Consider sentences from the fourteenth chapter as typical examples: "I am the way, and the truth, and the life; no one comes to the Father, but by me. If you had known me, you would have known my Father also. . . . He who has seen me has seen the Father. . . . Believe me that I am the Father and the Father in me." The observation that "*the*ology" in the New Testament is "*Christ*ology" is decidedly true of John's Gospel.

In attempting to portray the nature and meaning of God in Jesus' teaching and activity as set forth in John, we shall reduce the complex and abundant materials to several generalizations with reference to the Synoptic picture earlier portrayed. This is valid, because John in essence deals in generalities regarding a very few central ideas. The sovereignty of God is as emphatically assumed as in the Synoptics. A characteristic way of saying this employs the idea of God's "glory," Jesus' glorification being a manifestation of God's glory (ch. 13:31 f.). In many other ways, including Jesus' dependence upon God and his obedience to him, God's supreme sovereignty is acknowledged. Although God's judgment is largely exercised in a delegated manner by Jesus, God is its source and authority.

It is God's redemptive activity that is emphasized in John. God takes the initiative in seeking to provide salvation, most obviously by sending Jesus. His love (*agapē*) is the motivating force in all of this. His redemptive activity takes two forms. He reveals the truth about himself and about the meaning of human existence, offering light in darkness. He also provides the dynamic necessary to salvation, what Paul calls "the power of God unto salvation." Some of the most characteristic ideas of John's Gospel are set forth with reference to the dynamic of salvation embodied in Jesus. The "I am" sayings may be cited by way of example. The central idea is that Jesus is the answer to man's spiritual need, and this is said by means of various analogies: "bread of life" and the "living bread which came down from heaven"; "the light of the world"; "the door of the sheep" and "the good shepherd"; "the resurrection and the life"; "the way, and the truth, and the life"; "the true vine" in relation to God (the vinedresser) and to the disciples (the branches). It is through Jesus' glorification that the Counselor will be given, providing hope and confidence in the future. In other ways as well, especially in offering eternal life, God's power for salvation through Jesus is portrayed.

The paradox that characterizes the Synoptic picture of God is implicit in the Johannine picture. The abundance of love and mercy that characterizes God in the Johannine Gospel never compromises his ethical sovereignty or the unfortunate consequences that ensue when his gracious gift of redemption is refused. When his mercy is repudiated God is known as judge. The universal sweep of God's love, embracing all mankind, does not cause him to be less condemnatory of the consistent obduracy of the Jews in their confrontations with Jesus. Pilate replies with finality to their protests at the cross about the wording of the inscription: "What I have written I have written" (John 19:22). In the same spirit the Father speaks in unequivocal terms to those who, failing to sense that "grace and truth came through Jesus Christ," "received him not."

The story of the blind man in John, ch. 9, with its vivid portrayal of the obstinate blindness of the Jewish authorities, is clear enough in this respect. As elsewhere in the Gospel, it is the positive note that is struck, but it is made unmistakably clear that when one refuses to rise to the challenge of the good news, God's negative judgment is the only possible answer. So Jesus answers the Jewish leaders who had cast the blind man out of the synagogue, typifying the experience of some in John's environment: "If you were blind, you would have no guilt; but now that you say, 'We see,' your guilt remains." This reminds us of the blasphemy against the Holy Spirit which "never has forgiveness" for the same reason, because they said, "He has an unclean spirit." There is something very final in Jesus' statement, "You will die in your sins unless you believe that I am he" (ch. 8:24). This is just as final as the

pronouncement of "eternal punishment" in Matthew's judgment scene, except that, characteristically, the criterion of
judgment in John is an attitude toward Jesus as against the
treatment of one's fellowman in Matthew. In any case, Jesus
in John, as in the Synoptics, makes no effort philosophically to
resolve this paradox of mercy and justice. As in the Synoptics,
he leaves it in the hands of the Father.

The Johannine picture in this respect gives force to the observation of Bultmann that "Jesus' words never convey anything specific or concrete that he has seen with the Father. . . .
Never is the heavenly world the theme of his words. . . . His
theme is always just this one thing: that the Father sent him,
that he came as the light, the bread of life, witness for the
truth, etc.; that he will go again, and that one must believe in
him." This is all intended to signify that his word is "an
authoritative word which confronts the hearers with a life-
and-death decision."[31] It is an exaggeration to say that "as the
Revealer of God" Jesus *reveals nothing but that he is the
Revealer*,"[32] but it is true that many of Jesus' words are not so
much about God as about himself (as in the "I am" sayings).
Even his word, by itself or collectively as his words, is identi-
cal with himself. It is left to faith to open up further meanings
from responding to Jesus.

Even when we draw out implications about the nature of
God which go beyond this, as we have done in a simplistic
manner, this generally remains the impression that the Johannine picture gives. It is also the case when we ask about ideas
relative to doing God's will in the sphere of ethics, as John
views it. The running controversy between Jesus and the Jews
turns up few concrete issues except that of Sabbath observance, and this is subordinated to the question of Jesus' authority as one who has come from God (cf. John 9:14 ff.). However, we may still seek to be more specific about what John
portrays in this respect. It can be done summarily.

Regarding the nature of man, Jesus in John is as realistic and
as optimistic as he is in the Synoptics. Man's ability to make
right choices, primarily the right choice about Jesus, is pre-

supposed in every discussion of the response that God requires of him. It is presupposed that, if he wills, he can "sin no more" (ch. 5:14), that he can be "born anew," which is to be "born of the Spirit" (ch. 3:6–8). Repudiating a doctrine of strict retribution, it is assumed that sin consists of failure to believe in Jesus or to respond to him in faith or in any one of its synonyms. Jesus' coming has created a crisis, since with his coming men no longer have any excuse for not coming to the light, and their sin consists primarily of blindness to his meaning for salvation. This blindness is exemplified most vividly when he who is actually sinless is accused of being a sinner or of having a demon (chs. 8:46; 9:16; 10:20 f.). This dominant assumption of John with regard to man's freedom of choice refutes the view that he is seriously influenced by the magical view of conversion as a change of nature characteristic of some Hellenistic and Gnostic thought. As in the Synoptics, man's capacity for choice is a genuine one.

What is said positively about the ethical life, "realized discipleship," can be stated very briefly. We need not repeat much that has been said about the emphasis upon doing God's will except to note the form that it takes in ch. 14. Here this is expressed in terms of keeping Jesus' commandments as this is linked up with Jesus' own obedience. All that has been said about believing in Jesus, receiving him, and the like, coheres at this point.

The one essential characteristic of the ethical life is love (*agapē*): "A new commandment I give to you, that you love one another; even as I have loved you, that you also love one another. By this all men will know that you are my disciples, if you have love for one another" (ch. 13:34 f.). The inspiration to this practice of love is Jesus' love for the disciples, reproducing God's love for Jesus and the disciples. In this sense Jesus is "the reality in which the obedient one first learns the proper understanding of himself."[33] With the cross in focus it can be said that "greater love has no man than this, that a man lay down his life for his friends" (ch. 15:13), the disciples being designated as Jesus' friends. In this connection echoes of

Mark's martyr ethics are heard in Jesus' anticipation of persecution of the disciples (e.g., ch. 15:18 ff.). The commandment to love is called a "new commandment," meaning the anticipation of its coming to fulfillment in the new life of the Christian community.

Much is implied here about the kind of inwardness that is displayed in the Sermon on the Mount, although there are no specifics as in the Sermon. It would appear that the Jesus of John's Gospel presents in an oversimplified way the essential ingredient of love as set forth more explicitly by Jesus in the Synoptics, leaving its application to the disciples in concrete circumstances. The focus of attention in fact is upon the inner life of the Christian fellowship, not upon the outreach of the church into the world. In this respect it is like Ephesians, with its view of the church as the unified body of believers, setting before the world an example of God's purpose for all mankind. Since there is a proleptic outreach in the high-priestly prayer and since God sent his Son "into the world" because he loved it, it cannot be said that there is anything narrowly exclusive in John's view.[34] And there is concern for the effect of the inner unity of the church upon the world. The degree of such outward looking may be greater in I Peter, as one example, but it is not different in kind, nor is it different in kind from the universalistic implications of the message of Jesus in the Synoptics. Is it perhaps, corresponding to some extent with Jesus' concentration upon his own people in the Synoptics, that what John believes is called for in his circumstances is an emphasis upon the unity of love within the Christian fellowship? At least that is where the accent falls in the ethical teaching of Jesus in John's Gospel.

The Johannine Miracles

As implied in ch. 20:30–31 it is likely that John drew the miracle stories from a "Book of Signs" which was in existence before he wrote, making a selection and editing them for his own purposes.[35] We are concerned, however, only with the finished product as set forth in the Gospel. Thus we shall classify the miracles in John, following the outline of the preceding chapter, and concentrate upon the distinctive features of the Johannine picture as compared with the Synoptic picture. By way of anticipation we may cite Fuller's conclusion with the summary in ch. 12:37–43 in view: "The whole of the ministry, not the miracles only but also the discourses, had but one meaning: it interprets the revealing, saving action of God in the incarnation, death and resurrection of the Son." John simply makes explicit what is implicit behind the Synoptic sources, "namely that every unit of material, the miracles included, preaches in a nutshell the total redemptive act of God in Christ."[36] It is our task to indicate how this is the case with reference to the miracle tradition in John, realizing that this tradition is presented in the closest relationship to Jesus' message. It is so close in fact that one cannot be understood without the other.

John's miracles consist of three healings, one raising of the dead, and three nature miracles. The healings include an official's son at the point of death (ch. 4:46–54), corresponding to the centurion's servant in Matthew and Luke; a lame man at Bethesda (ch. 5:1–9); and a man born blind (ch. 9:1–34). The raising of Lazarus is the one raising of the dead (ch. 11:1–44). The nature miracles include the turning of water into wine at Cana (ch. 2:1–11), which is peculiar to John, and different versions of two Synoptic miracles: the feeding of the multitude (ch. 6:1–3) and the walking on the water (vs. 16–21).

We may get the proper perspective on the miracles in John by taking note of three distinctively Johannine features. First, there are no exorcisms of demons in John's Gospel. Not only so, but the whole framework of the cosmic struggle, so prominent in Mark's Gospel, has largely given way to the Johannine vertical dualism of two worlds instead of two successive ages. This is consistent with what has been said previously about John's eschatology. This is also indicated by the absence of typical Synoptic vocabulary such as "mighty works" and "unclean spirits," and by the relatively insignificant references to "kingdom of God," "Satan," "demons," and "angels." The only point of contact with the Synoptic tradition consists of references to the Spirit with which Jesus is permanently inspired and which he bestows upon those who believe in him.

The second distinctive Johannine characteristic is the way in which the portrait is impregnated with the Hellenistic divine man concept, so that to a certain extent the genuineness of Jesus' humanity appears to be qualified. This tendency is present in the miraculous knowledge that Jesus possesses of "all that was to befall him" (ch. 18:4). He knows ahead of time the sequel of his story. This is most clearly expressed in the language of "my hour has not yet come" (ch. 2:4, e.g.) and the subsequent recognition of its coming in the farewell discourses. He knows from the start that Judas will betray him. He knows that the death of Lazarus is not a tragedy at all, but a predetermined means by which God may be glorified. In a sense the appeal to believe Jesus' words is predicated upon this kind of knowledge rooted in the idea of Jesus as the divine epiphany. Echoing the Synoptic tradition in some of its parts, the disciples recognize that Jesus knows "all things."[37] This is why the note of tragedy is swallowed up in John's view of the death of Jesus, since from the beginning Jesus anticipates it with full knowledge of its character as the completion of his mission. Jesus' immunity to the plots of his enemies, as at his arrest in Gethsemane, is in this frame of reference.

In addition the Johannine miracles are "full of features which are common in pagan wonder stories to an even greater degree than the synoptic miracles." They have a more secular character and they make Jesus out to be more of a wonder worker by toning down Synoptic characteristics that distinguish their miracles from pagan parallels: "the specific Christian teaching in the dialogue and the colouring of the narrative with Old Testament motifs."[38] There is something of the character of a prodigy in the turning of water into wine. Also the sense of the miraculous is heightened in other events by certifying that the official's son was at the point of death, that the man at the pool of Bethesda had been lame for thirty-eight years, that the blind man had been blind from birth, and that Lazarus had been in the tomb long enough for decomposition to set in.

Connotations consistent with this outlook inhere in some of the appeals to Jesus' works as the basis of belief in him, especially in the contrast drawn between Jesus and John the Baptist who "did no sign." The stated purpose of the Gospel in ch. 20:30–31 is to inculcate belief in Jesus as God's Son by means of a selected number of signs. Although generally speaking these signs are more than miracles with evidential value, in contrast to Mark's attempt to tone down the divine man influence by means of the messianic secret John makes full use of the concept.

However, as a third feature of the picture of miracles in John, this divine man concept is put to positive use, as Fuller once again so well expresses it. By using the miracles as media for revelation discourses John "shifts the emphasis away from the miracles as displays of divine power and reinterprets them as signs of the revelation which the pre-existent is bringing into the world. The incarnate life is an epiphany not of a pagan wonder worker, but of the light and life and truth of God himself." In this way John seeks to meet the need for "a direct confrontation with the revelatory presence and saving action of God himself" which the kenotic Christology of Phil. 2:6–11, with all its devotional depth, is unable to satisfy. For John's readers the divine man concept serves this purpose as an effective instrument.[39]

It is not necessary to analyze every possible Johannine incident in order to demonstrate the creative way in which the miracles have been interpreted in order to serve a religious purpose. Only two are explicitly designated as "signs" (chs. 2:11; 4:54), but all of them have a symbolical significance, along with other features that are not miraculous in nature.[40] John's mind appears to move constantly on two levels, as is indicated by his use of symbolical characters: Nathanael as the type of the true Israelite; the beloved disciple as a type of the true disciple; the "Greeks" symbolizing the Gentile world; Mary of Bethany symbolizing the devout believer; Thomas symbolizing the more materialistically-minded believer; etc.

The device by which John brings out the symbolical significance of the miracles is an accompanying discourse or dialogue.

The first sign at Cana serves the purpose, like the Nazareth
sermon in Luke 4:16–30, of symbolizing the meaning of Jesus'
whole ministry. In contrast to what is offered in Judaism, Jesus'
glory is manifested by supplying the "wine" of the gospel,
God's presence and power being revealed in a saving act. The
revelation is not simply a word, but a redemptive act. There
is but one basic message reemphasized repeatedly by means
of different symbols, whether it be the healing of blindness,
the feeding of the multitude, or the raising of Lazarus. When
Jesus declares that he is the resurrection and the life he is not
saying something different from assertions that he is bread of
life, light of the world, or, what he is implicitly saying in the
Cana miracle or in the cleansing of the Temple. As we have
observed, John has a single message of salvation through Jesus,
and the miracles are turned to express that in their own way.
More specific things are implied, to be sure, as when the feeding of the multitude is directed toward an understanding of
the Eucharist as a messianic banquet made truly available
through the cross, even though the Eucharistic aspect of the
Lord's Supper is absent from John. The underlying message,
however, is always the same. The supreme sign, as we shall
soon see, is the passion and glorification of the Son fully docu-
mented at the Last Supper before it actually occurs.

This way of viewing the miracles as signs or symbols of spiritual reality may exist to some extent in the Synoptic tradition,
but it is not the prevailing Synoptic perspective. One marked
difference is the absence in John of the idea that the miracles
are the tokens of the Last Days, simply because the eschatological perspective is radically different. Eschatological signs,
as in Mark, ch. 13, are absent. To the extent that Jesus is portrayed as compassionate in a healing setting, it is more artificial in John, as when he weeps even though he knows that
he will raise Lazarus soon. But this too may be symbolical, a
weeping because of unbelief in general, and thus consistent

with the portrayal of his love for the disciples and the world. Obviously the secret Messiahship motif of Mark has no place in John's open declaration of Jesus' status from the beginning of the Gospel.

At the same time there is a pattern similar to that in the Synoptics which shows Jesus taking a negative attitude toward belief based upon miracles and which counters the divine man concept. The quotation of Isa. 53:1 and 6:10 in John 12:37-40 takes place with reference to the fact that the signs had failed to elicit belief, even though the sign comprehends the total meaning of the event. In ch. 2:23 f. Jesus does not trust himself to those who believe when they see his signs, and in ch. 6:26 he distinguishes this kind of response from a more genuine religious experience. On the highest level of belief is that which is contrasted with Thomas' need for external verification: "Blessed are those who have not seen and yet believe" (ch. 20:29). More often than not it is Jesus' word, comprehending his full significance, that elicits faith. This is graphically portrayed in the confidence that the official whose son was healed has in Jesus (ch. 4:48, 50).

Many of the references to Jesus' works may contain an element consistent with the divine man idea. On the other hand, the central motif in this area is the idea that Jesus accomplishes "the work" (singular) that God gave him to do, with his whole career and the full meaning of his message in view (ch. 17:4). This implies that to believe in Jesus for the sake of the works that God accomplishes in him transcends the kind of response that the wonder worker alone can elicit, especially since the belief of the disciples that the Father has sent the Son is also God's work. The "greater works" which the disciples will perform after Jesus' departure transcend miracle-working, if they involve it at all, since they carry forward Jesus' own work. At least the miracles, granting their unique features, merge into the total meaning of Jesus' mission as John sees it, preaching "in a nutshell the total redemptive act of God in Christ." Thus they call for faith in Jesus as God's Son, the bearer of spiritual reality and vitality, rather than in

Jesus the wonder worker. The real wonder is that he makes God known and effectively present as the power that overcomes the world.

The Death of Jesus

With C. H. Dodd, we consider John's Gospel to be divided into two distinct parts following the prologue in ch. 1:1–18, "The Book of Signs" (chs. 1:19 to 12:50) and "The Book of the Passion" (chs. 13 to 21). The latter is made up of the farewell discourses (chs. 13 to 17), the passion narrative (chs. 18 to 20), and the appendix (ch. 21). The farewell discourses, which are quite distinctive of John, contain two main classes of material: "first, material corresponding to the 'esoteric' teaching comprised in the Synoptic Gospels, but enlarged and developed in a Johannine sense; and secondly, material corresponding to certain parts of the Book of Signs, but developed upon a new plane of significance."[41] Apparently, fresh teaching under both heads is largely in the nature of an expansion of topics already presented.

Any completely systematic treatment of Johannine thought about the death of Jesus needs to develop the themes of the farewell discourses that are relevant, as Dodd has done. However, our purpose dictates a different procedure here. Recognizing the value of Dodd's observations, we shall concentrate upon the death of Jesus with the passion story primarily in focus, but with attention to data anywhere in the Gospel which contribute to our understanding. Actually the farewell discourses are included in the passion story proper, since the final plot against Jesus begins to take shape following the raising of Lazarus in ch. 11:45 ff. and since the setting of the discourses is the Last Supper.

We shall organize the material under headings that correspond to those employed in the treatment of the Synoptics in the preceding chapter: responsibility for the death of Jesus, prepassion story anticipations of death and resurrection, and theological interpretations of the death of Jesus. Our concern is to bring out distinctly Johannine traits and themes.

The Jewish opponents of Jesus in John's Gospel consist of the Jews, Pharisees, and chief priests. As against the Synoptic picture, scribes and Sadducees and elders are not named. It is the Pharisees who are viewed as working hand in glove with the chief priests. They appear before the passion story at the initiation of the final plot, and at Jesus' arrest. As in the Synoptics, however, they appear primarily in earlier stages of conflict with Jesus, while the chief priests, though mentioned (with Levites) once in ch. 1:19, figure alone mostly during the final stages of the plot. The chief priests named are Caiaphas and Annas, the former actually being in control. Pilate figures in the final scenes much as in the Synoptics with reference to the Jewish leaders.

The main question concerns the identity of "the Jews." In some references the expression appears as a vague generalization (e.g., ch. 7:1). In other references, however, it appears to be an equivalent for the Jewish leaders. In ch. 8, for example, Pharisees are mentioned in v. 13 and the Jews in four succeeding verses. In the final events it appears that the Jews are to be equated with the chief priests, even though some ambiguity remains. The protesters in John's version of the cleansing of the Temple are the Jews, but in the Synoptics they are the chief priests and elders. It appears reasonable to assume that John has the Jewish leaders in mind in this way of designating Jesus' opponents, probably in a representative as well as in an individual capacity. Historical reminiscence is combined with the opposition that the church in John's situation is facing from the Jewish synagogue after the destruction of Jerusalem in A.D. 70. The expulsion of the blind man from the synagogue, for example, is not simply a historical reminiscence, if it is that at all; it is an experience of at least some Jewish Christians in John's community.

Thus, in general, John takes the same view of the responsibility for the death of Jesus that characterizes the Synoptic accounts. It rests upon the Temple hierarchy, abetted by teachers of the law, in this case the Pharisees rather than the scribes, with Pilate unwillingly drawn in to carry out their ne-

farious designs. As in Luke's Gospel, the innocence of Jesus is
emphasized by Pilate's attitude toward him and toward the
proceedings. An apologetic motif is evident in the emphasis
that is placed upon the manner of Jesus' death as crucifixion
rather than stoning, necessarily involving the Roman authorities. This also supports the expression "lifted up" with its
double sense of raised up on a cross and elevated in exalted
dignity.

The charges against Jesus concern the main theme of the
Gospel as a whole, namely, Jesus' authority, his claim to be
sent from God. Even when the specifics of the Synoptic accounts are in focus, Sabbath observance and the cleansing of
the Temple, which is rarely the case, the question concerns
Jesus' status and significance. Although the term "blasphemy"
occurs only once (ch. 10:33), involving stoning, the problem
is that Jesus makes himself "God" or "Son of God" (ch. 19:7).
The plot takes shape in the first place because of the sign that
was accomplished in the raising of Lazarus, the question of
Jesus' authority and influence being the issue. John emphasizes
the political charge against Jesus as part of the strategy of the
Jewish leaders, and the confrontation with Pilate involves the
question of his kingship. However, the ultimate issue is the
extent to which Jesus witnesses to the truth. In other words,
the charges against Jesus at his trials are the same as those
made against him throughout the Gospel with reference to his
claim to come from God with light and life and truth. What
the passion story does is to put this in a historical context
which makes the incarnational nature of Jesus' revelation emphatic, as against a possible docetic view and as against the
opposition of Judaism. There is also some concern for the effect upon Roman officials. In this respect, granting that which
is unique in the materials and in the purpose of John, it is very
much like the Synoptic picture.

John's picture is also much like the Synoptic picture, again
with features quite unique to his outlook, in its portrayal of
Jesus' anticipations of his eventual death. John does not repeat
the passion predictions in Synoptic terminology, but he has his

own way of emphasizing Jesus' expectation. He introduces even more of an element of predeterminism than is evident in the Synoptics, and he does it from the beginning. As early as ch. 2:4 Jesus looks forward to his "hour" or to his "time" as "not yet come," and he is aware when it has arrived (ch. 12:23). The hour is more than the time of his death, since this will be the occasion of his glorification and return to the Father, but his death is the focal point of the predictions. This will also be the time when the localized worship of God in Jerusalem and in Mt. Gerizim is transcended (ch. 4:21–23). Foreknowledge of Judas' betrayal is also part of this predeterministic outlook. Corresponding to the anticipation of death and resurrection in the Synoptic passion predictions are Johannine references to Jesus' laying down his life in order to take it again, the lifting up of the Son of Man, and the double meaning of the term "ascend."

The Synoptic pattern of misunderstanding on the part of the disciples is also echoed within the context of John's method of introducing "stupid characters" whose failure to grasp Jesus' cryptic utterances permits him to elaborate upon his teaching. This involves the Jews in many references, Nicodemus, the Samaritan woman, and so forth. The disciples fit into this pattern in general (cf. ch. 4:27, 33). Peter's response at the footwashing is typical. Specific references to the passion are included (chs. 13:22; 16:17). The betrayal of Jesus by Judas and his denial by Peter, as in the Synoptics, highlight this feature of the story.[42] The equation of the verb "to know" with "to understand" also fits within this context.

C. H. Dodd contends that if we properly distinguish between apologetic and theological interpretation, the passion narrative of John's Gospel contains "only a minimum of intruded interpretative elements."[43] It is primarily of apologetic significance, for example, for John to emphasize the testimony of the empty tomb. "It does not proceed from the specifically Johannine theology."[44] On the other hand, "the repeated use of the verb *anabainein* ["to ascend"] (xx. 17) points back to passages in the Book of Signs (iii. 13, vi. 62) where it has a spe-

cific theological significance."[45] At the same time, the passion
story is intended to be understood "in the light of all that has
been said in earlier parts of the gospel, directly and indirectly,
about the meaning of Christ's death and resurrection."[46] With
these distinctions in mind, since they appear to be valid, we
shall content ourselves with bringing out summarily distinctive
features of the Johannine theological perspective on the death
and resurrection of Jesus. Since some of the facets of this picture have already been implied, it will suffice simply to recall
them here.

With the total event of the arrest, trial, and crucifixion of
Jesus in view, we can hardly improve upon C. H. Dodd's conclusion that here we have "a *semeion* ["sign"] on the grand
scale, to whose significance each detail contributes," yet a sign
that "differs from all other signs" as "a sign which is also the
thing signified."[47] Let us consider first the idea that certain details of the closing events call up "by association a chain of
ideas already expounded" and gather them up into the supreme sign. For example, we now perceive that the sign of
the wine at Cana is the blood of the true Vine, that the sign
of the bread is the flesh of Christ given for the world, that the
sign of Lazarus is the life victorious over death through the
laying down of that life, etc. The spear thrust in ch. 19:34 f.
recalls references to "rivers of living water" (ch. 7:38 f.), "a
spring of water welling up to eternal life" (ch. 4:14), and the
drinking of blood unto eternal life (ch. 6:54). The confession
of Thomas, "My Lord and my God!" recaptures the august
sentiments of "The Word was God" (ch. 1:1). The reference
to Jesus' kingship as not of this world, but a witness to "the
truth" (ch. 18:37), recalls numerous expressions of a similar
nature earlier.

In these and other ways the events of the passion coalesce
with the whole Gospel to give it a significance as a sign "on a
grand scale." But there is more, since all previous signs were
preliminary to their ultimate verification in the passion as "an
event in both worlds," something that happened in time "with
eternal consequences." "In it the two orders of reality, the tem-

poral, and the eternal, are united; the Word is made flesh."
Thus the passion is also "the thing signified," because the preliminary signs "are true—spiritually, eternally true—only upon
the condition that this Event is true, both temporally (or his-
torically) and spiritually or eternally."[48] Although this is the
language of faith speaking, it rests upon a solid conviction
about the reality of the historical crucifixion, thus turning
away from a docetic view of the history of Jesus of Nazareth.

This is brought out by the way in which John telescopes, as
it were, the death and the resurrection of Jesus. In the Synoptics, as in I Cor. 15:3 f., the crucifixion is followed by the
mighty act of resurrection which reverses the negative verdict
of crucifixion. For John, on the other hand, the hour of death
is anticipated as the moment of glorification, and Jesus' dying
words acknowledge the fact that at that point he has completed his divine mission to the world and is released from his
commission in order to return to the Father. In that sense the
resurrection as a subsequent event is unnecessary. The appearances simply serve to portray the way in which personal relations are renewed, as anticipated in the farewell discourses; or
they give attention to the fact that the Spirit was received on
one occasion in a way not true of any other occasion. The
resurrection does not reverse a defeat on the cross, however,
because in John the crucifixion is not a defeat; it is the moment
of Jesus' vindication. In John's unique outlook this carries to
an extreme the view of the New Testament that the cross has
redemptive significance. In the climax of the Gospel it is suggested that it is not even necessary to have an experience of
the resurrected Christ, at least not in a materialistic sense, so
long as one has eyes opened to the true meaning of Jesus'
death (ch. 20:29).

Various items peculiar to John's resurrection narratives might
be cited here, but they are not of primary interest. It is more
important to ask what it is about Jesus as represented by his
crucifixion that leads John to his view of things. We may recall
the deterministic motif that informs the Gospel and note the
Scriptural apologetic that supports it, as in the Synoptic ac-

counts, despite different quotations in John.[49] We begin to approach his mind more profoundly, however, when we note the way in which he brings out the voluntary nature of Jesus' suffering, however strong the deterministic note may appear to be. Jesus chooses to lay down his life, as he chooses to be obedient to the Father throughout the Gospel, and as he voluntarily surrenders himself in the garden. Another clue exists in the way in which terms of a metaphysical cast (life, light) recede in chs. 13 to 17 and are replaced by terms of a more distinctly ethical cast, primarily by the term "love" or *agapē*. Without abandoning for a moment the conviction that Christ brings life and light, nevertheless, John appears to want to emphasize the truth "that the final reality of life and light is given in *agapē*."[50] From this it is but a step to the conclusion that the glorification and exaltation of Jesus in his death are taken in an absolute sense, since "it is the absolute expression of the divine *agapē*."[51] Thus Jesus himself perfectly embodies that love of God which, for the sake of imparting eternal life to the world, had sent him into the world in the first place.

This is the Johannine way of saying that the death of Jesus has redemptive significance. It is not so much the sacrificial language of Paul, since this type of analogy is not prominent in John.[52] It is, rather, the evidence of love in a self-sacrificial sense, love in a supreme sense for one's friends and by implication for the whole world. It is also to a certain extent an "example," as in I Peter, since the "greater works" promised for the disciples of necessity consist of abiding in, and thus exemplifying, the love of Jesus (God) for them.

We have been concerned to portray the leading Christological themes and interests of John in his Gospel. We may believe that he did not express these ideas in a vacuum. Especially important are his anti-Jewish polemic[53] and his opposition to Gnostic Docetism. In the former case John is much like Luke. In the latter case, however, as against Luke's direct negative to Docetism, John "makes a positive approach to gnosticism, using some of its language in order to destroy its error."[54] To this may probably be added a polemic against the disciples of John the Baptist, and perhaps against others. However, these are all means to an inclusive end. The overarching aim is to create such an appreciation of the significance of Jesus that the life that is available in his name may be received through believing response. This is its offer to nonbelievers. To believers the challenge is so to embody that life within their fellowship that the church may be an effective instrument of its bequest to the world, which is the object of God's saving purpose.

Chapter IV

THE GOSPEL-PERSPECTIVE
IN THE NEW TESTAMENT

UP to this point we have been considering the Gospels largely
in isolation from the rest of the New Testament. However, if
the Gospel-perspective is to be fully appreciated, we must set
its "variety-in-unity" within the context of the New Testament
as a whole by means of a comparison with the perspectives of
the Epistles. Since our focus of attention is the New Testament rather than early Christian literature in general, references to extracanonical writings will be included only where
they appear to be particularly relevant.

In order to accomplish this comparative task we shall employ a fourfold scheme of New Testament Christology as a
basis after the manner of the following diagram:[1]

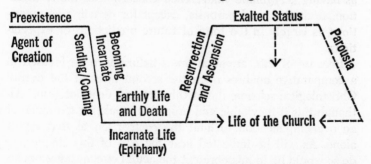

Accordingly, we shall treat the New Testament data
under four headings: Jesus' (1) pre-earthly status and activity,
(2) earthly life and death, (3) resurrection and exaltation,

(4) parousia. The transitions in the form of transfer from heaven to earth (becoming incarnate), and subsequently from earth to heaven (resurrection and ascension), will be absorbed into the major groupings of material.

Certain general observations of a more or less obvious nature may be made by way of anticipation. Both the Gospels and the Epistles are oriented in the postresurrection situation to the extent that both presuppose the resurrection and are mutually bearers of the proclamation and teaching of the church about the risen Jesus. However, their focus differs between the four facets of the total Christological pattern. In the Epistles the earthly life of Jesus is assumed to be either a preliminary stage to what follows it or an interim period between what goes before and what comes after it. There is little concern for details of Jesus' activity and teaching. This is as true of The Acts as of Paul, even though it is a difference in degree. The death of Jesus is emphasized, but in the form of its theological and soteriological significance. The great bulk of the material deals with the exalted Christ and, less so, with the pre-earthly and the parousia stages of the total event.

On the other hand, three of the Gospels completely ignore the pre-earthly period, and all four are distinguished by their concentration upon the details of Jesus' earthly life and death as having kerygmatic value. Their concern with the resurrection, exaltation, and parousia, except for certain presuppositions, is largely in the form of future predictions or expectations.

Because of this, attention tends naturally to be focused in a comparative analysis upon the second facet of the overall Christological scheme, the earthly life and death of Jesus. Although this is inevitable and proper, it would be too much of an oversimplification to limit the comparison to that aspect alone. As will be indicated near the end of this chapter, to do so would be to misrepresent the actual circumstances existing between the Gospels and the Epistles. The relationships are much more complex than this suggests.

In portraying the Christological perspectives of the New

Testament as a whole it will be in order at certain points, as in the treatment of the Gospels, to appeal to non-Christian contextual categories for help in understanding them. With great acuteness James M. Robinson states the rationale for this concern. "The original Christian message," he says, "was a flow of Jewish-Hellenistic language and hence was never 'pure' in the sense of being exclusively Christian. Except in the case of speaking with tongues, the Christian message was intelligible to the non-Christian because it was proclaimed in his language. Such proclamation always involved both an affirmation, usually only implicit, of the relative usefulness of a given non-Christian culture, represented by its language, and, by the proclamation of its subjection to Christ, a rejection, often explicit, of the same culture's orientation. The accuracy and adequacy of any historical analysis are measured in terms of these dialectical interrelationships."[2]

With the whole range of Christological speculation in view, John McIntyre speaks to an important point within this spectrum. Countering what he calls the myth of the theological wordbook approach, he says, "The meaning of words for speaker and listener, for writer and reader, is largely dependent upon the setting in which they occur and the purpose they were designed to serve."[3] Particularly pertinent applications of this principle to the New Testament are found in Moule's article, "The Influence of Circumstances on the Use of Christological Terms."[4] Along the same line is Werner Kramer's elaboration, as against a statistical procedure, of "theme-criticism" in seeking to discern the meaning of Christological terms within the context of different strata of New Testament thought.[5]

The non-Christian tools for interpreting the New Testament consist of a variety of sources representing a Jewish-Hellenistic syncretism, exceedingly complex and with many crosscurrents. Generally speaking, it may be broken down into Palestinian-Jewish, Hellenistic-Jewish, and Gentile elements.[6]

In the process of elaborating the details of the proposed diagram in the following pages the question of the precise dating of the New Testament documents is not of great concern.[7] For our purpose it is less important, for example, to date The Acts with precision than it is to see its dual relation to the Gospel of Luke, on the one hand, and to the period subsequent to the Gospel on the other hand. This applies as well to the "genuine" and the "disputed" letters of Paul, or to Paul and the Pauline tradition, and also to the relationship between John's Gospel and the Johannine Letters. We are not asking about the influence of one document upon another, which presupposes a definite chronological scheme, but only about comparative Christologies and related matters as they stand. In this comparative process it is hoped that the picture of the Gospel-perspective set forth in earlier chapters will be sharpened in its variety as well as in its basic unity.

THE PRE-EARTHLY STATUS AND ACTIVITY OF JESUS

In sharp contrast to the Synoptic Gospels, but with affinities with John's Gospel, limited sections of the Epistles concern themselves with ideas about a pre-earthly stage in the event of Christ. The most explicit data are found in fragments of Christological hymns: Phil. 2:6–11; Col. 1:15–20; Heb. 1:1–4; I Tim. 3:16; I Peter 1:20 and 3:18–22;[8] and occasionally elsewhere.

In a summary form the details are as follows: Paul's *kenōsis* view in Phil. 2:6–7 is unique. Jesus existed "in the form of God," which probably means in a state of "equality with God." It is not clear whether he refuses to grasp at something which he can have if he wants it or whether he declines to retain a mode of existence which he fully possesses. At least his status possesses a dignity greater than that of the "image of God" in Gen. 1:27.[9] This is the case even when the term "image" is used (II Cor. 4:4; Col. 1:15). Other expressions include "the firstborn of all creation,"[10] "before all things,"[11] "predestined before the foundation of the world."[12] Something about preexistence may be implied in references to the "mystery which was kept secret for long ages,"[13] and possibly in the idea that

Christ is the Rock in the wilderness during the time of Moses.[14] References to the preeminence or supremacy of Jesus, although they generally refer to the postresurrection stage, imply something about the pre-earthly situation.[15]

Jesus' agency in creation and in sustaining it are both found in I Cor. 8:6: "For us there is one God, the Father, from whom are all things and for whom we exist, and one Lord, Jesus Christ, through whom are all things and through whom we exist." Colossians 1:16–18 supports this idea, retaining the concept of instrumentality by using the preposition "through" (dia), but going beyond I Corinthians to add that "all things" are created "for him" and sustained "in him."[16]

The idea of Jesus as both agent of revelation and salvation bringer is expressed in the form of his descent to earth as the transition from pre-earthly existence to that of earthly life. Five different ways of describing this inception of Jesus' earthly career appear.

First, some passages speak simply of Jesus' "coming" without stating upon whose initiative this occurred. Typical of this idea are the following: "until Christ came" (Gal. 3:24) and "the Son of God has come" (I John 5:20).

Second, God's initiative is explicitly stated in the idea that Jesus was "sent." Galatians 4:4 is typical: "But when the time had fully come, God sent forth his Son."

Third, God's initiative, especially with reference to the death of Jesus, is expressed in the idea of his having "given up" the Son on behalf of man's salvation (Rom. 8:32). Elsewhere, however, the initiative is that of the Son himself (Gal. 2:20; Eph. 5:2, 25).

Fourth, the self-emptying or kenōsis of Phil. 2:7–8a makes the idea of incarnation explicit, especially in the expressions "taking the form of a servant" and being obedient unto "death on a cross." In other expressions, such as "according to the flesh" (kata sarka), Paul reinforces this incarnational thrust (Rom. 1:3 f.) In Rom. 8:3 we read that the Son is sent "in the likeness of sinful flesh" and in Gal. 4:4 that he is "born of woman, born under the law." Echoes of this idea appear as well in I Tim. 3.16 and I Peter 3:18. Hebrews 2:14 and 17 especially emphasize Jesus' likeness to all other men in partaking of "the same nature." This antidocetic motif reaches its climax in the view of the Johannine Letters that to deny the coming of Jesus Christ "in the flesh" is to speak as Antichrist (II John 7).

Fifth, most explicitly in the Pastoral Letters, a positive attitude toward the whole earthly life of Jesus, as against his death alone, is implied in the idea of his being "manifested in the flesh" as an epiphany (I Tim. 3:16). The idea is that in the form of revelation something hidden has now been made known in Jesus' whole career.

Among the Gospels, John alone, largely in the prologue, reflects this type of thought. The infancy stories of Matthew and Luke, consistently with the theme of Old Testament fulfillment, presuppose on God's part a pre-earthly intention and preparation for Jesus' career, but the world of concepts is quite different.

In John, references to the Word as present "in the beginning [en arche] . . . with God" recall "the before all things" of Colossians and the Melchizedek typology of the letter to the Hebrews. The term "fullness" reminds us of Colossians, although it is differently applied in John. The idea of Jesus as having been "in the bosom of the Father," the statement about his "glory," and the references to his being "from above" cohere with these connotations. That "life" equivalent to "the light of men," was "in him" and Jesus' agency in creation are also pertinent.

The overwhelming emphasis of John, however, falls upon the incarnational theme of Jesus' descent and involvement with the world as the agent of revelation and salvation. There are similarities between John's thought and that of Paul in Phil. 2:6–11, but John's is expressed in the form of the epiphany theme characteristic of the Pastorals rather than in that of the self-emptying idea peculiar to Philippians. The predominant form of thought relative to Jesus' appearance in history is that of sending. This is expressed some forty-two times, of which John 4:34 is typical: "My food is to do the will of him who sent me." This idea forms a complex that includes in addition the sending of John the Baptist, the eventual sending of the Paraclete, and Jesus' sending of the disciples. Although God "gave his only Son," most of the references to God's giving have in view the authority that he bestows upon Jesus. The idea of Jesus' "coming" appears to a limited extent in conjunction with the coming of the Baptist.

Jesus' agency in revelation is expressed in a number of different ways, beginning in the prologue with the idea of the light shining in the darkness. Echoing the "Johannine" Q saying in Luke 21:22, Jesus makes God known or he manifests the Father. The other Johannine term is "witness" (*martyria*) and its verbal form. Most of its uses in John concern the witness borne to Jesus by God, the Scriptures, his works, and others, but occasionally it is used of Jesus' witness to God (e.g., John 5:36).

In order for modern man to be able to set this type of thought within the milieu in which it originated, it is necessary to appreciate the presuppositions of ancient man. S. J. Case introduces us to this subject in these words: "The sky hung low in the ancient world. Traffic was heavy on the highway between heaven and earth. Gods and spirits thickly populated the upper air, where they stood in readiness to intervene at any moment in the affairs of mortals. And demonic powers, emerging from the lower world or resident in remote corners of the earth, were a constant menace to human welfare. All nature was alive—alive with supernatural forces."[17] In due course we shall have occasion to recall these words with reference to the idea of the exalted Christ overcoming the cosmic powers. For the moment we have in mind the specific type of thought within this general frame of reference which applies to ideas of preexistence and pre-earthly activity on the part of Jesus Christ.

Both in vocabulary and in ideas the New Testament concepts in this area have affinities with the Wisdom myth of Hellenistic Judaism. Beginning with Job and Proverbs and culminating in the Wisdom of Solomon and the writings of

Philo of Alexandria, we can trace the successive stages through which the Wisdom myth developed. It is summed up in I Enoch, ch. 42, with four facets. After much aimless wandering, an abstract and sometimes hypostatized or personified Wisdom is assigned a dwelling place in heaven. From there she descends to earth to dwell "among the children of men" in order to provide divine guidance or knowledge (*gnōsis*). Being rejected by men, however, she can find no congenial dwelling place. Thus, resigned to this rejection, she returns to her place in heaven to sit "among the angels."

The details of this mythological picture include several items relevant to the New Testament materials. We find the general idea of preexistence or hiddenness, although in different degrees and stages of development, the idea of agency in creation and activity in sustaining the created universe, the idea of descent to earth as agent of revelation. The vocabulary of the myth is significant. Wisdom (*sophia*) is fused with Word (*logos*), and in Philo in particular a further fusion takes place with the Heavenly Man, Adam, and High Priest. Other terms for Wisdom include "image (*eikōn*) of God," "reflection or effulgence (*apaugasma*) of God," "stamp" (*charaktēr*), "first-born" (*prōtotokos*), and the idea of "foreknowledge" or "predestination" (*prognōsis*).

Earlier we had occasion to observe the way in which the Similitudes of Enoch (I Enoch, chs. 37 to 71) also portray a Son of Man figure, somewhat fused with other supernatural figures, who existed before creation and shared something of God's glory (*doxa*). In contrast to the descent of Wisdom to earth, however, the Son of Man is an eschatological figure who is not revealed until the End.[18] The Gnostic dualism of the Qumran Scrolls and of the Nag Hamadi literature is also relevant, especially in the background of John, but in the former it has more to do with the future than with the pre-earthly period.

Two things may properly be said about this parallelism between the Wisdom myth (and related types of thought) and the New Testament views. It illustrates the dialectic between dependence upon and independence of the non-Christian contextual language which was stated earlier in these pages. On the one hand we observe some New Testament writers, including John, trying to find a handle by means of which to make the good news intelligible to Wisdom-oriented and Gnostic-oriented readers. In the process the figure of a historical person takes on some of the traits of a divine being after the pattern of a hypostatized Wisdom figure. At the same time, due to the primacy of the distinctly Christian memory and experience, Jesus' earthly appearance and career are understood, without docetic implications, as genuinely incarnational in nature. In John's form of thought the revelatory function of Jesus, including the idea of his coming which is more implicit in the Synoptics (cf. Luke 19:10), is upgraded within the context of his dualistic presuppositions. At the same time, despite metaphysical implications, it is the functional significance of the Word made flesh that John emphasizes. Using the language of the gnosticized Wisdom myth, John strives to show his readers that Jesus is the true Revealer so that they may come in their experience to know the life and light that, as such, he imparts.

Here is the origin of the mystery of Jesus' person which made the paradoxical formulation of the two-nature Chalcedonian model in the fifth century perhaps inevitable, a formulation that went far beyond the essentially elementary and nonphilosophical nature of New Testament thought on this issue. New Testament thought is more confessional than philosophical in its attempt to elucidate a conviction of experience about Jesus' saving power. Beyond the attempt to elucidate that conviction for themselves and their readers in the language of their environment, in this case in Wisdom concepts which they transcend and qualify in the process, the New Testament "theologians" do not go.

THE EARTHLY LIFE AND DEATH OF JESUS

As is obvious, the Gospels fit into the total Christological picture of the New Testament primarily as expansions and elaborations of those features of the initial proclamation which have to do with Jesus' life and death in the preresurrection period. Even though they adapt their materials to postresurrection situations, they accomplish this by appealing to detailed reminiscences of Jesus' teaching and activity in a way quite uncharacteristic of any other New Testament writing. Pertaining to form as well as content, this is the most obvious difference between the Gospels and the Epistles. At the same time there are points of contact between the two, and our task here is to point out the extent and the nature of these contacts. This can be accomplished simply by describing, without commentary, the essential features of the picture of the earthly Jesus in the Epistles. Since the data are relatively meager, they may be treated exhaustively.

The main distinction lies between the period prior to the crucifixion and the crucifixion itself, interest in the latter being predominant in the Epistles. In presenting the precrucifixion data we shall distinguish between the material in The Acts and in the other sources. On the assumption that Luke-Acts is by a single author, we may in this way get a better perspective on the interests of the writers completely outside the sphere of the Gospels.

The picture of Jesus' life prior to the crucifixion, exclusive of The Acts, is as follows: Of Jewish heritage and Davidic descent, Jesus is "born of woman" as one among several brothers of whom only James is specifically named. Of events prior to Jesus' public ministry the baptism is implied in I John 5:6 and perhaps in Heb. 5:5; the temptation, in Heb. 2:18 and 4:15. With regard to Jesus' public ministry, Peter alone is mentioned as a disciple, along with references to James as Jesus' brother. A vague reference to the transfiguration appears in II Peter 1:16. Hebrews 2:3 reflects the preaching and teaching activity of Jesus, and a series of allusions reflects sayings of Jesus, notably in Paul's letters, James, and The Revelation to John.[19] However, there is nothing comparable to the Synoptic sayings tradition. A comparatively large number of theologically oriented references attest the quality of Jesus' life: his obedience, sinlessness, humility, and, with more direct bearing upon his death, his completely self-sacrificing spirit.[20]

The picture of Jesus' life in The Acts supports all this and amplifies it at several points. Amplification appears in the form of the proper name "Jesus" used alone many times (but see Hebrews), the mention of Mary as Jesus' mother, Nazareth as Jesus' hometown, and especially, references to the ministry, message, and disciples of John the Baptist. Peter's speech in Acts 10:36-39 outlines the public ministry. It provides chronological and topographical references and indications of its nature as including healing and the teaching of the good news of salvation as well as an attack on the Temple and the law. References to Jesus' disciples are expanded, disciples in general and the inner coterie of the Twelve whose names correspond to the list in Luke 6:14-16. Among the latter Peter is most prominent along with mention of John Zebedee, Judas, and James the Lord's brother. Along with references to his righteous character, as in Paul, Jesus' prophetic stance and endowment with the Spirit are cited.

In portraying the picture of Jesus' death outside the Gospels it is unnecessary to cite the multitude of references to the fact of death, since they are so abundant. Nor does it serve any purpose to treat the material in The Acts by itself, since there are few significant differences. It will suffice simply to take note of the few historical details that The Acts and the Epistles contain. These include references to Gethsemane (Heb. 5:7), the betrayal (I Cor. 11:23; Acts 1:16 ff.), the arrest (Acts 1:16), and the Last Supper (I Cor. 10:16; 11:20, 23-26). With precedent in the Qumran Scrolls, the cup is singularly absent from The Acts in situations of the breaking of bread. Hebrews 7:27 and 9:14 emphasize the voluntary nature of Jesus' death. Personalities involved in the drama are Barabbas (Acts 3:14), Pilate (Acts 3:13; 13:28; I Tim. 6:13) and, by implication from The Acts, the Sadducees and Temple authorities, elders and scribes, and the Pharisees. Jesus' death in the form of a crucifixion, implying his condemnation as a criminal, is accented

(Gal. 3:1; I Cor. 1:23; etc.). It is viewed as having taken place
in Jerusalem (Acts 2:5, etc.), "outside the gate" (Heb. 13:12),
and followed by honorable burial (Acts 13:29; I Cor. 15:4).
The responsibility of the Jews is mentioned once by Paul
(I Thess. 2:14 f.) and often in The Acts, the latter explicitly
exonerating Pilate (ch. 3:13). Cosmic powers are blamed by
Paul in one place (I Cor. 2:8 f.).

It can be seen from this review that historical details are
of little interest to the New Testament writers outside the
Gospels except as they presuppose the actual life and death
of a particular Jesus of Nazareth. What matters to them is
the meaning of the cross with reference to redemption, and it
is this that they elaborate. Wrestling with the problem of the
cross in their communities, "a stumbling block to Jews and
folly to Gentiles," they go beyond the Gospels in the direction
of a theological apologetic.

In doing so they do not entirely differentiate themselves
from the characteristics of the Gospels. Gospels and Epistles
alike view the cross in the light of the resurrection as having
redemptive significance. Mark, it is said, began his Gospel
with the cross and worked backward, and he records the saying about Jesus' being a "ransom for many." However, John's
Gospel comes more specifically than the Synoptics into this
sphere of redemptive thought with its emphasis upon the
voluntary nature of Jesus' death. If an anti-Gnostic motif is
most explicit in John and the Johannine Letters, it is at least
implicit in the Synoptics and in Paul's letters. Scriptural apologetic exists in both units of the New Testament tradition,[21] as
well as the more general idea of Jesus' death being "according
to the definite plan and foreknowledge of God" (Acts 2:23).
In both groups of sources the innocence of Jesus in the face
of the Jewish charges against him is taken for granted.

Granting these and other similarities, the Epistles provide a
theological elaboration and extension of the question which
goes far beyond the Gospel-perspective. Paul treats the death
of Jesus as a truly vicarious self-giving, if also initiated by God,
"for us" or "for many" with the motivation of redemption from

sin: "Christ died for our sins" (I Cor. 15:3).[22] The benefits of salvation which are so prominent a part of the picture of Jesus' work in the Epistles in general are geared into this vicarious self-giving of Jesus for sin and sinners. It is "Christ crucified" who is "the power of God and the wisdom of God" (I Cor. 1:23 f.). Men are "sanctified through the offering of the body of Jesus Christ once for all" (Heb. 10:10). Forgiveness of sins, producing peace of mind and reconciliation between God and man and man and man, is a major effect of Jesus' death. Jesus' ability to act as mediator between God and man is effected by his sacrificial death, especially in I John and Hebrews. Particularly in Romans and Galatians, Jesus' death opens the way to genuine ethical freedom over against the stultification of a law economy. It is the death of Jesus as well that is the key to his triumph over the cosmic powers.

The fact of these effects is emphasized more than explanations of how they have come about, but at least two general answers are suggested. In one the emphasis falls upon the divine initiative and graciousness, with the language of sacrifice being predominant, inclusive of references to "the blood of Christ"[23] and technical terms like "expiation" or "propitiation" (*hilasmos* or *hilastērion*).[24] The precise theory of atonement envisaged in these references is not completely clear, but two elements are constant: God's provision for reconciliation as an "act of liberation" (Rom. 3:24, NEB) and its cost in "blood" as typified by I Peter 1:18 f. This is the New Testament source of the general idea of atonement involving both God and Jesus in a costly experience with reference to man's guilt, without which reconciliation could not be effected. This goes beyond the idea, while it includes it, that Jesus simply reveals the love of God as it has always existed and thereby clears up the "mystery" of God's eternal purpose. In any case the New Testament writers are more certain that a redemptive transaction has taken place than they are about how to explain or explicate it precisely. Their language and spirit, that is, are in the nature of confessions of faith rather than of theological erudition and definition.[25]

There is a second answer, however, to the question of how the death of Jesus produces a saving effect. This places more responsibility upon the recipient of God's grace, although this is implied in the former answer. I Peter 2:21 makes it explicit: "For to this you have been called, because Christ also suffered for you, leaving you an example, that you should follow in his steps." This is followed up by exhortations to "rejoice in so far as you share Christ's sufferings" and to be prepared to suffer "as a Christian." Echoing the Gospels, similar sentiments elsewhere cohere with references to Jesus' own obedience and faithfulness, as in Rom. 5:18 f. and Heb. 5:8 f.

As in the previous section, it is in order to ask about the extent to which the influence of non-Christian precedents can be discerned in this area of thought in the Epistles. So far as the period prior to Jesus' death is concerned, there is nothing much of significance to be noted. Messianic titles are used almost at random and without too much precision. They illustrate primarily the conviction, as in the Gospels, that the earthly stage was a significant part of the whole messianic event. Paul's statement in Rom. 1:4 suggests that in his view the resurrection simply served to make emphatic and obvious what was true before it happened, namely, that Jesus was the Son of God from the beginning. In this context the title "Jesus Christ" is used almost as a proper name. The Wisdom myth is perhaps presupposed to the extent that it contained the idea of a revelatory significance in Wisdom's earthly pilgrimage. As in John's Gospel, the Hellenistic divine man concept, with its idea of the divine essence being present in an earthly figure, may have been influential.[26] In both cases, however, the lack of interest in the details of Jesus' life do not suggest a very strong influence. It is more likely that the picture of the faithful Jew in the Wisdom of Solomon, only superficially influenced by the divine man idea, lent its general influence in the emphasis upon Jesus' obedience and faith in his vindication. Generally speaking, it is much easier to believe that the controlling element in the view of Jesus' life which is set forth in the Epistles is the common Christian memory of the events as they were viewed from a postresurrection vantage point.

With regard to Jesus' death, however, the non-Christian context provides several potentially significant precedents. These include the sacrificial system of Judaism, the prophetic example of Jeremiah, the vicarious suffering of Moses,[27] and especially the Suffering Servant of Isa., ch. 53. The most interesting fact in this area of thought is that no one precedent appears to dominate the scene. As far as the influence of non-Christian precedents can be traced the picture is a variegated one. The particular circumstances in each case apparently are the determinative factors. For example, in the context of Paul's faith/works controversy he appears to find sacrificial language most useful. For the author of Hebrews, Mosaic and priestly analogies seem best to serve the purpose. For the writer of I Peter the Servant of the Lord concept proves useful. There is no stereotyped frame of reference or practice.

As previously noted, the anomaly is that there are so few references to the precedent of the Suffering Servant in both Gospels and Epistles, especially to the redemptive phrases of Isa., ch. 53.[28] This would appear to be the most likely analogy for interpreting Jesus' death in the passion stories, in Rom., chs. 3 and 8, or in Heb., ch. 10. However, the evidence does not support the idea that it was of predominant importance to the New Testament writers.[29] If it did influence ideas about Jesus' death as one for sin and as having universal dimensions, specific evidence to that effect is strangely absent from the records.

Perhaps the best explanation, even though it does not fully solve the enigma, is that the unique feature of the Suffering Servant Songs, the idea of vicarious suffering *for many*,[30] was not a live messianic alternative in the background of the New Testament despite efforts to prove otherwise.[31] At least in some messianic interpretations of the Isaian Servant which employ the term "Servant" the distinctive feature of atoning suffering "for many" is omitted.[32] In other sources when the title "Servant" is used messianically it tends to coalesce with other concepts such as the Mosaic prophet, the Son of Man, or David. With regard to David, the Jewish extra-Biblical liturgy gives precedence to the idea of royal rather than suffering Servant in the form of God's servant David. Furthermore the Targums consistently give the title a collective interpretation in Palestinian Judaism, and in Hellenistic Judaism the title is deeschatologized to make it an equivalent of the supremely righteous "child of God" (cf. Wisd. of Sol. 2:14).

Generally speaking, the New Testament picture reproduces the coalescing tendency in Judaism, but mainly with reference to Jesus' exaltation rather than to his death. Acts 4:27 and 30 reflect Jewish liturgical practice in portraying David's Greater Son Jesus as Servant. This is consistent with the tendency in Christian worship to use honorific titles for Jesus rather than titles having to do with his humiliation and death. Other areas of thought in which the idea of Servanthood is absorbed include the finality of Jesus' accomplishment (e.g., Heb. 10:10; I Peter 3:18) and his victory over the cosmic powers (e.g., Rom. 5:18 f.; Col. 2:15).

Once again, in the light of these considerations, we are made aware of the creative nature of the Christian experience in interpretations of Jesus. The controlling factors in interpretations of the death of Jesus are the redemptive facts experienced in relation to his death and resurrection, along with the effect of a set of circumstances in any given case which did not encourage any one non-Christian precedent to dominate the scene. In this respect the focus of the Gospels upon the historical facts, despite apologetic interests, abides in the Epistles. This is the case even when the latter find it expedient to go beyond the Gospels in terms of theological elaboration of the meaning of Jesus' death. The controlling factors are the historical event and the experience of saving power that the Christian insight discovers in it.

RESURRECTION AND EXALTATION

In the Gospels the resurrection narratives appear as a sort of epilogue at the end of the story in anticipation of something important to follow. This is true, even though the Gospels also presuppose the resurrection and are influenced by thought about Jesus arising in the postresurrection setting.

Against this the Epistles focus in such a concentrated manner upon the "something important to follow" which has followed, that other considerations are practically engulfed by the abundance of the data. Because of this fact it is only in a very limited and restricted sense that we can talk about comparing the Gospel-perspective with that of the Epistles in this area of thought. On the other hand, since, by contrast as well as by comparison, our purpose is to highlight the distinctive features of the Gospel-perspective, some elaboration of the subject is in order. What is called for is a selective procedure that will accomplish the end in view without taking us too far afield from the main highway. To that end we shall consider three dominant features of the relevant material in a more or less cursory manner: (1) the pattern of transition from death to resurrection and exaltation, (2) the exalted status of Jesus, and (3) the functions and achievements of Jesus as exalted Lord.

Paul's formula in I Cor. 15:3-5 probably represents a widespread understanding of the first topic among Christians in his day. The basic elements are "Christ died" and "was buried," "he was raised," and "he appeared," with Scriptural support being added where it is considered to be relevant. As it appears in I Corinthians, this formula probably represents an advanced stage of a process of development. Originally separate, the references to death and resurrection have now become combined, with the title Christ placed at the head of a formula that originally read "God raised Jesus" (as in Acts 2:24).[33] A variation on the death/resurrection couplet, assuming but bypassing the resurrection, pairs death and exaltation as in Phil. 2:8 f. and elsewhere.

The Gospels reproduce this formula in expanded forms. They alone introduce the empty tomb tradition, although they share with Paul attention to the appearances. Luke alone specifies the ascension, which Paul presupposes, and John among the Gospels most explicitly introduces exaltation content into the crucifixion scene. In any case the formula has the value of indicating that the resurrection event, while standing in its own right, was generally viewed as a transition from the earthly period of Jesus' career to that of his exalted reign. Thus it served the purpose, like the incarnation in an earlier setting, of linking together separate elements of one total event.

The second topic, the exalted status of Jesus, brings to the fore various titles and related categories of thought by means of which the faith of the early Christians was expressed. Before dealing with these matters let us consider the significant variations between The Acts and Paul with regard to the way in which the Holy Spirit is viewed in relation to the exalted Jesus.[34] Luke and Paul both agree on the general sequence of events after Jesus' death: resurrection, exaltation, and expected parousia. Within that framework, however, The Acts generally pictures the "absentee Christ" functioning on earth in the interval between resurrection and parousia in the form of representation by the Holy Spirit. Its Christology is a highly individualized one, with Jesus and Holy Spirit clearly distinguished from each other.[35]

On the other hand, for Paul, as Moule says, "Christ is indeed 'in heaven' in the sense that he is no longer a limited individual 'on earth'; but Christians are limbs of his body and are incorporated in him in such a way that all sense of remoteness is completely obliterated."[36] With Paul's consistent "in Christ" and much else in mind, we may say that for Paul the Spirit is "not the representative and substitute of an absent Christ but the mode of his very presence."[37] Despite a different vocabulary the Johannine Letters are like Paul in this respect. Perhaps the difference between The Acts and Paul is that between different stages of development, but that is not the point at the moment. The point is a difference in conception that, insofar as any comparison at all is valid, finds the Gospels generally sharing the Lucan rather than the Pauline perspective.

Turning to the titles of the exalted Jesus, we face an exceedingly complex subject with regard to which it is practically impossible to arrive at secure conclusions. This is largely due to the fact that apparently, while in the beginning certain titles and models may have been used with some discrimination, the tendency was in the direction of a random and undiscriminating usage.[38] The situation today is comparable. Many ancient titles are employed for Jesus without any real point of reference beyond a positive or traditional feeling for him. In the light of this fact we shall concentrate upon certain features of the material with regard to which there at least appears to be a high degree of probability.

We may note, first of all, that the main titles used of Jesus were Christ, Lord, and Son of God, with a variety of others being used sparingly in a limited number of writings. Among the latter are Lamb in the Apocalypse, Servant (or child) in The Acts, High Priest in Hebrews, Savior in the Pastorals and II Peter, Shepherd in I Peter, and so on. We have already observed something of the use of these titles in the Gospels, including the distinctive use of Lamb and Shepherd in John's Gospel.

The main anomaly in this picture of the exaltation setting is the almost complete disuse of the title Son of Man outside the Gospels. This presents an enigma comparable to that due to the paucity of explicit references to the Suffering Servant in the New Testament as a whole, since the Son of Man figure in Daniel provided a ready precedent for the ultimate vindication of the martyr Jesus and, in line with Daniel's corporate interpretation, of God's martyr people (cf. Col. 1:24). Outside the Gospels, however, as we have noted previously, the use of Son of Man is confined to Heb. 2:6 and to three martyr contexts based on Daniel in The Acts (ch. 7:56) and Revelation (chs. 1:13; 14:14). At least for the interval between Jesus' resurrection and parousia many early Christians decidedly preferred other terms such as Lord or conceptions of a different kind such as the heavenly session in Ps. 110:1.

Various explanations for the disuse of Son of Man are offered. Although they do not really solve the problem, they contain degrees of plausibility. Like Shepherd in I Peter 5:4 and Lamb in Revelation, the association of the title with the parousia may have tended to unfit it for use with reference to the exalted reign of Christ during the interval. To the extent that Son of Man was viewed as an individualistic designation of

Jesus it was less appropriate as a collective term to signify a persecuted people than terms like Adam, Israel, or body. At least it apparently seemed too limited in scope to comprehend all that Jesus as exalted Lord could mean to his followers.[39] Whatever the explanation, the difference between its use in the Gospels and in the Epistles is a mark of distinction between them.

A more profitable line of inquiry is suggested by C. F. D. Moule in the article previously mentioned which has to do with distinctions between the main titles. We shall summarize his line of thought. The main distinction is related to the use of terms in a worship setting, on the one hand, and, on the other, in a setting of explanation and apology.

The demands of adoration and worship tended to call forth directly honorific terms, especially when the exalted Jesus was addressed directly. With emphasis upon the majesty of Jesus rather than upon his humiliation, the predominant term was Lord (*Kyrios*), which tended to swallow up other terms.[40] "Our Lord, come!" (I Cor. 16:22) is parousia oriented, but it illustrates the usage. The term "Christ" never appears in the vocative, and usually it is employed in the "faith-formulae" typified by I Cor. 15:3 f. as marking the transition from death to resurrection. The term "Lord," on the other hand, tended to embrace the thought of Jesus' Lordship over the whole cosmos as well as over the church, and its focus was always upon present and future rather than upon past events. Assuming this, Paul extended the sphere of Lordship to the secular world and the everyday affairs of Christians.

This general impression abides when we consider allusions to Christ in prayers addressed to God. Even though in the latter there was also a tendency for "Lord" to be fused with other terms in such a way as to blur the distinction between Jesus and God, and even though other terms were used independently, the use of honorific titles characterized worship settings. Terms relating to Jesus' humiliation were excluded except in special circumstances. Usage was also in part controlled by the Jewish Psalter and other liturgical forms. In this connection "the measure of adaptation applied to these was controlled by the tension set up by the growing tendency to transfer (OT) *kyrios* passages (and even *theos* passages) to Jesus while, at the same time, retaining a recognition of the role of Jesus as Messiah and Son of God."[41]

Settings of explanation and apology tended to lift up other terms, as we have observed to a certain extent in apologetic treatments of the death of Jesus. A case in point is the response of the Pastoral Letters and The Revelation to John to the challenge of emperor worship with the latter's use of Son of God, Savior, Lord, and even God (*theos*). Since the term "Lord" was widely used of pagan deities in general, if a direct challenge was to be made to the cult of emperor worship, other terms would be more appropriate. In Revelation the exalted "Christus Imperator"[42] is labeled "King of kings" (Rev. 17:14; 19:16), which is its only favorable application in the New Testament.[43] Only in Rev. 1:5 in the New Testament is "ruler" (*archōn*) used of Jesus. The term "Savior" (*sōtēr*) predominates in the Pastorals. "Lord" is entirely absent from Titus. In Titus 2:13 the correct text may equate "Jesus Christ" and "great God."

The term "Son of God" has less distinctive uses in the New Testament; the tendency is for it to be combined with other terms. Perhaps two basic ideas are associated with the term in the Epistles. One is the pre-earthly setting of Jesus with its ideas of preexistence and of his coming into the world which derive from Hellenistic Judaism. Philippians, ch. 2, suggests, however, that the idea of Sonship (not the term) in this setting became fused with that of Lordship.[44] The other idea is that of the solidarity between the Son and the Father which is characteristic of Paul's usage (and of John's), the emphasis here being an aspect of Jesus' Lordship as a permanent status.[45] As such it appropriates to itself the basic features of other terms.

Turning to the Gospels from this cursory survey, it would appear that in general the Gospels illustrate the undiscriminating use of Christological titles. For them, as for Paul, the term

"Christ" is often almost a proper name. At the same time the use of Lord in Matthew and Luke, the latter in particular, reflects its postresurrection significance in the church. On the other hand, John prefers Son of God in order to emphasize the solidarity between Jesus and God which is characteristic of one facet of Paul's thought. The predominance of "Son of man" on the lips of Jesus in the Gospels is the most distinctive thing about the titles in this area. This signifies their independence of, despite some dependence upon, currents of thought within the Christian communities at large.

One observation may be made with reference to the distinction between worship and apologetic motifs in the Gospels. Attempts to trace strong liturgical motifs in the Gospels are not very convincing.[46] This negative judgment on other grounds is fortified by the use of titles in the Gospels. While the use of Lord in Matthew and Luke might suggest otherwise, this title plays no significant role in Mark or John; and Matthew and Luke, like Mark, are in general concerned with apologetic interests of different kinds. The prevailing apologetic concern with the crucifixion of Jesus is common to them all. The term "Son of Man," once again, with its passion and eschatological orientations, points away from a liturgical to an apologetic interest. The term "Son of God" as used in the Gospels carries connotations of apology either in the direction of indicating that Jesus brings the prophetic line to its fulfillment (as in Heb. 1:1 f.), or, as in John, in the direction of a transcendence of the idea of nationalistic Davidic messiahship. There may be intimations as well, if least so in Matthew, of a setting in which the attitude of the Roman government toward the church is a matter of great concern, even though indications of official persecution are not as self-evident as in the case of the Pastorals, I Peter, and the Apocalypse.

The third topic to be considered here has to do, in addition to what has already been implied, with the functions and achievements of the exalted Lord in the interval between resurrection and parousia. This is a many-sided subject which contains many implicit points of comparison between Gospels and Epistles as well as many points of difference. In line with our primary interests we shall select one major item for consideration, the cosmic dimensions of the work of Christ, since it invites comparison with the exorcism activity of Jesus in the Gospels. Then we shall content ourselves with a summary statement about additional features of the picture.

The New Testament views of the cosmic dimensions of the work of the exalted Lord constitute an important emphasis which is difficult for many people today to grasp. A demythologized version of the ancient idea of demons and supernatural powers offers some light on New Testament conceptions. That is, we can grasp the idea of impersonal forces that influence our lives, the social forces that condition us and determine the atmosphere in which we live and work. These include the laws of nature, the economic or industrial organization of the country and world, its pervading secularization, the class or racial structure of society, even the psychological conditioning of every individual. Some of these are beneficent in the sense that they prevent the world from disintegrating, giving it organization and structure. On the other hand, they may put man in bondage unless he finds a way to make them slaves rather than masters. In part this analogy helps to define what the New Testament has in mind in talking about the cosmic dimension in the eternal struggle which goes on in every individual, in human society, and in the created universe. Fully to grasp this outlook, however, it is necessary to use our imagination in trying to think in ancient thought forms within the context of that age. In discussing this we shall concentrate primarily upon Paul's view of the situation.

Paul is mainly concerned with the dangers to man's freedom which the powers represent. In one set of symbols Paul speaks of Satan as the chief adversary[47] in a complex consisting of demons[48] and angels.[49] This is the familiar modified dualism of Jewish apocalypticism in which Satan and his minions, mysteriously by God's permission, oppose God and his heavenly battalions in the universe and in human life. The demons and angels are thought of as transcendental beings in the same

category as the "principalities" with which they are linked in
Rom. 8:38 and elsewhere.

The cosmic hierarchy is divided into categories designated
by a series of technical terms. Colossians 1:16 names "thrones
or dominions [a form of *kyrios*] or principalities [*archai*] or
authorities [*exousiai*]." Other terms are "powers" (*dynameis* in
Rom. 8:38, etc.), "elemental spirits" (*stoicheia* in Col. 2:8, 20),
the "names" contrasted with the "name of Jesus" in Phil.
2:9–10. Sin and death also belong in this hierarchy.[50]

These battalions of "principalities and powers," spearheaded
by Satan, constitute a "dominion of darkness" set over against
the "kingdom of [God's] beloved Son" (Col. 1:13). The force
of all of this for the Christian is expressed summarily in Eph.
6:11–12: "Put on the whole armor of God, that you may be able
to stand against the wiles of the devil. For we are not contend-
ing against flesh and blood, but against the principalities,
against the powers, against the world rulers of this present
darkness, against the spiritual hosts of wickedness in the heavenly places." This struggle becomes very bitter and intense
when sin enters into man's inner being to deceive and destroy,
forcing him to do what he does not want to do (cf. Rom.
7:8 ff.), or when "a messenger of Satan" becomes a "thorn in
the flesh" (II Cor. 12:7).

It is the Christian's triumphant conviction that this whole
"dominion of darkness" has been defeated by Christ's death
and exaltation (Phil. 2:9 f.; Eph. 1:21; Heb. 1:4 f.). If the complete victory of Christ over the powers is delayed until the future parousia, as portrayed in I Cor. 15:24–28, his resurrection
and exaltation are the earnest and guarantee to faith of that
final victory.

This is said in a variety of ways in the New Testament. Of
particular note are the ways in which Ps. 110 and 8 are employed with reference to Christ in this context. Psalm 110:1
supplies the idea of Christ as exalted or standing or, usually,
seated at God's right hand along with the servitude of his enemies. Psalm 8:6 supplements the latter idea with the thought
of "all things" subjected to Christ. In The Revelation to John

the "power over the nations" which is quoted from Ps. 2:8 f. has more than a political connotation in the apocalyptic frame of reference (Rev. 2:26; 12:5).

In some references the eschatological reservation of I Cor. 15:24 ff. is bypassed, the future victory being thought of as a present fact (Phil. 2:9 f., e.g.). This paradox simply implies the intensity of the conviction that, whatever "mopping up" remains to be done, sin and death cannot have the last word in God's universe under the dominion of his Son. Allied with this is the new order of humanity which has been inaugurated by Jesus as "last Adam" or "man of heaven" in reversing the effects of Adam's fall (I Cor. 15:45–50; Rom. 5:15–21). That this conquest rests in the ethical dimension of "one man's obedience" does not deprive it of cosmic significance any more than is the case in Phil. 2:8–10. Obedience may, in part at least, be the efficient cause, but the effect of that obedience unto death is the bestowal of "the name that is above every name," the latter probably designating the cosmic powers inclusive of sin and death.

The parousia expectations of the Christians are inherently involved in this subject, but we shall delay until later further treatment of this aspect of the subject. By way of summary let us simply suggest that "the power of God for salvation," which Paul believed the gospel to be, resided in no small part in his conviction about the way in which God had used the event of Jesus Christ to affect the very universe itself, the creation as well as the world of human intercourse. The letter to the Ephesians is the high point of this conviction.

The most obvious point of comparison in the Gospels with reference to this portrayal of the cosmic work of the exalted Christ is constituted by the exorcisms. The whole framework of Mark in particular presupposes proleptically what Paul believed had come to pass with the exaltation of Jesus. In each case the same world of concepts is presupposed, recalling the earlier quotation of Case, and the same view of one aspect of Jesus' work is made explicit. In this respect the Epistles, as it were, fulfill the Gospels. What Jesus began to do on earth with reference to demon-possessed persons and other forms of war-fare with Satan he now does more directly and decisively on a cosmic stage. Through his exaltation he is now in a position to strike at the root of the problem, and, as faith believes, he is doing so. Complete victory is still an anticipation, but it is as-sured. Even though the Gospels share the faith that character-ized Paul's outlook, they are still unique in confining attention to the preliminary stages of the contest before the resurrection and exaltation of Jesus had released him from human limita-tions so that he might complete the task.

Beyond this the Epistles develop in detail, depending upon the particular circumstances and conditions being dealt with in each case, the idea of Jesus as reigning in heaven over his people until the parousia. The details concern the blessings of salvation and the life and functions of the church. For our purpose there is no point in portraying these particulars in de-tail, since within that context the Gospels represent a distinctive response to situations in the early church which differentiates them from the kind of response characteristic of the Epistles. A few points of particular interest will suffice for characterizing the interrelationships of Gospels and Epistles.

Since the Gospels are kerygma, if in a unique form, they proclaim the good news about Jesus as they report what he himself said about many other matters. Although Jesus' own self-understanding is revealed, if obscurely, in this process, a sharp difference of focus still remains. In the Gospels Jesus is far more the Proclaimer than the Proclaimed. This is so even when legitimate conclusions are drawn regarding similarities between Jesus' religious and ethical message and that of Paul, and when parallels between Gospels and Epistles are ex-hausted.

A case in point has to do with ethics. We may recall that Jesus' ethical message in John lacks the kind of detailed expo-sition characteristic of the Sermon on the Mount and of the Synoptics in general. John simplifies the whole picture with a single emphasis upon *agapē* as the characteristic Christian virtue. This tendency to subsume the ethical message of Jesus under a single principle, the law of love, is also found in Rom. 13:9 and in James. The latter shows more interest than Paul in the details of Jesus' message. John also, consistent with Matthew, portrays Jesus' ethical teaching as a "new commandment" or a new law, and this, once again, is reflected in James. W. D. Davies, in a full treatment of this matter, points out that the striking thing about all these references outside the Synoptics (except for I John 4:21) is that "they refer to the love of neighbor *but not to the love of God.*" This is due to the fact that "the love of God has been defined in terms of the life of Jesus. The act whereby God sent his Son into the world to die for sinners has become the pattern, the paradigm of his love."[51] The same orientation is found in Paul, for example in Rom. 5:6 ff. and 8:32 (also in Eph. 5:1 f.). Paul "urges us not so much to love our neighbor and to love God as to look at Jesus and then to love our neighbor in his sight."[52] It is this emphasis which comes out most clearly in John's Gospel. Despite its gospel form this indicates its affinity with the Epistles in a way unique to John among the Gospels.

Another significant feature of thought in this area consists of the particular interests of Matthew which cause F. C. Grant to call it "the ecclesiastical gospel."[53] The key words here are those added to the Marcan account of Peter's confession, "I tell you, you are Peter, and on this rock I will build my church" (Matt. 16:18), and some related sayings. The Gospels in general reflect an interest in the institution of the church. This is evident in the Synoptic record of the institution of the Lord's Supper, the selection and mission of the Twelve, in John's concern for church unity under *agapē*, and so forth. As compared with the Epistles, however, there is relatively little ecclesiological interest. Granting some common concerns, as is to be expected, the interests of the Evangelists lie in another direction.

Perhaps the closest point of contact here is the mutual concern of Gospels and Epistles for the mission of the church. This is more subtle in Mark, as in the story of the Syrophoenician woman, more ambiguous in Matthew than in Luke, but it is a thread running throughout all three; and John as well is taken up with it. The constant factor throughout the New Testament, in Gospels and Epistles, is the running controversy with Jewish antagonists, often very overt and at times more disguised, as the church presses forward to become predominantly Gentile in composition. What is revealed in the Epistles is the story of this development following out the implications, more than the overt teaching, of Jesus' own outlook. The most radical shift in perspective in this regard is Paul's scheme in Rom., chs. 9 to 11. According to this the ancient pattern of "first the Jew, then the Gentile" is revised to make room for the (hopefully) temporary rejection of the Jews following the admission of Gentiles into the church. On the whole the Gospels presuppose the earlier formula as they reflect various stages in the movement of the church from a Jewish-Christian to a Gentile-Christian body.

These few items may point in a direction of thought that could be elaborated with profit. In the concluding section of this chapter we shall have occasion to return to the subject in the framework of a larger context of thought.

THE PAROUSIA

Since much has already been suggested with regard to the future expectations of Paul and other New Testament writers, we shall content ourselves, again in a somewhat impressionistic manner, with considering certain selected features of the subject. The entire range of New Testament eschatology is in view, but our concern is narrowly with patterns of thought that deal explicitly with the person and work of Jesus within that whole, and this largely as set forth by Paul.

In order to deal adequately with the eschatology of Paul, one would have to analyze carefully the different contexts in which his variegated utterances appear, judging what he says by the circumstances and his apparent purpose in each case.[54] Even when we think in more general terms we must distinguish between what he says about the new age of the Spirit or of Sonship having come in contrast to the age of the law (cf. Gal. 3:23 to 4:7; Rom. 8:15) and, on the other hand, what he says about the consummation of the new age which, having begun, has not yet fully arrived. Although in Paul's thought these periods overlap, there is a definite consummation (cf. I Cor. 11:26; 15:25; II Thess. 2:1; etc.). It is this future event that we have primarily in focus at this point.

We may note first somewhat different emphases between The Acts and Paul. The Acts has a minimal future expectation (chs. 1:11; 3:20 f.; 17:31); its emphasis falls upon the activity of the Holy Spirit in the present. The stage for this is set in the opening verses with the promise of the gift of the Spirit being the alternative to speculation about a future supernatural coming of the Kingdom of God (ch. 1:6 ff.). In Luke-Acts as a whole the indefinite delay of the parousia is implied, as in John's Gospel. In this way Luke appears to make a decided differentiation between the period of the church and previous stages of the gospel history.[55] Over against this, despite a sense in which Christ is viewed as making a present impact, Paul in general presupposes a more urgent future expectation. This is more fully explicated in some places than in others when the circumstances required it (as in I and II Thessalonians), but it is a consistent assumption of Paul (cf. Rom. 13:11; Phil. 4:5; etc.). In effect Paul holds present and future aspects in tension, as in the Synoptics generally, despite its weakening in Luke's Gospel. It is John, even more than Luke, that places a one-sided emphasis on the present, as by contrast The Revelation to John is equally one-sided in its almost exclusive future emphasis.

A summary of categories of thought that involve the exalted Christ in this context is as follows. The expected "coming" or "appearance" of Christ (his "visitation") finds frequent expression in the main body of Paul's letters, most frequently in the Thessalonian and Corinthian correspondence, but elsewhere as well.[56] It is also present in the Pastorals, I Peter, The Revelation to John, Hebrews, and elsewhere. The only explicit statement that Christ will appear "a second time" is in Heb. 9:28. Another form of expression is "the day of Jesus Christ" and related expressions, largely in the Pauline tradition[57] but also in Heb. 10:25. Outside the Pauline tradition references to "the day" are less directly and personally related to Christ. The agency of Christ in the final judgment is prominent in Paul's letters, most explicitly in I Cor. 15:23–28. Except for the Apocalypse, references to judgment in the balance of the Epistles tend to focus on God or to be general in nature.

The most noteworthy aspect of Paul's thought in this area is his conception of Christ as "the first fruits" of the general resurrection at the End, explicated in I Cor. 15:20, 23, and implied elsewhere. This shows how Paul's eschatology is conditioned by his view of the resurrection of Jesus (as in I Thess. 4:13–18). The resurrection is the hinge or fulcrum upon which everything about the future turns.

Another extremely significant view of Paul is the idea that in the End the Son will be subjected to God (I Cor. 15:28). Here the work of Christ is essential to the consummation of God's plans in the form of subduing the powers; it is just as essential as his present dealings with the church and the world. Yet he works instrumentally as the Son of the sovereign Father rather than entirely on his own.

This subjection of the Son appears on the surface to be inconsistent with many references to Jesus' exaltation, especially those in which the distinction between God and Jesus becomes fuzzy. However, there is no real inconsistency in such passages as Phil., ch. 2, or Col., ch. 1. In the former "the name which is above every name" is bestowed by *God* in the process of exaltation, and it is "to the glory of *God* the Father" that "every tongue confess that Jesus Christ is Lord." And in Colossians "the fulness of God" is something bestowed by *God* upon the one through whose agency *he* delivers mankind from "the dominion of darkness." Christ is *"God's* mystery" and in exaltation he sits at the right hand of *God*. As in the Gospel-perspective, the vindication of Jesus is *God's* act.

There is no real problem if we recognize that the New Testament authors are not thinking ontologically, if at points they tend in that direction, but rather confessionally and analogically, more religiously and ethically than theologically.[58] This applies across the board, but it appears most explicitly in the parousia-oriented passage in I Cor. 15:24–28. According to it, at the End the Son will be subjected to the Father so that "God may be everything to every one." The Son is always subjected to the Father in a willing and complete obedience.

The eschatology of II Peter is distinctive in that it represents a rather decided shift away from the prevailing Christ-centered emphasis of other parts of the New Testament. Rather than being the consummation of a process initiated by God's action in Jesus Christ, the Last Days are viewed as a second future event and as a scrapping of the universe (II Peter 3:10 ff.). This does not build firmly upon the whole Christ event as with Paul. In this sense at least the author did not understand Paul (ch. 3:16).

The future aspect of the eschatological crisis precipitated by Jesus' appearance is a Synoptic Gospel feature which links the Synoptics with one dominant emphasis of Paul's eschatology. John's present emphasis, on the other hand, links him with another dominant Pauline motif. To the extent that Paul holds future and present elements in tension, he is closer to the Synoptics than to John. John, along with Luke, assumes the kind of extension of the interim period that is characteristic of The Acts.

The Synoptic combination of ideas of visitation and vindication is reproduced in the balance of the New Testament. The latter is always presupposed whereas the former is most prominent in some of Paul's letters, I Peter, and The Revelation to John. Although the language is Paul's, Jesus as the "first fruits" of the general resurrection is an idea common to Gospels and Epistles. In both, Jesus is also viewed as judge in the consummation, although often God is viewed as acting by himself. The explicit reference to Jesus' subordination to God at the End is peculiar to Paul, but the idea of Jesus as *God's* agent in a monotheistic context, whether in the present or in the future, is a commonplace of New Testament thought.

FOUNDATION AND SUPERSTRUCTURE

By way of conclusion it is in order to consider the interlocking relationship that is exhibited in the New Testament between what we may call foundation (kerygma) and superstructure (*didachē*). C. F. D. Moule has properly warned against maintaining the distinction too rigidly. If we do, he says, "we shall not do justice to the real nature of all Christian edification, which builds, sometimes more, sometimes less, but always at least some of the foundational material into the wall and floors."[59]

On the level of the initial proclamation and appeal to nonbelievers, as defined by Moule, the Gospels at first glance appear to belong more in the category of proclamation than of appeal. Moule's definition is as follows: "Jesus' life and miracles and deeds of goodness were such as the following (extended examples). His clash with the Jews, his sentence and execution followed the following pattern (details). The resurrection was manifested like this (narrative). The relevant scripture are appropriately inserted throughout." On the other hand, the Epistles appear to conform more to the definition of the initial appeal, as follows: "Repentance, baptism, and the coming of the Spirit *mean* (a new life, a transfiguring outlook, the wearing of the new humanity, etc., etc.); they involve (details of character and conduct); they are related to Judaism and pagan religions as follows (discussion of the relevant issues)."[60]

In the entire New Testament, Luke-Acts alone appears to be explicitly addressed to nonbelievers, and even then the Christian community is on the sidelines. Judging by its stated purpose in ch. 20:31, John's Gospel would appear to be outwardly directed too, but much of its content surely has believers in view. Mark and Matthew are written to believers, but probably in part with the intention of supplying them with apologetic ammunition in their dealings with nonbelieving neighbors. As against this outward-looking factor the Epistles as a whole are addressed to believing communities, either to han-

dle internal problems or to encourage them in the face of persecution. Only by implication do they offer insight on the
nature of the initial appeal to nonbelievers.

With these factors in view the important consideration is not
so much the question of who is being addressed as it is of the
nature of the material that is employed. How are foundational
materials and superstructural materials related to each other
regardless of the situation of the ones addressed? The picture
is one of interlocking and interpenetration in both Gospels and
Epistles. Although addressed to the already evangelized, the
edificatory material in the Epistles constantly echoes the evan-
gelistic appeal, as it were in retrospect. Much is said about the
call to decision and the kind of response that the gospel requires. On the other hand, the Evangels, explicitly or implicitly
directed to nonbelievers, elaborate both foundation and superstructure. For example, at one and the same time the parable
of the prodigal son offers God's forgiving mercy and sets a
standard of conduct for the believer. Gospels and Epistles alike
are concerned with both "awakening faith and strengthening
faith."[61]

The difference is, in part, one of form as between literary
genres, but this involves a difference in perspective as well.
To a great extent the gospel form is dictated by its greater interest in historical reminiscences as a means of awakening and
strengthening faith. Though in both types of literature Jesus
is the Proclaimed, it is the unique distinction of the Gospels
to concentrate upon Jesus as Proclaimer, in both word and
deed, to the end of evangelization and edification. This distinction remains a clear-cut one even when we grant that the
Epistles, if in a minimum degree by comparison, take the historical facts of Jesus' life and death for granted. It abides when
we grant that the emphasis in the Epistles on the death of Jesus
presupposes a great deal about the quality of his life.[62] The
maximum emphasis of the Gospels on the historical reminiscences is not a difference in kind, since they also presuppose the resurrection, but it is an emphatic and a unique
difference.

The implication is that the Evangelists deliberately set out to correct what they considered to be a one-sided and incomplete presentation of the gospel. In doing so they were not challenging Paul's resurrection faith. They were simply seeking a better balance with reference to the circumstances confronting them. For them this meant serious attention to the origins of the Christian faith in the ministry of Jesus as well as with reference to his death and resurrection. Moule has correctly stated their implied outlook: "But Christians knew well that if they lost sight of the story behind that experience [of the risen Christ] their worship would be like a house built on sand; and that if they preached salvation without the story of how it came they would be powerless as evangelists; and that if they could not explain how they came to stand where they did, they would be failing to give a reason for their hope."[63] If we change "Christians" to "some" or to "many Christians," the statement is still valid. It is important, as well, in suggesting that the memory of the preresurrection Jesus was not completely merged with impressions of Christ received after the resurrection.

The distinctive nature of the canonical Gospels stands out when they are compared with the apocryphal gospels. The latter are more influenced by Hellenistic literary forms; they exaggerate the silences of the canonical Gospels about the periods prior to and following the ministry; and they do so by breathing an entirely different atmosphere from that of the New Testament Gospels.[64] As Maurer says of the comparatively sober Gospel of Peter, with its "massive apologetic reasoning" at the center rather than upon the fringe, "The passion and resurrection of Jesus, yea He himself, are loosened out of the soil of real history and transferred to the realm of legend and myth." The difference in climate is also apparent "in the misunderstanding of the scriptural proofs in the Gospels."[65] If John's Gospel shares with some apocryphal gospels an affinity for Gnostic ideas, its comparatively more serious concern for the actual facts of Jesus' human experience sets it decidedly alongside the Synoptics.

Having the uniqueness of the Gospels in mind, we may conclude by noting that the Epistles are in one sense as much concerned with "facts" as are the Gospels. In the words of Oscar Cullmann, "The question about Jesus was not answered by early Christianity in terms of a mythology already at hand, but in terms of a series of real facts." These facts included "the events of the life, works, and death of Jesus of Nazareth," but they also took in "the experience of his presence and continuing work beyond death within the fellowship of his disciples."[66] Granting that we are dealing here with two different categories of facts, historical knowledge and religious conviction, for the early Christians what happened in each category was factual.

The Gospels take this as much for granted as do the Epistles, despite their focus upon the preresurrection period. Gospels and Epistles are bound up in one package, not only by centering attention upon Jesus Christ as the unifying bond amid much diversity,[67] but also by their mutual concern for actual happenings. They both subject the "mythology already at hand," as well as all contextual precedents, to the facts of their Christian experience, so that no precedent is taken over unaltered.

At the same time the Gospels make a unique contribution within this frame of reference. They permit us to a limited degree to observe Jesus himself defining his own self-understanding in reaction to his milieu. We have to say "to a limited degree" because of the ways in which this picture has been affected by postresurrection Christological speculation and apologetic. With reference to messianic titles and some related matters the picture is confusing. This is a gain, however, in that the relative emphasis of Jesus upon the content of his message comes through clearly. The Evangelists show us a person far less concerned with the precise definition of his person than with the intrinsic salvation that he brings in his message and his deeds. Much more than in the Epistles, if only in degree, the Gospels place the emphasis upon the scale of values of the Proclaimer with reference to the question of his person as well as of his work.

This is another significant way in which the Gospels provide an indispensable appeal to origins as a means of keeping the various aspects of Christian thought in proper perspective. It clarifies the continuity between the preresurrection and the postresurrection situations and provides a perspective without which the total New Testament picture of Jesus would be seriously out of focus—as the framers of the New Testament canon apparently realized.

Chapter V

THE RELEVANCE OF
THE GOSPEL-PERSPECTIVE

IN and of itself historical study has its charms. It can be as fascinating for the addict as a double-crostic, even though, having no answers in the back of the book, it yields less certain results. On the other hand, if the historical enterprise is to justify the time and energy devoted to it, it must offer some wisdom to the present. On this premise we shall consider the relevance of the Gospel-perspective today, attempting only to suggest a direction of thought rather than to exhaust the possibilities.

In exploring this domain we are concerned with what J. M. Robinson depicts the twofold task of theology to be in our kind of world, a world in which the ideology of Christendom in the West is "being superseded by secular alternatives."[1] It must first address itself to the translation task of scoring "the Christian point in distinction from the traditional language." This is necessary because "in our situation what happens when traditional Christian language is used is often simply not Christian." An even more fundamental reason, in the words of Amos N. Wilder, is that "as the world changes with the passage of time nothing except things like the multiplication table can be merely repeated without translation or interpretation."[2] Because of this it is always true that "in order for God's Word to remain constant his words must constantly change."[3] What makes this question so urgent today is the vast difference between the modern world view, especially its scientific dimension, and that of every previous age.

Robinson's second point is that, with the help of historical study, theology must elucidate clearly "what our message is a translation *of*—the question of recognizable continuity of subject matter within the flow of change." As long as Christianity is considered to be a historical religion, which is its genius, it is required that it be defined with reference to its origins. This means determining what significance is to be attached to the Biblical evidence, especially the New Testament evidence, in relation to other pertinent data.

Except for purposes of precision in definition these two facets of the theological task should not be separated. They are two halves of a whole, and we shall assume this as we proceed.

Presuming the validity and pertinence of these observations, the question becomes that of *how* the Gospel-perspective is relevant in the light of *our* circumstances. This means thinking in terms of its implications rather than in terms of a literalistic transplanting of an ancient tradition into our modern garden. Does the Gospel-perspective contain insights that, when translated into our language, have significance for Christian faith and theology today?

We believe that, among others, two such insights are of indispensable value. Proceeding from the general to the particular, one is derived from the way in which history and theology are amalgamated, encouraging us to work toward an understanding of Christianity which reproduces this synthesis. The other is implied in the interest in Jesus' history, encouraging Jesus research in its modern form. These subjects overlap, but they are distinct enough to provide focal points for discussion. Let us proceed to take a closer look at them.

HISTORY AND FAITH

In previous pages we have observed the way in which throughout the New Testament, in both Gospels and Epistles, historical and theological elements are intermingled and synthesized. Employing the terminology of Norman Perrin, we may designate these two elements as "historical knowledge" and "faith-knowledge,"[4] the latter including both theological and experiential factors. Let us recall what has been said previously about the way in which the Gospels give maximum attention to details of Jesus' preresurrection history and the Epistles elaborate various aspects of postresurrection faith-knowledge, without the synthesis of the two being absent in either. Assuming that, our specific concern is to determine the value of each kind of knowledge in the Gospel-perspective.

It is the faith element that provides the dynamic for the recovery of the preresurrection details and the writing of the Gospels. It is the postresurrection experience of the living Christ that makes his death a subject of concern. Frederick Herzog has properly defined the content of this faith-knowledge, the emphasis falling upon faith in *God* as the underlying factor. Habituated to viewing history and God together, the disciples were nevertheless not prepared to see God at work in a man on a cross. The Emmaus story in Luke most clearly explains how this was overcome: "In the resurrection the meaning of the suffering was interpreted." But "on purely historical grounds it is quite unintelligible why a resurrection should tell us more about God than a cross." "Without a grasp of the unity of cross and resurrection interpreted by the reality to which they point the resurrection remains mute."[5] *God's* act in Jesus, as the early Christians saw it, stimulated an interest in the preresurrection history.

This also provided the dynamic for the kind of creative reinterpretation of history that characterizes the Gospel-perspective. This freedom in interpreting the reminiscences, which has been made abundantly clear in previous pages, is also suggested by the probability that Matthew and Luke did not so much intend to improve upon, as to replace, Mark. Each Evangelist, including John, thought that he was writing *the* Gospel. At least the combining of the four in the canon was motivated in part by the need to consider the demands of several different communities, each of which valued one of the Gospels above the others. The initial and continuing interest in creative retranslation at every stage of the development was inspired by sensitivity to God's action through the risen Christ. On this side of the shield the perspectives of Gospel and Epistle are the same. This dynamic operated, as we have observed, not only with reference to the historical element, but also included the way in which contextual materials were adapted to elucidate the Christian message.

It is important to remember in this connection that the difference between the two New Testament perspectives was not a chronological difference. The formation of the gospel tradition and the writing of Paul's letters coincided, and the finished Gospels appeared at the same time that other Epistles were being written. Nor was it primarily a cultural difference, since both perspectives recall Palestinian origins in a predominantly Gentile environment. The difference is one of emphasis with regard to substance, with circumstantial and experiential factors as causes. For the framers of the canon, echoing the sentiments of their predecessors, neither perspective had a monopoly upon the Holy Spirit. This may well represent wisdom for us, as we believe. The Holy Spirit employs many methods of expression.

There is more to be said, however, about the significance of the maximum concern for Jesus' history which the Gospels display. In this connection it is well to remember that, in the process of canon formation, "the Gospels early took that place in the Christian Testament which Torah won in the Hebrew canon."[6] In all canonical lists they stand first. Also, limiting the canonical Gospel to the original four was a deliberate repudiation of the trend toward a multiplicity of Gospels of a Gnostic character. At that stage, as well as at an earlier time, it was considered important to anchor the Christian faith securely in history—at least by those who won the fight over the canon. And for this purpose the gospel genre was indispensable.

Against this background it is in order to emphasize the integrity of the gospel genre as an expression of the kerygma. The canon does not encourage us to treat the Gospel as a "poor relation" to the Epistle. Nor is there any indication that the

Evangelists themselves thought that they were merely supplementing Paul's way of proclaiming the gospel. The implication of the Gospels is that they considered their way of doing it as the way it should be done, at least that in their circumstances they believed a maximum attention to the preresurrection Jesus to be essential for faith. Stressing the central place of the narrative mode in the whole New Testament period, Wilder may well be speaking for the Evangelists' outlook when he says that "the Christian movement stood or fell with the stories about Jesus, giving substance as they did to the larger history of God's dealings with men."

If we wish to be more reticent about the intentions of the Evangelists, we can at least find Wilder's further word instructive about the value of what they did. "As Jesus became little by little a figure of the past it was inevitable that gospels should be written, precisely to show the relation of his deed and deeds to the story of God with Israel and the world. At this later stage the written Gospels anchored the Greek Gentile churches in concrete Palestinian origins. . . . The Christian could now relate his own history to the Christ-history, and find his own difficult role in the world-drama meaningful and glorious, since his role was caught up in that of the Son of Man himself. By means of the Gospels each of them could, *and each one of us can,* move back in time and walk with him along his way of victory through defeat; or could, *as we can,* bring him forward as a contemporary in the pilgrimage of a later day. In either case our own stories take on meaning, since they find their place in the larger story of which God is the author."[7] This places the Gospels meaningfully within the framework of the entire Biblical drama with its prevailing assumption that God makes himself known to eyes of faith predominantly in his effective action in history.[8]

To be sure, the Gospels but elaborate the historical element in the kerygma reflected in the Epistles. Although receiving minimum attention, comparatively speaking, this historical element is the constant factor amid much Christological and ecclesiological variety. Paul's gospel is unthinkable without the

cross and the obedience of which it is the ultimate manifestation. In the Epistles generally it is taken for granted that it is
"this Jesus whom you crucified" whom God has made "both
Lord and Christ" (Acts 2:36). The difference between the two
perspectives is thus not one of kind. However, it is still an important difference in method and outlook on how to proclaim
the Christian gospel. Although both presuppose "the scandal
of particularity," more definitely than the perspective of the
Epistles the Gospel-perspective makes it less easy to substitute
an idea for a distinct individual in the content of the resurrection faith.

This brings into focus what is called the "new hermeneutic"
today. As a book by that title indicates, this expression is used
to characterize the thought of Ernst Fuchs and Gerhard
Ebeling. The book contains essays by these scholars, reactions
to them by some American scholars, the whole being introduced by James M. Robinson.[9] Fuchs and Ebeling are mem-
bers of the "Bultmann school" to the extent that they share
its existentialist presuppositions, although their new hermeneutic tends to qualify Bultmann's emphasis on the kerygma and
amounts to an alternative to his views on demythologization
of the Biblical text.[10]

These two scholars go about the translation task by posing
the problem of continuity of subject matter as that between the
Jesus of history, primarily his message, and the proclamation
about him in the form of the kerygmatic Christ. The solution
that they propose fastens upon the term "word event": *Sprach-
ereignis* ("speech event") or *Wortgeschenen* ("word happening"). This turns out to mean, as Ebeling defines it, that *faith*
is the element of continuity. What came to expression in Jesus
was faith. As "witness to faith" Jesus became, and becomes, the
"basis of faith" in the resurrection.[11] Jesus' personal decision
in the face of the reality of God constitutes a manifestation of
faith as a word event in him. When the believer echoes Jesus'
decision by making his own positive response to the call of the
gospel to decision, Jesus' witness to faith becomes the basis of
the believer's faith. Permitting the Scriptures to interpret him

by means of an existentialist hermeneutic, the believer experiences faith as a reality manifested in language.

In this approach, according to Perrin, "hermeneutic has, in effect, taken the place of kerygma and a concern for an existentialist interpretation of the kerygma has been modified by a concern for the historical Jesus until it has become a concern for an existentialist interpretation of the New Testament—now seen . . . as a means whereby that faith which came to word or language in Jesus may come to word- or language-event for us." This amounts to a new theological position, the result of pushing to an extreme a Lutheran emphasis upon faith and word, in which "faith is practically personified."[12]

Critics of the new hermeneutic are confused by the ambiguities that result from a failure by its exponents to clarify their prejudgments.[13] Of greatest revelance for us is the criticism that this hermeneutic empties faith of meaningful content, in effect, seriously compromising an alleged appeal to history. As Wilder puts it, revelation "reveals nothing! Thus Jesus himself, his person, has no special character. . . . The significance attaches to the time, not to him." The corrective is historical realism in presupposing that Jesus' person and work rest upon ideology and that the word is meaning as well as address. "Faith involves consent to truth as well as obedience to an invitation or a call."[14] Unless the address is informed with a meaningful truth aspect, it remains abstract and ambiguous, blowing where it wills without any necessary relation to *Jesus* Christ. Without the kind of clear-cut distinction between historical knowledge and faith-knowledge urged by Perrin there is no adequate norm by means of which to denote that which is distinctive of Jesus or unique in his message.

This ambiguity is very evident in Fuch's open-ended interpretation of the parables,[15] as contrasted with Joachim Jeremias' classic analysis.[16] Because the whole issue of the relationship between historical Jesus and kerygmatic Christ is separated from the ground of history, the parables are emptied of cognitive content.[17] Also, because of the erroneous presupposition that one can discern a "pure" word of God, unconditioned by the culture in which it is uttered, historical realism is absent. The net effect, despite the location by Fuchs of the language revelation in daily life, is that "the cognitive, persuasive, semantically meaningful terms of the divine address and self-impartation are sterilized away."[18] Contrary to the underlying assumption of the New Testament as a whole, the view of Jesus that emerges tends to be docetic, and the New Testament synthesis of historical knowledge and faith-knowledge, most clearly seen in the Gospel-perspective, is seriously distorted by a subtle devaluation of the historical factor.

As Herzog points out, the faith element as well is not adequately understood due to the failure to consider fully the implications of the Christological emphasis that is made. Proposing a hermeneutic of the word "God," Herzog believes that the new hermeneutic tends to beg the question in not making explicit hermeneutically that Christological language implies theological language, that "christology is concerned with Jesus in relationship to *God*."[19] By concentrating upon a hermeneutic of the word "God" Fuchs and Ebeling might avoid the untenable one-sidedness of their supposition that understanding is a one-way street: from text to man. They might view "the primal hermeneutical task in theology" as "the bridging of the gap between the christological interpretation of language and such prejudgments contained in man's language as are related to God."[20] As such, hermeneutic would be viewed not as equivalent to theology as a whole but, as it should be, as the first step in theological method. This would also be more consistent with the Godward orientation in the Gospel-perspective in general and in Jesus' message and bearing in particular.

JESUS RESEARCH

The question of the historical Jesus has already been introduced into the discussion. With the implications of the Gospel-perspective in view, we shall concentrate upon it here. This will be but to continue the previous discussion in terms of the question of "recognizable continuity of subject matter" in the translation task. There are two main issues. The first is that of the rationale of the quest. The second concerns its nature, primarily with reference to the caution that the method of investigation should be "appropriate to the nature of the sources."[21]

With regard to the first of these, it hardly needs to be said that the Evangelists were not historical scholars. One may be justified in speaking of "Luke the historian,"[22] if he means that in certain respects Luke, more than the other Evangelists, evidences some of the characteristics of ancient history writers. It is not legitimate, if it be taken to mean that Luke was primarily interested in reconstructing the past. Like the others, in form and content, he was an Evangelist. He was intent upon employing historical reminiscences in a creative way in order to make the good news intelligible and persuasive. This is the impression of the Gospel-perspective in general.

Furthermore, the sharp distinction between "Jesus of history" and "Christ of faith," especially the terminology, is the invention of modern scholars. The Evangelists apparently did not view this dichotomy in such a rigid manner. At least for them the message of Jesus transmitted in the Gospels was as much that of the resurrected Christ focused upon later situations as of the preresurrection Jesus relative to his original setting. Some tend to make this identification too absolute, but, in comparison with the presuppositions and thought forms of the modern historian, it has its point.

However, this need not detain us further. It is not only obvious; it is irrelevant. It is irrelevant, that is, in trying to answer the question whether or not the Gospel-perspective *implies* anything important for modern Jesus research. This lifts up the matter of consistency among interests, purposes, and methods, with the nature of the Gospel-perspective taking on great importance.

The fundamental reason for the quest is that it is implicit, and thus inevitable, in the tension between history and kerygma within the Gospel-perspective, as within the New Testament as a whole. Harvey K. McArthur is convincing on this

point. He clearly discerns the factors in the Biblical tradition
that make inevitable a tension between the Jesus of history and
the Christ of faith, which in turn produces the quest.[23] He
makes clear that "all periods show some trace of this tension
between the historical and the theological elements in the
Christian faith," and that it is "most acute in periods when the
church has been in intellectual conflict with the surrounding
culture."[24] The period of the early church was the first of these.
The challenge then was to formulate the Christian faith over
against the culture of the Greco-Roman world. The Gospels
stand at the beginning of this process, their creative way of
handling the problem being predetermined by their presuppositions and thought forms. Robert M. Grant has shown how
this process was continued by a series of early Christian scholars leading up to Origen.[25]

The other period of acute tension is the modern one. As
evidenced by the turmoil in theological thought today, the
Renaissance inheritance has forced the church again to rethink
and to reformulate its faith. Furthermore, the form that the
quest has taken in our times has been determined by the pre-
occupation of modern culture with the question of history and
its meaning. This means that for *us* modern historiography applied to Jesus research is the only adequate means of dealing
with the *historical* element in the Gospel tradition, if we wish
to keep faith with the intention and creativity of the Evangelists. Legitimate differences of opinion about how to "do" history are significant only on the basis of that premise.[26] Since
everyone who concerns himself with Jesus at all presupposes
some picture of Jesus of Nazareth, and is influenced by it, it
is important that, in delineating the features of that picture, the
best available historical tools be employed.

This, we believe, is the implication of the Gospel-perspective. It is also consistent with the logic of the historical religion
that Christianity is. This is put convincingly in summary form
by C. F. D. Moule. Arguing that blind faith is not real faith,
he writes: "For belief it is necessary to see—at least something.
The decision to accept Jesus as Lord cannot be made without

historical evidence—yes, historical—about Jesus. If it were a decision without any historical evidence it would not be about Jesus (a historical person) but only about an ideology or an ideal. . . . Before we can decide for Jesus we need to know what manner of man he was, how he was related to his antecedents, why he died, and what (so far as it can be indicated) lies behind the conviction that he is alive. To take all this unexplained is not Christian decision at all, even if it may be a moral or a religious decision."[27]

This is the thrust of Wolfhart Pannenberg's "theology as history," as of Cullmann's "salvation in history," in reaction against the "theology of the Word of God." According to Pannenberg the present-day forms of the latter, including the new hermeneutic, are inadequate to the extent that they represent only modern expressions of an authoritarian claim to revelation which exempts itself from questions of critical rationality. On the one hand, Pannenberg argues for the integrity of faith as necessary to knowing God's revelation in Jesus Christ. Faith, rather than preliminary knowledge of Jesus, unites us with God and imparts salvation. Furthermore, the only criterion of the truth of God's revelation in Jesus of Nazareth is that "again and again it subsequently proves itself true as we experience the reality in which we live."[28] On the other hand, "faith does not take the place of knowledge." Logically, if not always psychologically, the basis of faith is "the knowledge of Jesus' history, including his resurrection from the dead." Thus it is important to begin with Jesus of Nazareth, because "knowledge . . . leads into faith," and because "the more exact it is, the more certainly it does so." Furthermore, unless faith is to be simply "blind gullibility, credulity, or even superstition," it must have trustworthy historical grounding. "Faith can breathe freely only when it can be certain, even in the field of scientific research, that its foundation is true," since the idea of the unity of truth is necessary for intellectual and personal integrity.[29] The probability coefficient in historical study remains, in principle making it possible for research to remove the foundation for the certainty of faith. This is unlikely, however, and it is just as possible that "better" knowledge of Jesus could be forth-coming.[30]

On a more popular level the importance of appealing to the Jesus of history is illustrated by the travesty of Hollywood versions of Jesus, such as *The Greatest Story Ever Told* or the earlier *King of Kings,* as compared with Pasolini's *Gospel According to St. Matthew.* The finished Hollywood epic is paralyzed by its concern not to offend anyone, and it fails to effect a religious interpretation of life by its insertions of phony "religious" tidbits. Instead, such works "reveal ignorance and superstition, and combine banality of thought with vulgarity of intention." By contrast the *Gospel According to St. Matthew,* "a black and white film made on an economy budget by an Italian Marxist, . . . presents far more effectively the drama and mystery of the Passion."[31] And it does so, among other things, because it takes the historical foundation seriously.

This contrast has symbolical value. The Hollywood version of Jesus speaks for all the ways in which substitutions for a vital Christianity characterize the current scene. These include the cult of spiritual health with its "how-to-be-a-successful-Christian" appeal, evangelism viewing sin in terms of private wrongdoing while bypassing its terrible social dimension, and the equation of American civil religion with Christ. Pasolini's Christ, on the other hand, challenges us to realize that the only way to "get back on the main highway of the Christian faith" is to rediscover the "hard core of biblical religion" with the Jesus of the Gospels at the center of attention.[32]

This is all emphatic in reinforcing the importance of making a clear distinction between historical knowledge and faith-knowledge, so that the contributions of the former to the latter may be clearly discerned. As Perrin rightly sees it, there are three such contributions. First, historical knowledge provides the content required to give meaning to a faith in a certain Jesus of Nazareth as Lord and Christ. It makes the term *"Jesus Christ"* intelligible. Second, it tests the validity of the term "Christian" when it is used to characterize a proclamation of Christ's Lordship. Since not all such proclamations agree, some

norm is needed. If that norm involves more than the Jesus of
history, it does not involve less. Third, provided that the
method of "translation" is adequate, historical knowledge may
be applied directly to later situations in many instances.[33]

John McIntyre adds to this the value of historical knowledge
for Christology. The limitations of the revelation and the two
nature models, creating a serious crisis in Christological thought
today, require that the "psychological model" be brought realistically into the discussion. This term is the theologian's way
of designating the Jesus of history. It embraces Jesus research
on the premise that, "if we are unable to speak of the *personality* of Jesus, we are *ex vi terminorum* forbidden to speak about
Jesus."[34] In the course of arguing that enough can be learned
by historical research about Jesus' personality to make the
psychological model viable, McIntyre rightly points out that
some who theoretically discount this possibility actually assume it in practice.[35]

These citations will suffice to state a point of view, a view
that is not uncontested in the current debate,[36] but one which
makes sense to us. We are not concerned, however, to enter
into that debate except as certain facets of it emerge in the
ensuing discussion. Having sought to establish reasonable
grounds for taking the quest seriously, we shall now turn our
attention to a consideration of the potential contributions of
the Gospel-perspective to the nature of the quest. What can
be said, with our focus upon the precaution that method should
be "appropriate to the nature of the sources"? At least four
general observations appear to be in order.

First, the view that it is impossible to write a full-scale
biography of Jesus in the modern sense is indicated by the
Gospel-perspective itself. The Gospels indicate no such interest
and they do not provide sufficient materials for such an under-
taking. Instead, they encourage us to expect more accurate
information about the great common denominators of Jesus'
thought and typical impressions of his deeds than about details. This suggests a proper definition of the historical task
with reference to the probability coefficient. The problem is to

decide *which aspects* of the sources *most probably* represent *in essential respects* valid preresurrection reminiscences. Since practically all scholars assume that something can be learned about the Jesus of history, the only viable question is that of its extent and nature as determined by this understanding of the task.

This corresponds with what it is that we most need to know in the interests of faith-knowledge. Mary D. Shideler speaks to this point in dealing with the question of how we may hear God speaking today in the light of the first-century "scandal of particularity" and the peculiar character of our modern situation. We do not recognize God's word for today, she says, "by collating texts and abstracting principles from them," but rather by "discerning within the records of [Jesus'] ministry *the quality which is distinctly his own.*"[37] If this embraces respect for the truth aspect of the historical revelation, it points in the right direction.

Second, the reconstruction of the gospel tradition by means of form criticism and related methods is consistent with the *nature* of the Gospel-perspective. The interrelationships of the Gospels reveal the process by which they came into being, with the different strata resembling a mound that invites archaeological investigation. The strata appear to be single sayings and pericopes at the lowest oral level (except for passion stories), then collections of cycles of tradition, and finally the finished Gospels. The reconstruction of the history of this tradition is more successful with the Synoptics than with John's Gospel, but the latter can be compared to some extent with the Synoptics. At least the nature of the Gospels encourages the application of critical procedures, corresponding to archaeological method, in order to lay bare the forms of the tradition nearest to Jesus himself, so that we may "return to Jesus from the primitive Church."[38]

Since "facts" at every level are unavoidably interpreted facts, the problem is to determine which interpretations most probably represent with greatest accuracy the preresurrection Jesus. As it stands the tradition provides some clues in this respect.

For example, the parables appear to resist complete assimilation to the interests of the Evangelists, despite their readaptation in various ways to later situations. As Dan O. Via, Jr., says, having their own characters and their own autonomous world, "they cannot become merely subsidiary to the structure of the Gospels but rather contend inevitably with the latter for the focal attention of the reader."[39] This is to say that the original form of the parable as spoken by Jesus has not been lost in the process of transmission. By means of form criticism and adequate criteria of authenticity similar probability results can be obtained in the treatment of other types of material.

This presupposition is more consistent with the nature of the Gospel-perspective than is the view of Birger Gerhardsson, who discounts the form-critical approach.[40] According to Gerhardsson the early Christians were completely bound by Jewish and Hellenistic patterns for the transmission of oral and written tradition. On the premise that Jesus conducted a Rabbinic school of discipleship for the purpose of guaranteeing the preservation of his teaching, it is held that the Gospels contain condensed memory texts and interpretative expositions which in all essential respects go back to Jesus himself.

This view has value to the extent that it counters an extreme historical skepticism toward the authenticity of the tradition, but it has too many questionable features to be convincing. A major fault is the use of Rabbinic analogies that apply only after the time of Jesus.[41] Above all, in several respects it is not consistent with the implications of the Gospel-perspective. It ignores the evidences of creativity in the use of contextual materials, including their forms of expression. It ignores the differences in the form of Jesus' teaching between the Synoptics and John's Gospel and fails to recognize the influence upon Jesus of different rhetorics in the Synoptics. It fails to grasp the indications that discourses like the Sermon on the Mount represent an advanced, rather than an original, stage of the formation of the tradition. It gives the Twelve a prominence that the sources are not self-consistent about, and ignores the evidence that before the resurrection they did not comprehend

Jesus' teaching. It disavows the evidence that Jesus did not envisage the establishment of the church after his death. Of greatest moment, it places an emphasis upon Jesus' understanding of himself as a rabbi, which is not a major motif in the Gospels compared with his prophetic stance within the messianic category. Generally speaking, this view exaggerates the continuity between Jesus' message and the records, without sufficient concern for evidences of discontinuity and tension between them.

The third observation is that an inclusive and flexible conception of the criteria of authenticity is more consistent with the nature of the Gospel-perspective than one that absolutizes the "criterion of dissimilarity." Norman Perrin speaks for the latter view,[42] defining the criterion of dissimilarity as follows: "The earliest form of a saying we can reach may be regarded as authentic if it can be shown to be dissimilar to the characteristic emphases both of ancient Judaism and of the early Church."[43] When this has been established other less "authentic" sayings may be drawn into the picture by applying two additional criteria: "coherence" and "multiple attestation." The latter is more useful in discerning motifs in Jesus' message than in recovering specific sayings.

Compared to Gerhardsson's view this position takes seriously the creative interpretative aspect of the tradition in the Gospels. It also helps us to determine that which was unique in Jesus' teaching compared with the emphases of ancient Judaism. Perrin's exposition of the nature and significance of Jesus' table fellowship with the unorthodox in Judaism is convincing. This makes the crucifixion of Jesus intelligible as the inevitable result of the radical threat to the very existence of Judaism which he posed. This view is consistent with the ambiguity and inconsistency of the source materials since they imply that, after as well as before the resurrection, Jesus' disciples did not fully agree on his meaning in some respects.

With all of that, serious questions arise about the absolute priority that the criterion of dissimilarity is assumed to have. When one presumes to recover the *ipsissima verba* of Jesus, he must employ some literary criteria, yet Perrin discounts literary factors in favor of substantial theological considerations. Actually, his emphasis upon the theological content of a saying makes his concern for the most original form of a saying irrelevant, since the motifs that the criterion of multiple attestation allegedly turn up are just as pertinent. Furthermore, to equate authenticity with dissimilarity in a rigid way presupposes a questionable definition of originality. The Gospel-perspective is more realistic in viewing the "new" element in Jesus' teaching as a fulfillment of the old, by means of which, in the form of a new synthesis, Jesus makes clear "what the God of Israel really is and means."[44] Here the emphasis falls upon the unity of saying and deed characterized by the intensity of Jesus' devotion to God who is immediate in his experience.

Perrin's view, at the opposite extreme from that of Gerhardsson, exaggerates the discontinuity between Jesus and the records. It represents an arbitrary historical skepticism that discounts the possibility of valid historical reminiscence on the grounds that eyewitnesses, as well as others not in a position to observe for themselves, absolutely identified the risen Lord of their experience with Jesus of Nazareth and vice versa. Over against this the Gospel-perspective implies both continuity and discontinuity, as do the Epistles, and this perspective is more consistent with historical probability.[45]

This leads to the consideration of a more inclusive criterion of authenticity, such as that proposed by Paul Althaus. He is predisposed to believe that "Jesus and His character have left their stamp deeply on the secondary, even on the legendary material," inclusive of John's Gospel, and that the Jesus of history is to be apprehended in the "consensus" regarding "fundamental characteristics" which the whole tradition displays. With regard to the problem of Jesus' understanding of himself and his role, Althaus believes that "it is impossible to keep Jesus' teaching and Himself apart."[46]

This kind of approach appears more suited to the nature of the Gospel-perspective. The basic criterion becomes that of self-consistency with reference to Jesus' antecedents and internal self-consistency with regard to the "fundamental character-istics" of the picture of the Jesus of history. Within that frame-work the criterion of dissimilarity is useful, if not to rediscover the exact words of Jesus, at least to assist one in determining Jesus' most characteristic emphases.

In addition to this we must consider the necessity for the historian to argue to some extent "from faith to fact." This is inevitable simply because "the pictures of the past which his-torical research is able to establish on the basis of probability evidence are always *less* than the reality of the original events."[47] One cannot learn the whole truth about a person by means of a postmortem examination of his effects, let alone of his corpse. Because of this the gap is of necessity filled in by imagination, intuition, or existential encounter. Within the framework of adequate historical procedures it is legitimate to argue from faith to fact in the same way that we do in many areas of our lives, as long as we have the general features, and not the details, of the historical picture in view.[48] This is the large element of truth in the view that the historian is not, and cannot be, completely "objective." To this extent existentialist interpretation is valid, as long as the center of exegesis "lies in the use of evidence and not in the influence of presuppositions,"[49] and provided that in analyzing the evi-dence all the canons of historical method are respected. In its own way the Gospel-perspective provides precedent for this kind of appeal from faith to fact, without (again "in its own way") losing a realistic sense of the historical.

The fourth observation has to do with the question of au-thenticity in terms of relative degrees of probability when the norm of "consensus" or internal self-consistency is applied. In the picture of Jesus that the Gospel-perspective supplies some features are more ambiguous, some less so, than others. Generally speaking, the religious and ethical staples of Jesus' assumptions and message are more self-consistently evident than the use of titles and related categories designed to eluci-date the enigma of his person. The former are also easier to grasp as a self-consistent whole than certain features of his eschatology. Previous chapters provide the evidence for this, and they may simply be recalled at this point. Jesus' scale of values, resting upon his views of God and man, asserts itself not only in his teaching but in his actions as well.

On this matter the perspective of the Gospels coincides with that of the Epistles. In the latter a variety of Christologies explicate the conviction that Jesus is the salvation bringer, at the same time that the religious and ethical fundamentals that Jesus is believed to reveal are generally self-consistent. There is some variety, to be sure, but, comparatively speaking, there is greater self-consistency than in Christology. The inference to be drawn from this is that the Gospel-perspective, reinforced by that of the Epistles, encourages us in Jesus research to concentrate upon the reconstruction of the fundamental religious and ethical features of the picture of the Jesus of history.

This kind of distinction suggests something in analyzing the enigma of Jesus' self-understanding. By way of example and for its own sake, we may elaborate this somewhat. The attempt to answer this question by means of an analysis of titles and related forms of thought is baffling in the extreme, and there is no consensus among scholars. The continuing debate over the title "Son of Man" is a case in point.[50] The basic problem here is not primarily the ambiguity of the sources, however, although this is a vital factor. It is, rather, that no traditional title really suits Jesus' unprecedented sense of authority. The impression of the Gospel-perspective is that Jesus found the use of specific traditional messianic categories more of a problem than a help. On the other hand, when his unique sense of authority is analyzed in terms of its religious and ethical ingredients, a self-consistent and coherent picture emerges.[51] In this way of approaching the question a comparison of Jesus with the Jewish scribe and the Hebrew prophet yields better results than speculation about messianic titles. At the center of the picture, as the focal point of everything else, is the impression of an immediate awareness of God which defies categorization. It is a prophetic self-consciousness, yet more than the prophet's sense of delegated authority. In the thought forms of Jesus' environment it can only be labeled "messianic," yet without clarity regarding the precise way in which this is formulated or felt in the mind of Jesus.

All things considered, the impression of the Gospel-perspective encourages us to think that Jesus' intimacy with God and his sense of commission from God constituted a mystery that he accepted as such without attempting to define it more explicitly. If he did employ one or more traditional terms or ideas in the process of thinking about it, which the sources imply, the ambiguity of the records leaves the secret with him. This is the messianic secret par excellence! This general impression is consistent with the logic of the situation. That is, it is consistent with the idea, as John Knox well expresses it, that "the greater the depth and mystery in Jesus' consciousness of vocation, and the more uniquely personal it was to himself, the less likely that he would have been able to define it."[52] Of even greater significance is the implication of the records that, as compared with the intense desire to make God real to men in his message and actions, the precise definition of his person was of secondary, at least of instrumental, importance. The Gospel-perspective thus suggests that this is the place for historical reconstruction to begin. This is its wisdom, however much further the historian may need to go in analyzing messianic categories and the theologian in thinking through a Christology for today.

Recalling earlier consideration of patterns of thought relative to Jesus' passion, historical probability permits us to say something about Jesus' thought of his death. The general impression of the "facts" behind the passion predictions and related data speaks with clarity, however much in their present form they undoubtedly represent hindsight after the event. They suggest that as a minimum basis for historical reconstruction it should be taken for granted that circumstances forced Jesus to think about the hazards of the hostility that his aggressive actions aroused, and that in a realistic way he did so. It should also be taken for granted that his motivation was consistent with the impressions of his character and unwavering faith in God which the Gospels generally portray, and which the Epistles also reflect. This is to believe, as reliable historical evidence, that Jesus foresaw the possibility of his death, that he forecast its possibility, even probability, and that he faced it with complete confidence that, if it occurred, as it probably would, God would ultimately vindicate him—as he did!

This is a far more reasonable conclusion from the evidence, in the light of historical probability, than the agnosticism of an extreme historical skepticism. It is also more realistic than the fanciful interpretation of an unbridled imagination that insists, regardless of the evidence, upon coming up with something novel.[53]

The evidence does not permit us to penetrate very far into the mind of Jesus beyond this generalized version of his self-understanding, but it doesn't really matter. If this is not all that we would like to know, it is all that we need to know in the interests of faith. This too is the wisdom of the Gospel-perspective.

EPILOGUE

ALBERT SCHWEITZER concluded his classic work on the quest with the memorable words: "He comes to us as One unknown, without a name, as of old, by the lake-side, He came to those who knew Him not. He speaks to us the same word: 'Follow thou me!' and sets us to the tasks which He has to fulfil for our time. He commands. And to those who obey Him, whether they be wise or simple, He will reveal Himself in the toils, the conflicts, the sufferings which they shall pass through in His fellowship, and, as an ineffable mystery, they shall learn in their own experience Who He is."[1]

This is witness to a reality that Schweitzer and many others have known, and still know, in their experience. It is this dimension of Jesus Christ which has inspired prophets and martyrs, poets and artists and musicians, as well as the rank and file of devout disciples over many generations. It reminds us that attention, as historians, to the preresurrection period of Jesus' story is not enough for vital Christian experience. There is in Jesus Christ a transcendental dimension which, mysteriously and compellingly to eyes of faith, manifests itself in the language of every time and place. This is because in confronting Jesus Christ men become aware of God on whose initiative and by whose power Jesus became what he was, and is.

However, this does not make the historical dimension, and the Jesus research that concentrates upon it, irrelevant for faith. As Moule says, "The nearer you push the inquiry back to the original Jesus, the more you find that you cannot have him without a transcendental element."[2] This is the impression of the Gospel-perspective in both its Synoptic and its Johannine thrusts, not more so, if differently expressed, in the latter than in the former. The genius of the Gospel-perspective is that it refuses to permit us to settle for a one-sided or exclusive emphasis upon either the historical or the transhistorical element. It constantly reminds us that "the Word became flesh and dwelt among us."

Granting this, the focus of this book makes it fitting that our final word should emphasize the indispensable contribution of the Gospel-perspective within that synthesis. With Mark's Gospel primarily in view, Eduard Schweizer has addressed himself discerningly to this point. He writes: "The historical Jesus does not convey faith to us—that is the work of the kerygma of the church—but . . . he keeps our faith from becoming unfaith or distorted faith. If man were a computer, he would need nothing except the shortest and most theoretical kerygma, and even that in the form of some holes punched into a cardboard. Since man is no computer, but a being of flesh and blood, he needs the manifestation of God's revelation in flesh and blood in order to continue believing, that is, following Jesus."[3] That is, man needs the dynamic of a person whose quality is such that, confronting him, he knows that God has drawn near.

We cannot fathom this person. In that sense he comes as one "unknown." He is always more than we can grasp by the study of the initial stage of his story, of his impact on history, or by existential encounter. But he does not come "without a name." As the Christ of our experience he is still Jesus of Nazareth, impressions of whose earthly story we can observe in the Gospel-perspective and which we can to some extent reconstruct by historical method. Recalling the task he set himself and his followers in days long gone but not forgotten, we are the better prepared to discern "the tasks which he has to fulfill for our time." Remembering the earliest impressions of who he was and what he did, our impressions of who he is and what he is doing are more likely to be realistic than fanciful. This, in part at least, is the relevance and the promise of the Gospel-perspective.

NOTES

INTRODUCTION

1. Oscar Cullmann, "The Plurality of the Gospels as a Theological Problem in Antiquity," *The Early Church*, ed. by Angus J. B. Higgins, tr. by Stanley Godman (The Westminster Press, 1956), p. 45.

2. Cf. Charles F. D. Moule, *The Birth of the New Testament* (*Birth* hereafter) (Harper & Row, Publishers, Inc., 1962), pp. 4–8; Amos N. Wilder, *The Language of the Gospel* (*Language* hereafter) (Harper & Row, Publishers, Inc., 1964), pp. 36–43.

3. H. J. Schoeps, *Paul: The Theology of the Apostle in the Light of Jewish Religious History*, tr. by Harold Knight (The Westminster Press, 1961), pp. 73 f. Our italics.

4. Cf. Harvey K. McArthur, *The Quest Through the Centuries* (Fortress Press, 1966), pp. 17–19; John Knox, *The Humanity and Divinity of Christ* (Cambridge University Press, 1967).

5. Cf. John A. T. Robinson, *Honest to God* (The Westminster Press, 1963), p. 65; Oscar Cullmann, *The Christology of the New Testament* (*Christology* hereafter), tr. by Shirley C. Guthrie and Charles A. M. Hall (The New Testament Library; The Westminster Press, 1959), pp. 306n1, 330n3.

6. Ernest C. Colwell, *Jesus and the Gospel* (Oxford University Press, Inc., 1963), p. 41.

7. Cf. essays by Rudolf Bultmann and Van A. Harvey and Schubert M. Ogden in *The Historical Jesus and the Kerygmatic Christ*, tr. and ed. by Carl E. Braaten and Roy A. Harrisville (Abingdon Press, 1964), pp. 15–42, 197–242.

8. Cf. Norman Perrin, *Rediscovering the Teaching of Jesus* (*Rediscovering* hereafter) (Harper & Row, Publishers, Inc., 1967), pp. 234–248; Wolfhart Pannenberg, "The Revelation of God in Jesus of Nazareth," *Theology as History*, ed. by James M. Robinson and John B. Cobb, Jr., tr. by Kendrick Grobel (New Frontiers in

Theology, Vol. III; Harper & Row, Publishers, Inc., 1967), pp. 101–133, 221–276, esp. p. 273.

9. Cf. Reginald H. Fuller, *The New Testament in Current Study* (*Current Study* hereafter) (Charles Scribner's Sons, 1962), Chs. V to VII.

CHAPTER I THE SYNOPTIC VIEW OF JESUS: WHO WAS JESUS?

1. On *exousia*, see Walter Bauer, *A Greek-English Lexicon of the New Testament and Other Early Christian Literature*, tr. and ed. by William F. Arndt and F. Wilbur Gingrich (The University of Chicago Press, 1957), pp. 277 f.

2. Cf. Eduard Schweizer, "Mark's Contribution to the Quest of the Historical Jesus," *NTS*, Vol. X, No. 4 (July, 1964), p. 428.

3. *Logoi:* Mark 10:22, 24; Matt. 7:28; 19:1; 26:1; Luke 4:22, 32, 36; 5:1; 7:17; 9:28; 22:61. On Luke, see Charles K. Barrett, *Luke the Historian in Recent Study* (*Luke* hereafter) (London: The Epworth Press, 1961), pp. 68, 71 f. On Matthew, see Moule, *Birth*, p. 91; Rudolf Bultmann, *The History of the Synoptic Tradition*, tr. by John Marsh (Harper & Row, Publishers, Inc., 1963), pp. 350 ff.

4. Cf. Zech. 13:3–6; Ps. 74:9; I Macc. 9:27. Cf. Cullmann, *Christology*, pp. 13–50; Franklin W. Young, "Jesus the Prophet: A Re-examination," *JBL*, Vol. LXVIII, No. 4 (Dec., 1949), pp. 285–299; Charles Scobie, *John the Baptist* (London: SCM Press, Ltd., 1964), p. 118.

5. Scobie, *op. cit.*, p. 123.

6. Cf. Norman B. Johnson, *Prayer in the Apocrypha and Pseudepigrapha* (*JBL* Monograph Series, Vol. II; Society of Biblical Literature & Exegesis, 1948).

7. Cf. Gerhard von Rad, *Old Testament Theology*, tr. by D. M. G. Stalker (London: Oliver & Boyd, Ltd., 1965), Vol. II, pp. 52 ff., 59 ff.; Abraham J. Heschel, *The Prophets* (Harper & Row, Publishers, Inc., 1962), Chs. I, XXIV.

8. Von Rad, *op. cit.*, pp. 195 f., 206–208. Cf. Jer. 43:3–5.

9. On Enoch, Baruch, and Jeremiah, see Cullmann, *Christology*, pp. 17 f.

10. Cf. Reginald H. Fuller, *The Foundations of New Testament Christology* (*Foundations* hereafter) (London: Lutterworth Press, 1965), p. 46.

11. Cf. Theodor H. Gaster, *The Scriptures of the Dead Sea Sect* (London: Martin Secker & Warburg, Ltd., 1957), pp. 353–355; also Scobie, *op. cit.*, p. 122; Fuller, *Foundations*, pp. 50–53. Cf. John 1:21, 25; 6:14.

12. Cullmann, *Christology*, p. 19.

13. Cf. Fuller, *Foundations*, pp. 47, 50–53, 59; Matthew Black, *The Dead Sea Scrolls and Christian Doctrine* (London: Athlone Press, 1966), p. 5. Isaiah 53:11 f. is never used in quotations from Second Isaiah (Cf. IQH 8:26, 35 f.).

14. Cf. Luke 1:5–25, 39–80 (ch. 3:2, 5 f.); and in Q: 7:24–38; 16:16. Cf. Fuller, *Foundations*, p. 91.

15. Scobie, *op. cit.*, pp. 127–129.

16. E.g., Ulrich W. Mauser, *Christ in the Wilderness* (SBT No. 39; Alec R. Allenson, Inc., 1963).

17. Cf. Moule, *Birth*, pp. 38, 40; also Luke's use of "Moses" in a context of Scriptural fulfillment (ch. 24:27, 44). Does Luke, chs. 9 to 18, follow an outline of Deut., chs. 1 to 26?

18. See in addition Matt. 10:41; 21:4, 46; Luke 7:13, 39; 24:19.

19. On the Servant theme in Matthew, see Edward P. Blair, *Jesus in the Gospel of Matthew* (Abingdon Press, 1960), pp. 79 ff.

20. Josephus, *Antiquities*, XX.5.1; *The Jewish War*, II.13.5.

21. Cf. Rom. 11:3; Heb. 11:32; James 5:10; Rev. 16:6; 18:24.

22. Cf. Test. Reub. 6:5–12; Test. Levi 8:11–15; Test. Jud., ch. 24; IQS 9:10 ff.; and n. 11, above. Cf. Karl G. Kuhn, "The Two Messiahs of Aaron and Israel," *The Scrolls and the New Testament*, ed. by Krister Stendahl (Harper & Brothers, 1957), pp. 55–64.

23. Fuller, *Foundations*, p. 32.

24. E.g., the individualizing of the term and its use for famous persons other than officials, *gnōsis* for the LXX *synesis* in quoting Isa. 53:11 (Wisd. of Sol. 2:13).

25. Fuller, *Foundations*, p. 69.

26. Cf. Philo, *De agricultura* 51.

27. Taking *huios theou* in Mark 15:39 to mean "*the* Son of God." Cf. Charles F. D. Moule, *An Idiom Book of New Testament Greek* (London: Cambridge University Press, 1953), p. 116.

28. On the link between Spirit and Sonship in Luke-Acts see Barrett, *Luke*, pp. 35, 67, 73; Paul Feine and Johannes Behm, *Introduction to the New Testament* (*Introduction* hereafter), ed. by Werner G. Kümmel and tr. by A. J. Mattill, Jr., (14th rev. ed.; Abingdon Press, 1966), p. 602.

29. James M. Robinson, *The Problem of History in Mark* (SBT No. 21; Alec R. Allenson, Inc., 1957).

30. Cf. John A. T. Robinson, "The Temptations," *Twelve New Testament Studies* (SBT No. 34; Alec R. Allenson, Inc., 1962), pp. 53–60.

31. Cf. Mark 7:24–30; 11:17; 12:1–12; 13:10; 14:9, 24.

32. Matt. 2:15; 14:33; 16:16; 27:40, 43; 28:19. Cf. Blair, *op. cit.*, pp. 55 ff.; Kümmel, *Introduction*, p. 76.

33. Cf. "Abba, Father" (Mark 14:36) and other references to "Father," especially in M materials: Thomas W. Manson, *The*

Teaching of Jesus (*Teaching* hereafter) (2d ed.; London: Cambridge University Press, 1935), pp. 94 ff.; Joachim Jeremias, *The Prayers of Jesus*, tr. by J. Bowden (SBT No. 6, 2d Series, Alec R. Allenson, Inc., 1967), Ch. I.

34. On the problem of authenticity, see Frederick H. Borsch, *The Son of Man in Myth and History* (The New Testament Library; The Westminster Press, 1967), pp. 145–156; Matthew Black, "The Son of Man Problem in Recent Research and Debate," *BJRL*, Vol. XLV, No. 2 (1963), pp. 305–318; Perrin, *Rediscovering*, pp. 167 ff.

35. Perrin, *Rediscovering*, pp. 164 ff.

36. Cf. Borsch, *op. cit.*, pp. 132 ff., 149, 153; Heinz E. Tödt, *The Son of Man in the Synoptic Tradition*, tr. by Dorothea M. Barton (The New Testament Library; The Westminster Press, 1965); Fuller, *Foundations*, pp. 34–43.

37. Fuller, *Foundations*, pp. 233 f.; Borsch, *op. cit.*, pp. 240–256, also 233–239.

38. Cf. classification and discussion of sayings in Manson, *Teaching*, pp. 211 f.; Borsch, *op. cit.*, pp. 320–364. Cf. Bibliography in Perrin, *Rediscovering*, pp. 259 f.

39. E.g., Luke 12:40 and Matt. 24:44; Mark 13:35 f., par.; Matt. 16:28; 19:28; 24:30.

40. Morna Hooker, "Jesus and the Son of Man," *The Finality of Christ*, ed. by Dow Kirkpatrick (Abingdon Press, 1966), pp. 32–54, and *The Son of Man in Mark* (Montreal: McGill University Press, 1967). Cf. Borsch, *op. cit.*, pp. 230, 87, 121; Sherman Johnson, *The Theology of the Gospels* (*Gospels* hereafter) (Studies in Theology; London: Gerald Duckworth & Co., Ltd., 1966), pp. 31, 57, 158 ff.

41. Hooker, "Jesus and the Son of Man," pp. 48 f.

42. *Ibid.*, pp. 52 f.

43. Borsch, *op. cit.*, pp. 230, 201, 218; 132, 145, 153 f.; 127–129, 175–177; 132.

44. Perrin, *Rediscovering*, pp. 172 f.

45. Cf. I. H. Marshall, "The Synoptic Son of Man Sayings in Recent Discussion," *NTS*, Vol. XII, No. 4 (1966), pp. 327–351; Borsch, *op. cit.*, pp. 21–54.

46. E.g., "bridegroom" (Mark 2:19 f.); "head of the corner" (Mark 12:10, par.); the "name" (Mark 11:9; Luke 13:35).

47. In addition, Matt. 1:22 f.; 2:5 f., 17, 23.

48. Matt. 4:14–16; 8:17; 12:17–21; 13:14 f., 35; 21:4 f.

49. William Wrede, *Das Messiasgeheimnis in den Evangelien* (3d unveränderte Aufl.; Göttingen: Vandenhoeck & Ruprecht, 1963). Cf. Rudolf Bultmann, *Theology of the New Testament* (*Theology* hereafter), tr. by Kendrick Grobel (Charles Scribner's Sons, 1951 and 1955), Vol. I, p. 32.

50. Leander E. Keck, "The Introduction to Mark's Gospel," *NTS*,

Vol. XII, No. 4 (1966), pp. 368, 370. Cf. Fuller, *Foundations,*
p. 232. Acts 1:1 characterizes the Gospel of Luke as "all that Jesus
began to do and teach."

51. Cf. Moule, *Birth,* pp. 20, 32.

52. Cf. Fuller, *Foundations,* pp. 195–197. On the Spirit with ref-
erence to Luke's purpose as a whole see Harry H. Oliver, "The
Lucan Birth Stories and the Purpose of Luke-Acts," *NTS,* Vol. X,
No. 2 (1964), pp. 225 f.

53. Günther Bornkamm, *Jesus of Nazareth* (*Jesus* hereafter), tr.
by Irene and Fraser McLuskey with James M. Robinson (Harper
& Row, Publishers, Inc., 1961), p. 187.

CHAPTER II THE SYNOPTIC VIEW OF JESUS: WHAT DID JESUS DO?

1. Schweizer, "Mark's Contribution to the Quest of the Historical Jesus," pp. 422 f.

2. *Ibid.,* p. 428.

3. Cf. Keck, *loc. cit.,* pp. 352–370.

4. Cf. Wilder, *Language,* pp. 9–25. On a wider stage see Cor-
nelius Loew, *Myth, Sacred History, and Philosophy* (Harcourt,
Brace and World, Inc., 1967).

5. Wilder, *Language,* p. 22.

6. *Ibid.,* pp. 79 ff.

7. Arndt and Gingrich, *op. cit.,* on *engizō* and *engus,* pp. 212 f.;
C. H. Dodd, *The Parables of the Kingdom* (3d ed.; London; James
Nisbet & Co., Ltd., 1935), pp. 44 f.

8. Luke 11:51 and Matt. 23:36; Luke 17:24, 26; cf. Matt.
24:27, 37.

9. Cf. David S. Russell, *The Method and Message of Jewish
Apocalyptic, 200* BC–AD *100* (London: SCM Press, Ltd., 1964);
Oscar Cullmann, *Salvation in History,* tr. by Sidney G. Sowers
(Harper & Row, Publishers, Inc., 1967), pp. 74–83.

10. Cf. my article, "Prophetic and Apocalyptic Eschatology in
the Synoptic Gospels," *RIL,* Vol. XXX, No. 1 (1960–1961), p. 109.

11. John A. T. Robinson, *Jesus and His Coming* (London: SCM
Press, Ltd., 1957), p. 39.

12. Norman Perrin, *The Kingdom of God in the Teaching of
Jesus* (*Kingdom of God* hereafter) (The Westminster Press, 1963).
Cf. Cullmann, *Salvation in History,* p. 32.

13. II Sam. 12:1–7. Cf. Manson, *Teaching,* pp. 64 f.

14. *Ibid.,* pp. 94 ff.; S. Johnson, *Gospels,* pp. 129 ff.

15. Bornkamm, *Jesus,* p. 57.

16. Manson, *Teaching,* pp. 160 f.

17. Joachim Jeremias, *The Central Message of the New Testament* (Charles Scribner's Sons, 1965), p. 30.

18. Bultmann, *Theology,* Vol. I, pp. 6 f.

19. *Ibid.*, p. 25.

20. Perrin, *Rediscovering*, pp. 54 ff., etc.

21. Thomas E. Lawrence, *Seven Pillars of Wisdom* (Garden City Publishing Co., Inc., 1938), p. 38.

22. Bornkamm, *Jesus*, p. 105.

23. *Ibid.*, p. 101.

24. Surveys of redaction criticism with ample bibliographies: Kümmel, *Introduction*, pp. 31–175; Moule, *Birth*, pp. 86 ff. and throughout; Fuller, *Current Study*, pp. 70–132.

25. Cf. Kümmel, *Introduction*, pp. 76, 83; Frederick C. Grant, *The Gospels: Their Origin and Their Growth* (*Gospels: Their Origin* hereafter) (Harper & Brothers, 1957), Ch. XI.

26. Cf. Matthew Black, "Review Article" on *The Judean Scrolls* by G. R. Driver, *NTS*, Vol. XIII, No. 1 (1966), pp. 87 f.

27. Bornkamm, *Jesus*, pp. 16 f. In *Rediscovering*, p. 31, Perrin makes this identification too absolute.

28. E.g., Luke 15:7 and Matt. 18:13 f.; Luke 16:8–13; 10:29, 36; Mark 10:11 f. compared with Matt. 19:9; 5:32; and Luke 16:18.

29. Cf. S. Vernon McCasland, "Miracles," *IDB*, Vol. III, pp. 392–402; James L. Price, *Interpreting the New Testament* (Holt, Rinehart and Winston, Inc., 1961), pp. 26–65; Reginald H. Fuller, *Interpreting the Miracles* (The Westminster Press, 1963).

30. On the question of classification see Bultmann, *The History of the Synoptic Tradition*, pp. 209–243; Vincent Taylor, *The Formation of the Gospel Tradition* (2d ed.; London: Macmillan & Co., Ltd., 1935), pp. 119–141; Charles F. D. Moule, "The Classification of Miracle Stories," *Miracles*, ed. by C. F. D. Moule (London: A. R. Mowbray & Co., Ltd., 1965), pp. 239–243.

31. Cf. Günther Bornkamm, Gerhard Barth, Heinz J. Held, *Tradition and Interpretation in Matthew* (*Matthew* hereafter), tr. by Percy Scott (The New Testament Library; The Westminster Press, 1963), pp. 52 ff., 275 ff.

32. Fuller, *Interpreting the Miracles*, p. 76.

33. M. E. Glasswell, "The Use of Miracles in the Marcan Gospel," *Miracles*, p. 162.

34. Cf. Price, *op. cit.*, p. 151; Wilder, *Language*, pp. 72 f.

35. Wilder, *Language*, p. 70.

36. Bornkamm, *Jesus*, pp. 132 f.

37. McCasland, *loc. cit.*, p. 392.

38. Luke 23:4, 13–16, 20, 22b, 25b, 47.

39. Cf. also Matt. 26:52–54; Luke 22:37; 24:46.

40. Accepting the shorter text of Luke 22:15–19a and omitting vs. 19b–20. On Luke's view in general see Barrett, *Luke*, p. 59; S. Johnson, *Gospels*, pp. 160 f.

41. Assuming that parallels between Mark and Paul are mainly due to their common dependence upon the primitive kerygma, as

in Martin Werner, *Der Einfluss Paulinische Theologie im Marcus-Evangelium* (Giessen: A. Töpelmann, 1923).

CHAPTER III THE JOHANNINE VIEW OF JESUS

1. Cf. Charles H. Dodd, *The Interpretation of the Fourth Gospel* (*Fourth Gospel* hereafter) (London: Cambridge University Press, 1955), pp. 444 ff., and *Historical Tradition in the Fourth Gospel* (London: Cambridge University Press, 1963), pp. 315 ff.; Wilbert F. Howard, *The Fourth Gospel in Recent Criticism and Interpretation*, rev. by C. K. Barrett (4th ed.; London: The Epworth Press, Publishers, 1955), pp. 213–227, 306–309; Kümmel, *Introduction*, p. 145.

2. John 1:14 as in I John 4:2 f.; II John 7. Cf. John A. T. Robinson, "The Relation of the Prologue to the Gospel of St. John," *NTS*, Vol. IX, No. 2 (1963), pp. 127–129.

3. Cf. Edgar Hennecke, *New Testament Apocrypha*, ed. by Wilhelm Schneemelcher, English ed. tr. by R. McL. Wilson (The Westminster Press, 1963), Vol. I, pp. 363 ff.

4. E.g., compare Mark 6:5 and Matt. 13:58; Mark 10:18 and Matt. 19:17.

5. Cf. John 1:38, 49; 3:2; 4:31; 6:25; 9:2; 20:16. The term "scribe" is never used in John's Gospel.

6. Dodd, *Fourth Gospel*, pp. 230–238.

7. Cf. I Enoch 90:6–19; 89:46; Test. of Joseph 19:8 *arnies* in Rev. 22:1, 3; 7:17; 14:1–5; 17:14; 6:16 (also as the sacrificial Lamb in Rev. 5:6, 12, etc.).

8. Dodd, *Fourth Gospel*, p. 255.

9. Cf. John 10:10, 28; 17:2; etc.

10. Cf. John 5:22, 27, 30; 8:16, 26; 9:39.

11. Dodd, *Fourth Gospel*, p. 262.

12. Cf. Dom J. Howton, "'Son of God' in the Fourth Gospel," *NTS*, Vol. X, No. 2 (1964), pp. 233 f.

13. As in Edwin D. Freed's "The Son of Man in the Fourth Gospel," *JBL*, Vol. LXXXVI, No. 4 (Dec., 1967), pp. 402–409. Cf. qualifications in Borsch, *op. cit.*, pp. 258, 266.

14. Dodd, *Fourth Gospel*, pp. 243 f.

15. Cf. Kümmel, *Introduction*, pp. 154–161; Raymond E. Brown, *The Gospel According to John I–XII* (The Anchor Bible; Doubleday & Company, Inc., 1966), pp. cxxii ff.

16. Thorleif Boman, *Hebrew Thought Compared with Greek*, tr. by Jules L. Moreau (The Westminster Press, 1960), p. 60.

17. Dodd, *Fourth Gospel*, p. 283.

18. J. A. T. Robinson, "The Relation of the Prologue to the Gospel of St. John," pp. 120–129.

19. *Ibid.*, p. 128.

20. Cf. Eric L. Titus, *The Message of the Fourth Gospel* (Abingdon Press, 1957), pp. 43–50; Ernest C. Colwell and Eric L. Titus, *The Gospel of the Spirit* (Harper & Brothers, 1953).

21. Dodd, *Fourth Gospel*, p. 284.

22. *Ibid.*, p. 285.

23. *Ibid.*

24. Cf. Edwyn Hoskyns, *The Fourth Gospel*, ed. by Francis N. Davey (2d rev. ed.; London: Faber & Faber, Ltd., 1947), p. 164.

25. Cf. Moule, *Birth*, pp. 66–70, 73; Herbert Braun, "The Problem of a New Testament Theology," *The Bultmann School of Biblical Interpretation: New Directions*, (JTC, Vol. I; Harper & Row, Publishers, Inc., 1965), p. 172; Barrett, *Luke*, pp. 15 ff.

26. Cf. Christopher R. North, "The Works of God," *IDB*, Vol. IV, p. 873.

27. Kümmel, *Introduction*, p. 143.

28. Bultmann, *Theology*, Vol. II, p. 37.

29. Cf. Moule, *Birth*, pp. 98 f., 170; Barrett, *Luke*, p. 65. For an emphasis on the future element see Alfred Correll, *Consummatum Est: Eschatology and Church in the Gospel of St. John* (London: S.P.C.K., 1958).

30. Perrin, *The Kingdom of God*, Chs. 3 to 4, 7 to 8.

31. Bultmann, *Theology*, Vol. II, p. 62.

32. *Ibid.*, p. 66.

33. Braun, *loc. cit.*, p. 170.

34. Cf. the view of John A. T. Robinson that the Gospel was aimed exclusively at Hellenistic Jews, in "The Destination and Purpose of St. John's Gospel," *Twelve New Testament Studies*, Ch. VIII.

35. Cf. Fuller, *Interpreting the Miracles*, pp. 88–96; Dodd, *Fourth Gospel*, pp. 297 ff.

36. Fuller, *Interpreting the Miracles*, p. 108.

37. Cf. John 16:30; also 2:25; 13:19; 14:29. On Jesus' "knowledge" in Matthew see Blair, *op. cit.*, pp. 86 ff.

38. Fuller, *Interpreting the Miracles*, p. 92, etc.

39. Fuller, *Foundations*, pp. 228 f.

40. Cf. Dodd, *Fourth Gospel*, pp. 133–143, 297 ff.

41. *Ibid.*, p. 390.

42. Cf. unconscious testimony to Jesus, most clearly in John 11:49–52; Titus, *The Message of the Fourth Gospel*, pp. 34 f.

43. Dodd, *Fourth Gospel*, p. 431.

44. *Ibid.*, p. 429.

45. *Ibid.*

46. *Ibid.*, p. 432.

47. *Ibid.*, pp. 438 f.

48. *Ibid.*, p. 439.

49. John 19:24 (Ps. 22:18); 19:28 (Ps. 69:21, 29); 19:36 (Ps. 34:20); 19:37 (Zech. 12:10); etc.

50. In John, chs. 13 to 17, *agapē* is used 31 times and "life" only 6 times. Cf. Dodd, *Fourth Gospel*, pp. 398 f.

51. *Ibid.*, p. 441.

52. On the debate over a sacramental principle in John see Fuller, *Current Study*, p. 123; Braun, *loc. cit.*, p. 174; and previous discussion of "Lamb." Even in the most relevant references (John 3:1–21; 6:51 ff.; etc.) John's religious and ethical emphasis overshadows the sacramental interest.

53. Cf. Kümmel, *Introduction*, pp. 79 f.; Moule, *Birth*, pp. 87 f.

54. Barrett, *Luke*, p. 62. On the question of gnosticism in John see Fuller, *Current Study*, pp. 119 ff.; Kümmel, *Introduction*, pp. 162 ff.; Moule, *Birth*, pp. 166 f.; F. Grant, *Gospels: Their Origin*, pp. 160 ff. On Jewish gnosticism see Kümmel, *Introduction*, pp. 160 f.; Black, "Review Article," pp. 86 f.; Fuller, *Current Study*, pp. 125 ff.

CHAPTER IV THE GOSPEL-PERSPECTIVE IN THE NEW TESTAMENT

1. Adapted from Fuller, *Foundations*, pp. 243–247. Cf. Knox, *The Humanity and Divinity of Christ*, p. 17.

2. James M. Robinson, "Hermeneutical Theology," *The Christian Century*, Vol. LXXXIII, No. 18 (May 4, 1966), pp. 580 f. Cf. S. Johnson, *Gospels*, pp. 148 ff.

3. John McIntyre, *The Shape of Christology* (The Westminster Press, 1966), pp. 38 f. Cf. James Barr, *Biblical Words for Time* (SBT No. 33; Alec R. Allenson, Inc., 1962), pp. 153–162.

4. C. F. D. Moule, "The Influence of Circumstances on the Use of Christological Terms" ("Christological Terms" hereafter) *JTS*, New Series, Vol. X, No. 2 (1959), pp. 247–263.

5. Werner R. Kramer, *Christ, Lord, Son of God*, tr. by Brian Hardy (SBT No. 50; SCM Press, Ltd., 1966), pp. 13–15.

6. Cf. Fuller, *Foundations*. Cf. James Barr, *Old and New in Interpretation* (London: SCM Press, Ltd., 1966), Ch. II, and S. Johnson, *Gospels*, pp. 4 ff., who warn against drawing the line too rigidly between Palestinian- and Helenistic-Jewish thought.

7. On questions of authorship and date see Kümmel, *Introduction*, and other standard Introductions to the New Testament. We presuppose a date before A.D. 65 for Paul's letters; before A.D. 100 for the Gospels, Hebrews, The Revelation to John; after A.D. 100 for the rest, including the Pastorals.

8. On the hymnic nature of these passages see Fuller, *Foundations*, pp. 204 ff. Cf. Knox, *The Humanity and Divinity of Christ*,

pp. 20–23. Explicit references to preexistence are absent from Galatians, II Thessalonians, Philemon, The Acts, James, Jude, II Peter, Johannine Letters.

9. Contrasting human "form" (*morphē*) with "equality with God" (*isa theōi*) and translating the verb in Phil. 2:6 "to be retained."

10. Col. 1:15; cf. Rom. 8:29.

11. Col. 1:17.

12. I Peter 1:20a; cf. Rom. 8:29 f.; Eph. 1:4, 12; II Tim. 1:9 f.; Heb. 11:40.

13. Rom. 16:25; cf. I Cor. 2:2, 7; Col. 1:26; Eph. 3:9; 6:19; 1:9.

14. I Cor. 10:4; cf. Heb. 11:26. Cf. the unconvincing argument of Anthony T. Hanson on I Cor. 10:4 in *Jesus Christ in the Old Testament* (London: S.P.C.K., 1965), p. 7.

15. Cf. Col. 1:18; Heb. 1:4; Col. 1:19; 2:9; Rev. 1:8; 21:6; 22:13; Heb. 1:2–3; 7:3.

16. Cf. also Col. 1:17; Heb. 1:2 f.; 11:3. If "church" in Col. 1:18 is a gloss, creation is in focus; *archē* has connotations of preexistence even though here it refers to the firstfruits of the resurrection. Cf. Fuller, *Foundations*, p. 215; and Eduard Schweizer, *TWNT*, VII, pp. 1035–1039 on *soma*.

17. Shirley J. Case, *The Origins of Christian Supernaturalism* (The University of Chicago Press, 1946), p. 1.

18. On the debate over the authenticity of the Son of Man term in I Enoch, chs. 37 to 71, see Fuller, *Foundations*, pp. 37 f., which represents the positive answer of most continental and American scholars, and, representing a negative verdict, Black, "The Son of Man Problem in Recent Research and Debate."

19. E.g., Rom. 12:14 (Matt. 5:44; Luke 6:28); James 5:12 (Matt. 5:37); Rev. 3:5 (Matt. 10:32). Cf. Raymond E. Balcomb, "The Written Sources of Paul's Knowledge of Jesus," unpublished doctoral dissertation (Boston University, 1951).

20. Typical are Rom. 5:18–21; II Cor. 5:21; Phil. 2:8; Heb. 4:15; I Peter 2:22; Eph. 5:2; I Tim. 6:13.

21. Cf. I Cor. 15:3; Rom. 15:3; Gal. 3:13 f.; I Peter 2:24 f.; Acts 8:32–35. Cf. E. Earle Ellis, *Paul's Use of the Old Testament* (London: Oliver & Boyd, Ltd., 1957); Barnabas Lindars, *New Testament Apologetic* (The Westminster Press, 1962).

22. Also Rom. 5:6, 8; 8:3; Heb. 9:28; I Peter 3:18; I John 3:5.

23. Cf. Rom. 3:25; 5:9; Heb. 9:12; I Peter 1:2, 18 f.; I John 1:7; Acts 20:28 (exceptional in The Acts). On sacrificial vocabulary see in addition I Cor. 5:7; Eph. 5:2; Heb. 1:3; 9:12; 10:10; etc. Cf. Markus Barth, *Was Christ's Death a Sacrifice?* (*SJT* Occasional Papers No. 9; London: Oliver & Boyd, Ltd., 1961); C. F. D. Moule,

"The Christology of Acts," *Studies in Luke-Acts*, ed. by Leander E. Keck and J. Louis Martyn (Abingdon Press, 1966), pp. 171 f.

24. Rom. 3:25; I John 2:2; 4:10; *elutrōthēte* in I Peter 1:18 f.; *antilutron* in I Tim. 2:6; *ēgorasas* in Rev. 5:9.

25. Cf. representative treatments of the atonement in the New Testament such as Donald M. Baillie, *God Was in Christ* (Charles Scribner's Sons, 1948); John Knox, *The Death of Christ* (Abingdon Press, 1958); Vincent Taylor, *The Atonement in New Testament Teaching* (London: Macmillan & Co., Ltd., 1940) and *Forgiveness and Reconciliation* (2d ed., London: Macmillan & Co., Ltd., 1960); and New Testament theologies by Rudolf Bultmann, Millar Burrows, Frederick C. Grant, Leonhard Goppelt, A. M. Hunter, Alan Richardson, Rudolf Schnackenburg, Ethelbert Stauffer.

26. Cf. Fuller, *Foundations*, pp. 68–72; *Letter of Aristeas*, 140; Josephus, *The Jewish War*, VII, 344; Philo, *Life of Moses*; etc.

27. Cf. the influence of the Qumran figure of Moses as eschatological prophet in Acts 3:22 and 7:37, with *pais* in chs. 3:13, 26; 4:27, 30; (22:14).

28. The Servant Songs are found in Isa. 42:1–4; 49:1–6; 50:4–9; 52:13 to 53:12. The main New Testament references are Acts 8:32 f.; 13:47; I Peter 2:24 f. Acts 3:13 may refer to Isa. 52:13, but elsewhere *pais* probably means "child."

29. Cf. Moule, "Christological Terms," pp. 251 f., 256.

30. Cf. Isa. 42:1, 4; 49:6; 52:15; 53:11 f.; and von Rad, *Old Testament Theology*, Vol. II, pp. 261 f., 273 ff. Cf. Borsch, *op. cit.*, pp. 127–129, 175–177.

31. As in Walther Zimmerli and Joachim Jeremias, *The Servant of God*, tr. by Harold Knight (SBT No. 20; Alec R. Allenson, Inc., 1957); Cullmann, *Christology*, p. 79; Hendrikus Berkhof, *Christ, the Meaning of History*, tr. by Lambertus Buurman (London: SCM Press, Ltd., 1966), pp. 57 ff.; Black, *The Dead Sea Scrolls and Christian Doctrine*, pp. 12 ff., 16. Cf. criticisms of this view by Fuller, *Foundations*, pp. 44–46; Moule, "Christological Terms"; Morna Hooker, *Jesus and the Servant* (London: S.P.C.K., 1959), pp. 55 f.; Borsch, *op. cit.*, p. 48.

32. Cf. Eduard Lohse, *Märtyrer und Gottesknecht* (Göttingen: Vandenhoeck & Ruprecht, 1955), pp. 66–78; as against Hooker, *Jesus and the Servant*, pp. 56–71. On I and II Maccabees: Black, *The Dead Sea Scrolls*, pp. 16 ff. On the problem of the death of the Righteous Teacher at Qumran: Fuller, *Foundations*, p. 53; and Black, *The Dead Sea Scrolls*, p. 5.

33. Cf. Kramer, *op. cit.*, pp. 19–65, 113 f., 149 f.

34. Cf. Moule, "The Christology of Acts," pp. 165 f., 179.

35. The qualifications do not alter the prevailing emphasis of The Acts. Cf. Acts 16:7; 8:26 and 10:7 and 27:23; 9:10, etc.; 2:38 f.,

etc.; I Thess. 1:10 and Phil. 3:20. On Luke's idea of a new era of the church beginning with Jesus' ascension, see Hans Conzelmann, *The Theology of St. Luke,* tr. by Geoffrey Buswell (London: Faber & Faber, Ltd., 1960).

36. Moule, "The Christology of Acts," p. 180.

37. *Ibid.* Cf. Neill Q. Hamilton, *The Holy Spirit and Eschatology in Paul* (SJT Occasional Papers No. 6; London: Oliver & Boyd, Ltd., 1957), pp. 83 f.

38. Cf. Kramer, *op. cit.,* pp. 26, 190 f.

39. Cf. Borsch, *op. cit.,* p. 403.

40. Moule, "Christological Terms," pp. 250 ff. *Kyrios* was used to translate YHWH, *marana,* and *adon.*

41. *Ibid.,* p. 255.

42. Hanns Lilje, *The Last Book of the Bible,* tr. by Olive Wyon (Muhlenberg Press, 1957).

43. Used of God in I Tim. 6:15 (Ps. 135:3, LXX; Deut. 10:17).

44. Cf. Kramer, *op. cit.,* p. 121.

45. *Ibid.,* p. 185. Cf. Rom. 1:4.

46. Cf. Moule, *Birth,* pp. 28 f., 86; C. F. D. Moule, "The Intention of the Evangelists," *New Testament Essays,* ed. by Angus J. B. Higgins (Manchester: Manchester University Press, 1959), pp. 165 ff.; C. F. D. Moule, *Worship in the New Testament* (Ecumenical Studies in Worship; London: Lutterworth Press, 1961); Leon Morris, *The New Testament and the Jewish Lectionaries* (London: The Tyndale Press, 1964).

47. E.g., I Cor. 5:5; II Cor. 12:7; I Thess. 2:18. Cf. "antichrist" in I John 2:18; 4:3—here only in the New Testament.

48. E.g., *daimonia* in I Cor. 10:20 f; I Tim. 4:1; James 2:19.

49. E.g., *angeloi* in Rom. 8:38 f.; Gal. 1:8; II Cor. 11:14; Col. 2:18; I Tim. 5:21; Heb. 1:4 f.; I Peter 3:22; Rev. 9:11.

50. Sin: Rom. 5:12, 21; 6:22; 7:11; 8:2; etc. Death: Rom. 5:12, 21; 8:2, 38; I Cor. 15:26; etc.

51. William D. Davies, *The Setting of the Sermon on the Mount* (London: Cambridge University Press, 1964), pp. 405 f.

52. *Ibid.,* p. 406. Is I Cor., ch. 13, based upon a sketch of Jesus himself?

53. F. Grant, *Gospels: Their Origin,* pp. 134 ff. Cf. Bornkamm *et al., Matthew,* pp. 15–51; S. Johnson, *Gospels,* pp. 183 ff.

54. Cf. C. F. D. Moule, "The Influence of Circumstances on the Use of Eschatological Terms," ("Eschatological Terms" hereafter) *JTS,* New Series, Vol. XV, No. 1 (1964), pp. 1–15, attributing the variety in Paul's emphases to circumstances rather than to a "development" in his thought.

55. As with Conzelmann's *The Theology of St. Luke,* pp. 207 ff.

56. Cf. Rom. 11:26; 15:12; Phil. 3:20; Col. 3:4; also Heb. 10:37.

57. E.g., Rom. 2:16; I Cor. 1:8; II Cor. 1:14; II Thess. 1:10; Phil. 1:10; Col. 1:5. Cf. Eph. 1:21; II Tim. 1:12; and four additional references in the Pastorals.

58. Fuller, *Foundations*, pp. 247 ff.

59. Moule, *Birth*, p. 130.

60. *Ibid.*, p. 132.

61. Kümmel, *Introduction*, p. 32.

62. Cf. Knox, *The Death of Christ*, pp. 134–137.

63. Moule, "The Intention of the Evangelists," p. 173, compared to the view that this distinction was completely obliterated, as in Perrin's *Rediscovering*, p. 26.

64. Cf. Moule, *Birth*, p. 193; Kümmel, *Introduction*, p. 33.

65. Hennecke, *New Testament Apocrypha*, Vol. I, pp. 181 f.

66. Cullmann, *Christology*, p. 316.

67. Cf. Moule, *Birth*, pp. 156, 165, 176 f., 178 f.

CHAPTER V THE RELEVANCE OF THE GOSPEL-PERSPECTIVE

1. J. M. Robinson, "Hermeneutical Theology," pp. 579 f.

2. Wilder, *Language*, p. 130. Cf. Pannenberg, "The Revelation of God in Jesus of Nazareth," p. 222.

3. Mary D. Shideler, "God Speaks to a Godless World," *The Christian Century*, Vol. LXXXIII, No. 21 (1966), p. 678.

4. Perrin, *Rediscovering*, pp. 234–248. A third kind of knowledge, the "historic," is absorbed into the "historical." Cf. Krister Stendahl, "Contemporary Biblical Theology," IDB, Vol. I, pp. 418–432, on distinguishing between what the text "meant" and what it "means." On this distinction see also Otto Kaiser and Werner G. Kümmel, *Exegetical Method*, tr. intro. by. E. V. N. Goetchius (The Seabury Press, Inc., 1967), pp. 35 ff.

5. Frederick Herzog, *Understanding God* (Charles Scribner's Sons, 1966), pp. 60–63.

6. Colwell, *Jesus and the Gospel*, p. 41.

7. Wilder, *Language*, p. 78. Our italics.

8. Cf. Dan O. Via, Jr., *The Parables* (Fortress Press, 1967), pp. 200–202; Floyd V. Filson, *A New Testament History* (The Westminster Press, 1964), Ch. XIV; Pannenberg, "The Revelation of God in Jesus of Nazareth," pp. 118 ff.

9. James M. Robinson and John B. Cobb, Jr. (eds.), *The New Hermeneutic* (Harper & Row, Publishers, Inc., 1964); Robert W. Funk, *Language, Hermeneutic, and Word of God* (Harper & Row, Publishers, Inc., 1966), pp. 47–71.

10. Rudolf Bultmann, *Jesus Christ and Mythology* (Charles Scribner's Sons, 1958).

11. Gerhard Ebeling, *The Nature of Faith*, tr. by Ronald G.

Smith (Muhlenberg Press, 1961), Chs. IV to V, and *Word and Faith*, tr. by James W. Leitch (London: SCM Press, Ltd., 1963), pp. 238–246; cf. Cullmann, *Salvation in History*, p. 53.

12. Perrin, *Rediscovering*, pp. 228 f. Cf. Herzog, *op. cit.*, p. 99.

13. Cf. Herzog, *op. cit.*, pp. 97, 99 f., 103; John B. Cobb, Jr., "Faith and Culture," *The New Hermeneutic*, p. 231.

14. Amos N. Wilder, "Word as Address and Word as Meaning," *The New Hermeneutic*, pp. 212 f., expressing a criticism that applies as well to the views of Schweizer on Mark's Gospel in Ch. II. Cf. also Funk, *op. cit.*, pp. 61 f.; my article, "Jesus in History and in Faith," *JBR*, Vol. XXIV, No. 1 (1961), pp. 35–38; Pannenberg, "The Revelation of God in Jesus of Nazareth," pp. 227–229; Cullmann, *Salvation in History*, pp. 21, 64–74, 319–328; Borsch, *op. cit.*, pp. 403 f.

15. Cf. examples throughout Ernst Fuchs, *Studies of the Historical Jesus*, tr. by Andrew Scobie (SBT No. 42; Alec R. Allenson, Inc., 1964). Also see this tendency in Funk, *op. cit.*, pp. 124–249; and in Via, *op. cit.*

16. Joachim Jeremias, *The Parables of Jesus*, tr. by S. H. Hooke (rev. ed.; Charles Scribner's Sons, 1963).

17. Cf. Richard N. Soulen, "Biblical Hermeneutics and Parable Interpretation in the Writings of Ernst Fuchs," unpublished doctoral dissertation (Boston University, 1964).

18. Wilder, "Word as Address and Word as Meaning," p. 209. Cf. Cullmann, *Salvation in History*, p. 45, etc.

19. Herzog, *op. cit.*, p. 93. This criticism applies equally to the "death of God" theology and to Carl Michalson's tacit substitute of history for God.

20. *Ibid.*, p. 98.

21. Cf. Perrin, *Rediscovering*, p. 52.

22. As Barrett, *Luke*. Cf. S. Johnson, *Gospels*, p. 34.

23. McArthur, *The Quest Through the Centuries*, Ch. I.

24. *Ibid.*, pp. 2, 23.

25. Robert M. Grant, *The Earliest Lives of Jesus* (Harper & Row, Publishers, Inc., 1961).

26. Cf. Cullmann, *Salvation in History*, p. 328.

27. C. F. D. Moule, *The Phenomenon of the New Testament* (SBT, Second Series No. 1; London: SCM Press, Ltd., 1967), pp. 78 f.

28. Pannenberg, "The Revelation of God in Jesus of Nazareth," p. 133; cf. pp. 232, 240 f.

29. *Ibid.*, pp. 128–131. Cf. McArthur, *The Quest Through the Centuries*, pp. 138 f.; Cullmann, *Salvation in History*, pp. 57 f., on Pannenberg, and in general.

30. Pannenberg, "The Revelation of God in Jesus of Nazareth,"

cf. pp. 272–276. Cf. the amplified treatment in *Jesus—God and Man,* tr. by Lewis L. Wilkins and Duane A. Priebe (The Westminster Press, 1968).

31. Donald Whittle, *Christianity and the Arts* (Fortress Press, 1967), pp. 141–143.

32. Oliver Powell, *Household of Power* (United Church Press, 1962), pp. 14–16.

33. Perrin, *Rediscovering,* pp. 242–248. Cf. Cullmann, *Salvation in History,* pp. 19 f.

34. McIntyre, *The Shape of Christology,* p. 124. Cf. my article, "The Psychological Model in Christology," *Theology,* Vol. LXX, No. 559 (Jan., 1967), pp. 8–17; Knox, *The Humanity and Divinity of Christ,* Chs. V to VI.

35. McIntyre, *The Shape of Christology,* p. 127. Cf. James M. Robinson, *A New Quest of the Historical Jesus* (SBT No. 25; London: SCM Press, Ltd., 1959), p. 68; Cullmann, *Salvation in History,* pp. 52 f.; Knox, *The Humanity and Divinity of Christ,* Ch. V, pp. 28 ff., 40 ff.

36. Cf. Introduction, n. 7; Hugh Anderson, *Jesus and Christian Origins* (Oxford University Press, Inc., 1964), esp. Chs. III to IV.

37. Shideler, *loc. cit.,* p. 678. Our italics.

38. Cf. Jeremias, *Parables,* Ch. II.

39. Via, *op. cit.,* p. 179. Cf. Wilder, *Language,* pp. 90 f.

40. Birger Gerhardsson, *Memory and Manuscript: Oral Tradition and Written Transmission in Rabbinic Judaism and Early Christianity,* tr. by E. J. Sharpe (2d ed.; Lund: C. W. K. Gleerup, 1964). Cf. also Harald Riesenfeld, *The Gospel Tradition and Its Beginnings: A Study in the Limits of "Formgeschichte"* (London: A. R. Mowbray & Company, Ltd., 1957).

41. Perrin, *Rediscovering,* pp. 30 f.

42. *Ibid.,* pp. 39–49.

43. *Ibid.,* p. 39.

44. Cf. Pannenberg, "The Revelation of God in Jesus of Nazareth," pp. 104, 109, 117, 123 f.; S. Johnson, *Gospels,* pp. 133, 167.

45. Davies, *op. cit.,* pp. 416–418; Frank W. Beare, "The Sayings of the Risen Jesus in the Gospel Tradition: An Inquiry Into Their Origin and Significance," *Christian History and Interpretation,* ed. by W. R. Farmer, C. F. D. Moule, R. R. Niebuhr (London: Cambridge University Press, 1967), pp. 178–181.

46. Paul Althaus, *The So-called Kerygma and the Historical Jesus,* tr. by David Cairns (London: Oliver & Boyd, Ltd., 1959), pp. 73 f.

47. McArthur, *The Quest Through the Centuries,* pp. 135 f. Cf. James McLeman, *Jesus in Our Time* (J. B. Lippincott Company, 1967), p. 146.

48. McArthur, *op. cit.*, p. 146. Cf. Colwell, *Jesus and the Gospel*, Ch. I.

49. Barr, *Old and New in Interpretation*, p. 187. Cf. Perrin, *Kingdom of God*, Ch. VII.

50. Cf. Borsch, *op. cit.*, pp. 15–54; Perrin, *Rediscovering*, pp. 164–198; Angus J. B. Higgins, *Jesus and the Son of Man* (London: Lutterworth Press, 1964).

51. Cf. my *Jesus the Religious Ultimate* (The Macmillan Company, 1956), pp. 35–48.

52. Knox, *The Death of Christ*, p. 118.

53. Cf. Borsch, *op. cit.*, pp. 330–332, against Bultmann and in contrast to fictitious "lives" of Jesus such as Hugh J. Schonfield's *The Passover Plot* (Bernard Geis Associates, 1965) and, earlier, as in Albert Schweitzer, *The Quest of the Historical Jesus*, tr. by W. Montgomery (2d ed.; London: Adam and Charles Black, Ltd., 1945), Ch. IV.

Epilogue

1. Schweitzer, *The Quest of the Historical Jesus*, p. 401.

2. Moule, *The Phenomenon of the New Testament*, p. 80. Cf. Pannenberg, "The Revelation of God in Jesus of Nazareth," p. 129.

3. Schweizer, "Mark's Contribution to the Quest of the Historical Jesus," p. 432. On modern gnosticism, see Cullmann, *Salvation in History*, pp. 23–28, 48 ff.; Knox, *The Humanity and Divinity of Christ*, pp. 17, 63 ff., 70 ff., 86; W. Rordorf, "The Theology of Rudolf Bultmann and Second-Century Gnosis," *NTS*, Vol. XIII, No. 4 (July, 1967), pp. 351–362.

INDEX

Subjects

Acts, The, 40, 44, 45, 51, 137, 140, 142, 149 f., 155, 156, 157, 167, 170, 203, 208, 209

Agapē, 72, 115, 121, 124 f., 137, 164 f., 207

Apocalyptic, 59–62, 92, 96, 102. *See also* Cosmic struggle

Atonement, 27, 52, 63, 96, 100, 101, 137, 150–152, 208, 209

Canon, New Testament, 13, 15, 16, 174, 178

Christ: in Judaism, 30 f.; title of Jesus, 18, 29–32, 38, 47, 49, 53, 75, 87 f., 94, 100, 101 f., 103, 143, 145, 152, 155, 156, 157, 158, 159 f., 161, 162, 163, 167 f.

Christ of faith, 14, 183

Christological models, 187; *kenōsis*, 87, 128, 142, 143, 155, 159, 162 f., 167 f.; psychological, 208, 213; two-nature, 15, 147

Christology, New Testament, 14 f., 121, 147, 154, 169,

207. *See also* Jesus' person; Jesus' titles

Colossians, 142, 143, 162, 168

Corinthians, I, 51 f., 151, 155, 158, 168 f.

Cosmic struggle, 24, 37, 52, 59 f., 85, 89, 126, 145, 160–163, 210

Daniel, 31, 39 ff., 61

Death/resurrection pattern, 52 f., 95, 104, 136, 155 f.

Docetism, 15, 102, 137, 144, 147, 180, 182

Enoch, I, 25, 31, 39 f., 43, 146, 205, 208

Ephesians, 162, 163

Epistles, 13 f., 142, 170 ff., 179 f., 207

Eschatology, 166–169; in Acts, 115 f.; Synoptic, 57 ff., 68, 81, 89, 115 f.; John's, 113–116, 129; Paul's, 115 f. *See also* Apocalyptic; Parousia; II Peter; Revelation to John

Ethics, New Testament, 77–83, 123–125, 164 f.

NAMES